New CLAiT 2006

for Office XP

ALAN CLARKE

WITHDRAWN FOR SALE

Hodder Arnold

WEST SUSSEX COUNTY COUNCIL	
200259705	
Bertrams	16.09.06
004.16	£14.99
WS 5/12	

Orders: please contact Bookpoint Ltd, 130 Milton Park, Abingdon, Oxon OX14 4SB. Telephone: (44) 01235 827720, Fax; (44) 01235 400454. Lines are open from 9.00–5.00, Monday to Saturday, with a 24 hour message answering service. You can also order through our website: www.hoddereducation.co.uk

British Library Cataloguing in Publication Data
A catalogue record for this title is available from The British Library

ISBN-10: 0 340 91537 4
ISBN-13: 978 0 340 91537 0

First published 2002
Impression number   10   9   8   7   6   5   4   3   2   1
Year   2009   2008   2007   2006
Copyright © 2006 Alan Clarke

All rights reserved. No part of this publication may be reproduced or transmitted in any form or by any means, electronic or mechanical, including photocopy, recording, or any information storage and retrieval system, without permission in writing from the publisher or under licence from the Copyright Licensing Agency limited. Further details of such licences (for reprographic reproduction) may be obtained from the Copyright Licensing Agency Limited, of 90 Tottenham Court Road, London W1T 4LP.

Every effort has been made to trace and acknowledge ownership of copyright. The publishers will be glad to make suitable arrangements with any copyright holders whom it has not been possible to contact.

Figure 1.6 reproduced with permission of Photodisc
Figure 1.7 reproduced with permission of Dell Corporation Ltd
Figure 1.8 © Jose Luis Pelaez Inc./CORBIS
Figure 1.10 © Simon Belcher/Alamy

Typeset by Fakenham Photosetting Limited, Fakenham, Norfolk
Printed in Italy for Hodder Arnold, an imprint of Hodder Education, a division of Hodder Headline, 338 Euston Road, London NW1 3BH.

Contents

Acknowledgements	iv
Introduction	1
Chapter 1 File management and e-document production	2
Chapter 2 Creating spreadsheets and graphs	53
Chapter 3 Database manipulation	99
Chapter 4 Producing an e-publication	128
Chapter 5 Creating an e-presentation	149
Chapter 6 E-image creation	175
Chapter 7 Web page creation	200
Chapter 8 Online communication	224
Glossary	253
Index	256

Acknowledgements

To my wife and sons for their help and support during the writing of the book and particularly to Christine for improving my grammar and spelling and Peter for checking the technical content of the book.

The author and publisher wish to acknowledge the following for use of on-screen images: CorelDRAW, Atomz.com, NIACE, The National Archive, Google and the Microsoft Corporation.

Screenshots reprinted by permission from Microsoft Corporation.

Screenshots are copyright Corel Corporation and Corel Corporation Limited, reprinted by permission.

Microsoft and Corel Trademarks are acknowledged.

OCR does not endorse the use of one software package over another, and all CLAIT qualifications are written in generic form. This book is written using the Microsoft® Office suite as examples, simply to provide clear support to the majority of candidates who will be using that package. The use of any of software is equally appropriate and acceptable to OCR.

Introduction

New CLAiT is an initial information and communication technology course and does not assume that you have any prior experience of using computers, applications (e.g. word-processing) or the Internet. It is suitable for people new to computing and is a qualification offered by OCR, who are a major qualification awarding body. The qualification conforms to the National Qualifications Framework.

In August 2005 New CLAiT was revised to produce a straightforward structure of eight units. You can achieve a Certificate by completing three units or a Diploma by completing five units. All eight units are covered within this book. For both the certificate and diploma you must complete the core unit (Unit 1) amongst your chosen units.

The book is based on Microsoft® Office XP and Microsoft® Windows® XP operating system. However, the exercises have been selected so that they are in many cases suitable for other versions of Microsoft® office. Only the e-image creation unit employs an application not based on Microsoft® Office. This is the drawing package CorelDRAW® 10.

The assessment of each unit is based on a practical test which places an emphasis on undertaking a task by accurately following instructions. For most units there is a choice of assessment methods such as local or computer-based. Your tutor will be able to provide you with detailed guidance about the nature of the assessment.

Chapter 1

Unit 1

File management and e-document production

This chapter will help you to use a computer, manage your data and produce documents. You will be able to:

- identify and use a personal computer, monitor, keyboard and mouse
- identify and use operating system software
- use an operating system to create and manage files and folders
- identify and use a word processor to enter text, numbers and symbols
- format basic paragraphs and document properties

The chapter covers the contents of the New CLAiT mandatory unit. It contains information and helps you practise the skills which are essential to the successful completion of the unit.

Assessment

This unit does not assume any previous experience of using a computer. You will be assessed through a practical realistic assignment which is designed to allow you to demonstrate your knowledge and skills against each objective. Your tutor can provide you with more guidance.

What is a computer?

A computer consists of two main components: hardware and software. The hardware is the physical element of the equipment that you can see when you look

Figure 1.1 Desktop computer

at a computer. Figure 1.1 illustrates a desktop computer, Figure 1.2 shows a tower computer and Figure 1.7 a laptop computer. These are some of the variations of personal computers. In the first two examples you will see a monitor which resembles a television, a box that contains the electronic heart of the computer (Central Processing Unit), a keyboard (Figure 1.6) and a mouse (Figure 1.8). The laptop computer integrates these features into a single structure. The views of the computer may seem complicated and you may wonder what the purposes of all the parts and connections are. For OCR New CLAiT you do not need to know but if you are interested you will find an explanation in the summary section at the end of the chapter.

All computers are different so when you look at your own computer it will be similar but not identical. The on-switch is often positioned on the front of the computer but in many models there is a second switch on the back of the computer. The second switch is usually the power supply control so it needs to be on in order for the front switch to operate. When the computer is switched on a small light near to the on-switch is sometimes illuminated.

Software is the set of instructions that controls the hardware. It controls the operations of the hardware such as saving information, electronic communications, word processing and many other applications. Software is divided into two main types.

The operating system – this is the program that controls and connects the application software and hardware. It provides all the standard features of the computer (e.g. saving information, printing and display of information on the monitor screen). This book is based on the Microsoft® Windows® XP operating system. However, there are other Microsoft® operating systems and also other completely different systems (e.g. Linux).

Figure 1.2 Tower computer

Applications – these are programs that help you carry out specialist tasks (e.g. word-processing, drawing pictures, communicating and designing presentations). The later chapters consider applications in considerable detail.

> ## Exercise 1
>
> ### Investigate the hardware
>
> 1. Before you switch on your computer, and with all the hardware disconnected from the power supply, carry out a visual inspection of the equipment. Observe the different connections and pieces of hardware.
>
> 2. Identify whether the computer is a desktop, tower or laptop, then locate the printer, keyboard (Figure 1.6) and mouse (Figure 1.8). These are the main components of a computer system's hardware. If you are considering a laptop then identify how these features are incorporated into the structure.
>
> 3. Inspect the back of the computer and you will observe a number of connections and cables. These link the different parts together and allow information to pass between the different elements (e.g. the computer sends information to the printer so it can produce a document).
>
> 4. Locate the on-switch or switches.

Switching on

When you switch on a computer you are instructing the operating system, which is software stored on the computer's hard disk, to start the computer following a set procedure. If the computer is connected to the power supply then you will hear the hard disk making noises while searching for instructions. The monitor will display some of the instructions but these are probably meaningless to all but those users at an expert level.

You may notice that the light on the floppy disk drive or other parts of the computer are illuminated. The standard start up (or 'boot up') procedure involves checking the floppy drive for a disk. If you have left one in the drive then the start-up sequence will be interrupted. This seems unusual but is actually a safety feature – if you have a hard disk failure it allows you to investigate the problem.

After a few moments the Microsoft® Windows® logo will apear on the screen. The system will continue to make noises until eventually the logo disappears and is replaced by what is known as a dialog box in the middle of the screen. This will ask you for your ==user name== and ==password==. You can change both once you have access to the computer. Once you have entered the correct name and password you click on to the OK button using the mouse pointer. This will present you with the Microsoft® Windows® desktop (Figure 1.3). This illustration has been kept very simple but on many desktops there will be many small pictures (known as icons) representing different software applications.

Figure 1.3 shows some icons on the main desktop area. Three important ones are:

- My Computer – this links you to the areas of the computer where information is stored (known as drives). Drives include the hard disk which stores the bulk of the information as well as CD-ROM and floppy disk drives which allow information to be placed in portable form. My Computer also links you to resources connected to the computer, such as printers
- Recycle Bin – this is a place where deleted files are kept so that if you make a mistake you can reclaim them
- Application icons – these allow you to load the application (e.g. Microsoft® Word)

Figure 1.3 Microsoft® Windows® desktop

At the bottom of the desktop there is a grey bar – the taskbar. At the right end of the taskbar is an area called the status area in which a range of small icons are shown. These represent programmes that are currently working. Other icons on the toolbar allow you to access the applications they represent while on the left end is the button called Start. Clicking on this provides access to a range of applications and other services and is also the way to switch off the computer.

Exercise 2

Switching on (booting up) your computer

1 With the computer, monitor and other hardware connected to the power supply, press the on-switch on the front of the computer and on the monitor. In both cases a small light will be illuminated and you will hear the whirring and clicking sounds of the computer starting.

2 If nothing happens then check that the power switch at the rear of the computer is in the on position.

3 Observe what happens – the time to start (boot) the computer can vary considerably depending on what is connected to the machine and how it is configured, so do not be concerned if it takes a few minutes.

4 Eventually you will see the dialog box requesting your user name and password. Once these have been entered you will see something similar to Figure 1.3 appear.

Opening applications

There are several ways of loading an application such as a word processor (Microsoft® Word) or a spreadsheet (Microsoft® Excel®). The two most used are:

- the Start button
- the application icon displayed on the Windows® desktop

In the bottom left-hand corner of the Windows® desktop (Figure 1.3) is a button called Start. This allows you to access many applications and standard features of the operating system. If you single click on Start, a menu will pop-up, which is shown in Figure 1.4. If you place the mouse pointer over the All Programs item it will become highlighted (i.e. the background will change colour) and a new menu, the programs menu, will appear alongside. This is shown in Figure 1.5.

Figure 1.4 Start menu

The programs menu will vary in length and number of items depending on what applications you have installed on your computer. In this case all the Microsoft® Office XP applications are available to you. You should notice that All Programs and other items sometimes have a small black triangle next to them. This indicates that if you highlight this item by placing your mouse pointer over it, then another menu will open.

To load Microsoft® Word single click on the Microsoft® Word option on the All Programs menu (Figure 1.5). The Microsoft® Word application will open. An alternative way of loading Microsoft® Word is to double click on the Microsoft® Word icon on the Windows® desktop.

Figure 1.5 Programs menu

Switch off

Switching off a computer must be done in the correct way or you run the risk of damaging your system. To switch off a computer using the Microsoft® Windows® XP operating system requires you to click on the Start button. A menu (list of options) will appear (Figure 1.4) and if you select the Turn Off Computer option then a small box entitled Turn off computer will appear.

The Turn off computer box provides several options and in most cases you will want to select Turn Off. You select an option by clicking on its icon. If you click on the Cancel button you will return to the desktop. If you position your pointer over an option then a short statement will appear explaining its purpose.

The process of shutting down involves the computer making noises and the screen showing a variety of images. The time required to complete the process varies but does not take very long. When the shut down is complete, the light on the computer will be switched off. However, the light on the monitor will still remain on until you press its switch.

Input

Users communicate with computers using input devices such as:

- a keyboard (Figure 1.6)
- a mouse (Figure 1.8)

There are a variety of input devices depending on how you need to interact with the computer system. When you input information into the computer it usually responds by displaying the information on the monitor screen.

A keyboard is similar to a typewriter and is designed to allow you to enter text into the computer. A keyboard and a typewriter have alphabetical keys and are laid out identically. There are also other keys which are common to them both, for example:

Figure 1.6 Keyboard

- space bar
- capital lock
- shift
- punctuation keys

The major difference, however, is that the keyboard has a number of additional keys. These are:

- a row of number keys towards the top of the keyboard and a separate number pad on the right
- enter keys which are used to confirm that you want to enter information into the computer
- a top row of keys labelled F1 to F12 which carry out particular functions
- a number of other special purpose keys whose role will gradually emerge as you work through the book

Exercise 3

Exploring the keyboard

1 Take a look at the keyboard. You will notice that it is divided into four main areas:

   - function keys across the top of the keyboard
   - number pad on the right of the keyboard
   - main alphabetical keys – notice the QWERTY layout (this is the sequence of alphabetical keys along the top left of the lettered keys)

continued

- various other keys some sandwiched between the QWERTY keys and number pad areas (e.g. Delete)

2 Identify the following keys: Ctrl, Alt, Home, Pg Up and Num Lock. These are special purpose keys, and eventually you will learn their purposes. For the moment you simply need to know where they are. This will help you once you start to use applications.

3 To enter uppercase letters requires that the shift and character keys are pressed together. This is also the way symbols on the top half of some of the keys are entered.

4 Some keyboards have a small Microsoft® Windows® symbol on a key. This is a shortcut equivalent to pressing the Start button on the taskbar. This might not seem useful at the moment but its importance will become apparent later.

There are other types of keyboard and various specialist ones have been devised for particular tasks.

Figure 1.7 illustrates a laptop computer keyboard. This is smaller and so is suitable for a laptop computer which is designed to be portable. The main difference from a desktop keyboard is the lack of a number pad.

A mouse is a small palm-sized device which is usually connected to your computer by a cable, although wireless mice are now becoming very popular. Many new computers are now supplied with a wireless mouse. The mouse is linked to an on-screen pointer which normally appears as an arrow and mirrors the movements made by the mouse.

Figure 1.7 Laptop Computer

Figure 1.8 shows a two-button mouse which is the type most widely used, but single and three-button mice are also available. This book will only discuss a two-button mouse.

If you move the mouse, the on-screen pointer moves in the same way. If you move right, the pointer goes right, if you move left then the pointer goes left, and so on. The buttons on the mouse allow you to communicate with the computer.

Other input devices exist which will also control a screen pointer. A trackball works by manipulating a ball and clicking buttons to control the pointer and make selections. Laptop computers have a variety of devices using touch buttons, pads and thumb balls to control on-screen pointers.

Figure 1.8 Mouse

Note: The mouse often sits on a small mat which is called, not surprisingly, a mouse mat. This helps the mouse move smoothly across the surface.

Exercise 4

Using a mouse – right-handed users

1. Place your right hand with your index finger on the left-hand button and your middle finger on the right button.

2. Move the mouse and watch how the pointer responds on the screen.

3. Practise using the mouse until you are comfortable – move the pointer up, down, left, right and diagonally until you can accurately control the pointer. Notice where you move the mouse to achieve the desired result.

Alternative Exercise 4

Using a mouse – left-handed users

1. You can adjust a mouse to make it suitable for left-handed people. This involves clicking on the Start button and Control Panel to reveal the Control Panel window. Double click on the Mouse icon. This will reveal the Mouse Properties window and you can select the left-handed option by clicking on the radio button labelled Switch primary and secondary buttons and then the OK button.

2. Place your left hand with your index finger on the right-hand button and your middle finger on the left button.

3. Move the mouse and watch how the pointer responds on the screen.

4. Practise using the mouse until you are comfortable – move the pointer up, down, left, right and diagonally until you can accurately control the pointer. Notice where you move the mouse to achieve the desired result.

Note: remember that if you select the left-hand mouse options then you will need to take this into account when reading the instructions in this book.

It is very important that you learn to use a mouse accurately and effectively. This will take practice. The main skills are:

- accurately moving the on-screen pointer until it touches objects on the screen. Often they will be animated or a text box will appear to explain their purpose.
- single clicking the left mouse button to communicate a command to the computer to select something
- single clicking the right mouse button to communicate a command to the computer to show some extra features such as revealing an extra menu of choices
- double clicking the left mouse button which communicates a command to the computer to start a process

- clicking and dragging (if you press the left-hand mouse button but do not release it while the pointer is resting on an object on the screen and then you move the mouse, the object will be dragged across the screen until you release the button)

Exercise 5

Practising your mouse skills

1 You can practise your mouse skills in many ways but it can be fun to play a game which is supplied as part of the Windows® operating system. This is a card game called Solitaire played using the mouse pointer to move the cards.

2 To load the games program requires using the mouse and can be quite a challenge if this is the first time you have used a mouse – but do keep trying.

3 The first step is to single click with the left mouse button on the Start button. A list of options will appear above the button. This is called a menu and is a standard way of presenting an option in Microsoft® Windows® and in applications.

Step 1: Slide the mouse up the menu until you highlight the All Programs option (the background changes to a new colour).

Step 2: At the end of the word Programs you will see a small pointer (triangle) which tells you that there are more options available. If you leave the mouse pointer over All Programs a new menu will appear to the right.

Step 3: Slide your mouse pointer in a straight line to the right until you highlight an option in the new menu, then move the pointer up the menu until you reach the option Games.

Step 4: If you leave your pointer over Games another menu to the right will appear. Again, in a straight line slide your pointer to the right until a new option is highlighted. Move the pointer until it is now over the option Solitaire.

Step 5: With the option highlighted, single click the left mouse button and you will see the Solitaire game appear. It will provide you with an opportunity to practise moving and controlling the precise direction of the mouse pointer.

4 Figure 1.9 illustrates the Solitaire game after a few cards have been played. The game has the same rules as the card game. You turn cards over by single clicking on the pile. Move cards by clicking the left mouse button on the one of your choice and holding the button down and dragging the card to its new location.

5 Try to play a game. If you find that every time you drag a card to a new location it returns to its original position, it is because you are making an illegal move.

6 Keep playing until you are confident about dragging and dropping and clicking with the left button. These are key elements in using a mouse but there are two further important actions. These are double clicking and single clicking with the right mouse button and there will be opportunities to improve these skills in other parts of the book. However, double clicking (which is clicking the left mouse button twice rapidly) needs practise. People often find it difficult initially to click twice quickly enough. If you find that after

> **continued**
>
> double clicking no action results, it is probably because you are leaving too long an interval between the clicks. Keep trying to click twice as quickly as you can. You will eventually get it right.
>
> 7 To close the Solitaire window you need to single click with the left mouse button on the button marked with an X in the top right-hand corner of the Solitaire window. Figure 1.9 shows the three buttons that allow the window to be minimised to a button on the Desktop taskbar, maximised to fill the entire display, or closed (i.e. buttons left to right). Experiment with expanding the window to fill the whole display and minimising it to a button. When the window is maximised you can reduce it in size by using the same buttons.
>
> 8 These controls appear on all windows. It is a standard part of the operating system. Applications can be displayed as a window (a rectangular area), the whole display or a single button on the taskbar.
>
> 9 When you have finished playing Solitaire, close the window.

Graphic User Interface

Microsoft® Windows® and the vast majority of modern software uses a Graphical User Interface (GUI). A GUI is a highly visual interface combining the use of a pointing device (e.g. a mouse) with visual links to applications, commands and options. The visual links take the form of small pictures called icons, buttons (small rectangles) or menus (i.e. lists of options). GUIs are easy to learn and to use since you do not need to remember a large number of commands, but only to recognise them when they appear on the screen. Most GUIs are consistent meaning that you can work out what to do even when you are using a new part of the system.

A key feature of a GUI, Microsoft® Windows® and Office is the window. This is a rectangular enclosed area in which applications, files and messages are displayed. Windows can be moved and resized (i.e. a window can fill a whole screen or be reduced to small picture on the edge of the display). Windows can be stacked on top of each other so that at first you can sometimes lose a window because it is hidden under another one.

While you are still learning about Windows®, using a mouse and GUIs, you probably feel confused and uncertain but this will change with practice. GUIs have made learning about using information and communication technology far easier than earlier computers based on command interfaces.

Figure 1.9 Solitaire

Storing and locating information

Computers have a permanent store for information, programs (applications) and data. This is called the hard disk or hard drive and it can hold an enormous amount of information. It is often designated by the letter C with a colon, so drive C: is the hard drive. The hard disk is normally a permanent part of the computer, although there are computers that allow you to remove a hard drive, but these are relatively rare. Information can be stored in smaller amounts on a floppy disks which is a portable storage device that you can carry from one computer to another. The floppy drive is often designated as the A: drive.

Figure 1.10 illustrates a floppy disk. The disk is inserted into the drive with its label on the top, the metal slider entering first. The disk is firmly pushed into the drive until it clicks. It is not possible to insert a disk the wrong way round so if it does not go in, you are holding it the wrong way up.

There are other portable storage devices that can hold far more data than a floppy disk. The memory stick is a small device which you can plug into a computer's USB port. It then becomes a new drive on to which you can store information. Memory sticks are sometimes called flash or pen drives and even dongles. Some computers have CD-RW (i.e. compact disc read write) or DVD-RW (i.e. DVD read write) drives which enable you to save information on to disks.

Figure 1.10 Floppy disk

Exercise 6

Inserting a floppy disk

1 Try to insert a floppy disk into the drive (Figure 1.1 and 1.2). Remember to push the disk firmly into the drive, but if it will not enter then check you are inserting it the right way (i.e. label on top and metal slider first).

2 The floppy will make a noise when it is in place and it will be inside the computer so that you cannot reach it. To remove the disk you need to press the button which is located near to the drive. This button will pop out as the floppy disk is pushed in.

3 Press the button and see the disk emerge.

4 Repeat the action of inserting and removing the disk until you are confident.

The Windows® operating system provides you with the means to search the hard disk and floppy disks when they are inserted into the drive. Windows® Explorer lets you view the contents of the computer drives. Figure 1.11 illustrates Windows® Explorer showing the contents of the C: drive (hard drive).

Windows® Explorer is a file management application provided within Microsoft® Windows®. The Explorer's application window is divided into a number of areas. These are:

- Title bar (e.g. Local Disk (C:))
- Menu bar
- Toolbar
- Address (i.e. shows the location or path of the highlighted folder)
- Folders (left-hand side of the display) – showing the structure of folders stored on the hard disk, floppy disks, CD-ROMs or other storage media. A plus sign indicates that the folder has more folders stored within it. If you click on the plus sign, the structure will be opened up to show these folders. The revealed folders can also be marked with a plus sign, indicating further folders stored within the revealed one.
- Contents of the folder (right-hand side of the display). This shows the files and folders stored within the highlighted folder.

Information is stored in a computer in what are known as files. All files have a unique name and they are normally grouped with related files and stored within folders. This is rather similar to the storage of paper records in cardboard files and it is intended to help you locate them again when you have a large number of files. In the computer it is also possible to store folders within other folders. In Figure 1.11 you will notice many small plus signs in the left-hand area of the display. This indicates that these folders contain other folders. Clicking on the plus sign will open up the folder to reveal what it contains. These are shown in the right-hand window. Figure 1.12 shows a group of folders within the Documents and Settings folder each with a unique name.

Figure 1.13 shows the folders stored within the Alanc folder. Two folders are revealed and if the My Documents folder is highlighted then the files stored in the folder are shown. The different types of files take on different forms or formats depending on the information they contain. Here we see examples of Microsoft Word, Text Document, PUB file (i.e. desktop publishing) and Bitmap Image.

Figure 1.11 Windows® Explorer

Windows® Explorer provides functions in the File menu to delete or rename your files. You highlight the file you need to work on by single clicking on it, then select the File menu and the options Delete or Rename. In the Edit menu you are also provided with options to copy (Copy and Paste) or move (Cut and Paste) the file to another folder.

Figure 1.12 Folders

Figure 1.13 Files

It is not always easy when you first start to use a computer to distinguish between different types of files. Applications (e.g. word processors) are stored as files, documents produced by the applications are also stored as files and so on. In a way everything is a file. You distinguish between them by considering the small picture (icon) in front of the file name and the extension at the end of the name (i.e. the letters following the full stop – .bmp, .gif, .doc and .txt). There are many different types of files.

You can change the appearance of folders and files in Windows® Explorer and in other Microsoft® applications. They can appear as:

- Icons
- Tiles (e.g. Figure 1.12)
- Details (e.g. Figures 1.11 and 1.13)
- List (i.e. similar to details but without the information about size, type and date of modification)
- Thumbnails (i.e. useful if you are viewing pictures since each appears as a small image making it easy for you to select the one you want)

In order to change the appearance within Windows® Explorer select the View menu and choose the appropriate option (i.e. icons, tiles, list, details and thumbnails). Alternatively choose the View icon on the toolbar and the options will be displayed allowing you to select one. The selected option is shown by a black dot placed alongside the item.

Exercise 7

Windows® Explorer

1 Open Windows® Explorer by clicking on the Start button, then highlighting All Programs and then Accessories to reveal a menu of options. Click on the Windows® Explorer item. This will open Explorer (Figure 1.11).

2 Explore the application by clicking on the plus signs to open up the folder structure. Keep clicking on new plus signs that are revealed and observe what changes.

3 Highlight a folder in the left-hand list and observe the changes in the right-hand area of the window. This area shows what a highlighted folder contains. You can also click on folders in the right-hand area to open them. Again notice any changes this causes.

4 When you click on a folder in the left-hand list you will notice the picture of the folder itself changes to look like an open folder.

continued

5 Use Explorer to investigate what is stored on the computer's hard disk. However, do not select Delete or Rename or any option within the menus since you may cause changes that harm your computer.

6 When you have investigated the structure, close Explorer by clicking on the Close button in the top right-hand corner of the window or select the File menu and the Close option.

Figure 1.14 Search Companion

If you use a computer regularly, you will find that you have many hundreds of folders and files. Although they all have individual names, in order to find them you will need to remember the name of the file and in which folder you stored it. This is further complicated by storing folders inside other folders. The Windows® operating system provides you with a way of finding files and folders, if you cannot remember a particular file location.

If you click on the Start button, a menu will pop up containing an option called Search (in other versions of Windows® this is sometimes called Find). If you click on Search, the Search Companion window appears (Figure 1.14).

Exercise 8

Finding a file

1 Load the Search Companion window (Figure 1.14). On the left-hand side of the window are a series of options to help you search for different types of files and folders (e.g. Documents). Select the Documents option by clicking on it and observe what happens (Figure 1.15). The display changes to ask you to specify the nature of the file you are seeking (e.g. name or

Figure 1.15 What do you want to search for?

File management and e-document production

continued

part of the name of the file and the last time you changed it). Enter the name of a file (e.g. clait) and select the **Don't remember** option and click on the **Search** button. If you make a mistake you can go back a step by selecting the **Back** button.

2 Observe what happens and you should see the search results on the right-hand side of the display fill with a list of files and folders. These all have your search term in their titles.

3 When the search is completed you will need to review the list to identify the particular file you are searching for. If you want to open the file, double click on the chosen item. The file will open inside the application which created it (e.g. text files in a text editor).

4 Explore the search function by entering new names, selecting different modification dates and try the advanced search functions (i.e. click on **Use advanced search options**). Try the different options and see what happens.

5 The advanced search options let you search specific drives and offers two additional features:

   – What size is it? (i.e. lets you specify the size of the file you are seeking)

   – More advanced options

   The more advanced options include allowing you to specify case sensitivity (i.e. match file name with lowercase or capital letters).

6 Continue until you are confident in locating files. Try locating files on a floppy disk (A:) as well as on the hard disk (C:).

7 Close the function by using the **Close** button in the right-hand corner of the window.

Create and manage files and folders

In addition to being able to find files and folders it is important that you are able to manage them. The Microsoft® Windows® operating system provides a range of functions to allow you to:

- Create and name folders (directories)
- Open, close and save files
- Delete files and folders
- Rename files and folders
- Print the file structure
- Cut, copy and paste
- Move files and folders
- Copy files and folders

Windows® Explorer is designed to manage your files and folders. It allows you to create, delete and rename files and folders. The **File** menu (Figure 1.16) offers you functions to Create, Delete, Open, Close and Rename files and folders. The **Edit** menu has the options of Cut, Copy, Paste, Move and Copy files and folders.

Figure 1.16 shows the following functions:

- **New** – create a new folder in the folder currently being viewed in Windows® Explorer
- **Delete** – deletes the file or folder highlighted
- **Rename** – allows you to change the name of the file or folder highlighted

Other options are available within the Edit menu:

Figure 1.16 Manipulating files and folders

- **Move To Folder …** – moves the highlighted file or folder to a new folder (this is the same process as Cut and Paste)
- **Copy To Folder …** – copies the highlighted file or folder to a new folder (this is the same process as Copy and Paste)
- **Undo** – this lets you change your mind, since it undoes the last action you have undertaken
- **Cut** – enables you to cut out a file or folder with the intention of moving it to a new location using the Paste option
- **Copy** – allows you to copy a file or folder to a new location using the Paste option but leaving the original file or folder unaffected.
- **Paste** – lets you place a copied or cut file or folder in a new location

Exercise 9

Manipulating folders

1. Insert a floppy disk into the drive.

2. Open Windows® Explorer by clicking on the **Start** button, highlighting **All Programs** and then **Accessories** and selecting **Windows® Explorer**. The application will appear (Figure 1.11) either in a window or filling the whole screen.

3. Click on the 3½ Floppy (A:) option (Figure 1.17). If the floppy is empty then no files or folders will be shown on the right-hand side of the

Figure 1.17 Drives

continued

display. If you cannot see the 3½ Floppy (A:) option, scroll up and down the window or click on My Computer folder to display the drives. 3½ Floppy (A:) is at the top of the list.

4 You are going to create a new folder so select the File menu, highlight New and click on the Folder option. A new folder will appear on the right-hand side of the display with the name New Folder. The cursor (a cursor is a small flashing bar that shows you where your text will appear when you enter it from the keyboard) will be flashing in the name box and you should type a name for the folder using the keyboard. In this case call it Master.

5 The Master Folder is stored on the floppy disk because this was the drive selected when the folder was created.

6 Double click on Master in the left-hand side and you will see the right-hand side is empty because this folder is empty. However, on the left hand side the Master Folder will appear (Figure 1.18) and because it has been selected, the folder icon is shown open.

7 Create a new folder and name it Master1. Open Master1 and create another new folder called Master2. You now have three folders stored one within another. Figure 1.19 shows the structure.

8 Highlight the Master1 folder by clicking on it, then select File menu and the Rename option. You can change the name to New Master. Repeat the process for Master2 and rename it Modern Master.

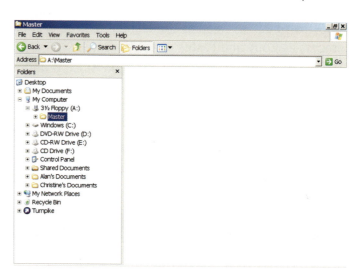

Figure 1.18 Master folder open

9 Highlight Modern Master (single click) and then select the Copy tool (alternatively select the Edit menu and the Copy option). Highlight the Master folder and select the Paste tool (alternatively select the Edit menu and Paste option). You will see the Modern Master folder copied into the Master Folder. The original Modern Master folder is still in place. Figure 1.20 shows the new structure.

Figure 1.19 Structure

continued

10. The process of using a function has now been illustrated. You must highlight the folder you wish to operate on and then select the function. Now practise using the other functions. The undo function lets you remove your last action so none of your changes need to be permanent:

    - Delete a folder
    - Cut and paste a folder
    - Copy To
    - Move To

Figure 1.20 New structure

11. When you select either Copy To or Move To a new window appears called Move Items or Copy Items (Figure 1.21). This allows you to find the folder you want to copy or move the file or folder to. Notice that in the Copy Items or Move Items window, you can create a new folder using the Make New Folder button in the bottom left-hand corner of the window.

Figure 1.21 Copy Items window

12. Continue trying the different functions until you are confident.

13. Close Windows® Explorer by clicking on File menu and the Close option.

Creating and printing documents

The Windows® operating system includes other applications in addition to Windows® Explorer. These include:

- Microsoft® Paint – a straightforward drawing application
- Microsoft® WordPad – a basic word processor

- Microsoft® Notepad – a text editor which is a limited word processor
- Microsoft® Calculator – an on-screen calculator
- Address Book – this allows you to keep details of peoples names, email addresses and telephone numbers

These can be accessed in a similar way to Solitaire by clicking the Start button, highlighting the All Programs and Accessories options in the menu and then single clicking on the application of your choice. In addition to these applications you can install other ones. This book is largely based on Microsoft® Office XP which is an integrated suite of products.

Word processors are one of the most widely used computer applications. In the next exercises, you are going to use Microsoft® Word (Figure 1.22) to create a short document, save it to floppy disk and print it. Microsoft® Word is a powerful word processor though there are many other word processors available and other applications such as text editors. The difference between a word processor and a text editor is mainly the degree of sophistication. Text editors are used principally for producing simple messages while a word processor provides the tools for writing a wide range of documents (e.g. from a letter to a book). Word processors provide tools for presenting and formatting information and are often WYSIWYG, which stands for What You See Is What You Get. This means that the way the words are presented on the screen is how they will be printed. They help you write by providing a wide range of features and functions such as spelling and grammar checkers and offer you considerable freedom to change the words, presentation, layout and appearance of your documents.

If you have never used a keyboard to enter text it may feel strange at first, but you will rapidly realise how useful a word processor is. Windows includes a text editor called Notepad which is shown in Figure 1.23.

Figure 1.22 Microsoft® Word

The Microsoft® Word display consists of three main areas:

- menus and toolbars which provide you with access to the word processor controls (e.g. Standard, Formatting and Drawing toolbars)
- the working area where you enter your words to create documents

Figure 1.23 Microsoft® NotePad

- the status bar (reading from left to right) shows:
  - Page 1 – the page you are on (e.g. the first page)
  - Sec 1 – the section of the document you are on
  - 1/1 – shows you that you are looking at the first page of your document which is one page long
  - At 2.5 cm – this tells you that you are entering text that will be 2.5 cm below the top of the page when it is printed
  - Ln 1 – you are entering text into the 1st line of your document
  - Col 1 – you are entering text in the first character position of the document

Exercise 10

Creating a document

1 Open Microsoft® Word by clicking on the Start button, highlighting the All Programs option to open a menu of options and single clicking on Microsoft® Word. The application will open (Figure 1.22). Maximise the window using the control buttons in the top right-hand corner of the window.

2 On the first line of the work area you will see a flashing upright line. This is called the cursor and indicates where any text or numbers that you enter will appear on the screen. Press any letter or number on the keyboard. You will see your selected character appear and the cursor move one space to the right, indicating where the next character will be entered. To remove your character press the backspace key. This is marked with a left-pointing arrow and will delete any character to the left of the cursor. There is another delete key which removes characters to the right of the cursor. This is located in the bottom right of the keyboard below the number pad.

3 Move the mouse pointer around the display and you will see that it changes shape. It is no longer shaped liked an arrow when it moves across the work area but is like the letter I.

4 Using the keyboard type:

My name is .... I live in .... and I am .... years old.

Fill in the blanks with your own details – name, town/city and age.

To enter a capital letter (upper case character) you need to hold down the shift key and then press the letter of your choice. If you want to enter everything in upper case press the Capitals Lock (i.e. Caps Lock) key once. To return to lower case, press Caps Lock again. For the current exercises you only need to enter single upper case letters.

5 If you make a mistake then you can remove it using the backspace key.

6 When you have entered the text then move your mouse pointer until it is immediately in front of 'I live in ....' and then single click. You will see the cursor move to this new position. This is how you move the cursor using the mouse, although there are other ways such as by using the arrow keys on the keyboard.

7 If you press the enter key then the text will be broken into two parts as shown below.

continued

My name is ....

I live in .... and I am .... years old.

The Enter key inserts a new line, but if you continue typing text the words will automatically go to the next line when you reach the end of the previous one. This is called text wrapping. If you hold down any key you will see the character appear many times and wrap around when it reaches the end of a line.

8 If you single click on the menu item File (Figure 1.24) a menu will drop down. This provides a number of standard features which, if you click on them, give you access to useful functions such as:

- New – creates a new document
- Open – opens an existing document so that you can read it and amend it if you wish
- Save – allows you to save your document to the computer's store on the hard disk, on a floppy disk or on another storage medium
- Save As – allows you to save an existing file under a different name
- Print – allows you to print your document on a connected printer
- Exit – an alternative to using the Close button

You will notice that the menu covers part of the text you have entered but will disappear if you click your mouse anywhere outside of the menu area or when you select an option. Above the Exit option is a list of files (e.g. C:\..\Chapter One File Management an...). These are the most recent documents that have been opened in Microsoft® Word. You can access them by clicking on them.

Figure 1.24 Microsoft® Word file menu

9 Close Word by selecting the File menu and the Exit option unless you want to progress immediately to Exercise 11.

Printing

Printers provide you with the means to output your computer work to produce letters, reports and other paper documents. There are several different types and three widely available types are:

- monochrome laser printer
- monochrome and colour inkjet printer
- colour laser printer

A laser printer uses magnetic toner to produce text and images on paper whereas inkjet printers work by squirting small drops of ink onto the page. They can provide both black and white and colour printing. Laser and inkjet printers are widely used in the work place and at home. Colour printers are more expensive than monochrome ones but the price of colour inkjets is now in reach of most computer users.

Printers are manufactured in a variety of sizes and shapes. Two key features of any printer are the on-switch and the paper holder. The on-switch can be positioned in a range of locations including the back corners, front panel and the sides of the printer. In a similar way, the paper can be fed into a pull-out drawer or pushed into an opening. Each manufacturer has their own design and it is important to study the printer's manual before using it.

Exercise 11

Printers

1. It is important to familiarise yourself with the printer you are going to use, so in this exercise you are going to explore your printer.
2. First make sure it is not connected to the power supply. Inspect the printer and see if you can locate the on-switch and where the paper is loaded.
3. Remove the paper and inspect it. In most cases the paper is A4 size and is loaded as a block. Replace the paper carefully. When you load paper it is useful to fan the edges of the block since this will help stop it sticking together. A problem with all printers is that the paper will sometimes jam inside (rather like a photocopier).
4. Connect the printer to the power supply and switch it on. Each printer will start in its own individual way but you are likely to hear some noise and see control lights flash. If you are using a large laser printer it will have a display panel and you will probably see a message appear, such as Warming Up. When the printer is ready, this message will change (e.g. Ready). Smaller laser and inkjet printers might have only a few lights. Inspect the labels near the lights and you may see error, paper and data lights. The meaning of the lights being illuminated depends on the type and model of your printer.
5. Observe the printer's start up process.
6. Some printers have a demonstration or test function. This is indicated by a button labelled Demo or Test. If your printer provides this function press the button and see what happens. Often a short document will be printed. In some cases this provides background information about the printer.
7. Once you are confident that you know how to switch the printer on and load the paper, switch the printer off if you are not going to use it.

Exercise 12

Create, save and print a document

1 Open Microsoft® Word by clicking on Start, highlighting the All Programs option to reveal a menu of options and single clicking on Microsoft® Word. The application will open (Figure 1.22). Maximise the window using the control buttons in the top right-hand corner of the window if the display does not fill the screen.

2 When the application is open you will notice that in the work area there is a small flashing vertical line in the top left-hand corner. This is called a cursor and it is here that your text will appear when you begin to enter it.

3 Type the following:

This is a short passage to help me understand how to create, save and print a document. The keyboard has many keys to enter text and numbers. The number keys are 1, 2, 3, 4, 5, 6, 7, 8 and 9. The symbol keys are =-/#.,:@?!£&%+*.

Observe the movement of the cursor and how the text wraps around at the end of each line. Remember to use the shift key to access symbols on the top of keys and to insert upper case letters.

4 Once you have created a document you can save it as a file by selecting the File menu and the Save option. The Save As window (dialog box) opens (Figure 1.25). This shows a view of a folder called Documents and Settings in which is stored a variety of folders (i.e. Administrator, Alan, Alanc, All Users, Christine and Peter).

To save your work you need to enter a file name in the box File name and then click on the Save button. Windows® inserts a a file name based on the text you have entered (i.e. This is a short passage to help me understand how to create). You can use this name or enter a new one by clicking in the File name box and entering a name. You may have to delete the automatic name. Your file will then be saved in the Documents and Settings folder. If you would like to save your file elsewhere you have to change the name in the Look in box. You change this box by clicking on the down arrow button at the end of the box, and a list of other choices where you can store your file appears (Figure 1.24).

Figure 1.25 Save As window

In many of the exercises you are instructed to save your file to a floppy disk. However, you are free to save them to any drive or folder.

continued

5 Notice that below the file name box is another called Files of type. This allows you to save your file as a particular file format. Since you are saving from the Microsoft® Word application, it automatically defaults to Word Document.

6 Insert a floppy disk into the drive. Enter your file name as Document, select Save in as 3½ Floppy (A:) and click on the Save button. You will hear the disk drive and see the mouse pointer turn into an hour glass for a few moments. This tells you that Windows® is working on a task.

Figure 1.26 Save As locations

7 If you now change your document by adding more text and want to update your saved file all you need to do is select the File menu and option Save. The Save As window will not appear since the system assumes you want to update your file Document stored in the same place (i.e. floppy disk).

8 Add extra text in order to test saving again. Your passage should now read:

This is a short passage to help me understand how to create, save and print a document. The keyboard has many keys to enter text and numbers. The number keys are 1, 2, 3, 4, 5, 6, 7, 8 and 9. The symbol keys are =-/#.,:@?!£&%+*. This is extra text to test saving again.

9 Select the File menu and the Save option. You may hear the drive start up but the Save As window will not appear. It is good practice to save your document early and then update it at regular intervals. Some applications can be set to save your work automatically every few minutes. However, you should establish the habit of saving at regular intervals. There are few things worse than losing all your work due to a problem with the computer or an electricity failure because you have not saved your work for a few hours.

(Microsoft® Word can automatically save your work – select the Tools menu, Options item to reveal the Options window. Choose the Save tab and consider the choices).

10 Another useful feature of saving in Windows® is that you can save the same document many times under different names. If you select File menu and the Save As option then the Save As window will appear and you can choose to save the document again under another name and in another folder. In this case save your document as Document2 on the floppy disk. You should see the original Document file (Figure 1.27).

11 You can repeat this operation as many times as you like and it is useful as a means of keeping an original document while revising its contents for another purpose (e.g. using

continued

a letter to the electricity company as a template for one to the gas supplier).

12 Having created a document you can print it by selecting the **File** menu and the **Print** option. A Print window will appear and you can print immediately if your printer is connected by clicking on the OK button. This will print your document using the printer's default settings. These are the standard settings which establish factors such as the number of copies, which pages to print if your document is longer than a single page, orientation of the paper (i.e. portrait or landscape) and quality of the printing. In many cases the defaults produce a perfectly acceptable printed document.

13 Print your short document using the default settings. Repeat the printing actions until you are confident you understand the process.

14 Close Microsoft® Word by selecting the **File** menu and the **Exit** option.

Figure 1.27 Saving several files with different names

Spell Checking

Microsoft® Word provides you with a function to check your spelling and grammar. This is carried out by selecting the **Tools** menu and **Spelling and Grammar** option. This opens the Spelling and Grammar window. In the window are displayed mistakes and suggested corrections that you are asked to decide on. You can choose to ignore them or accept the change.

The Spell Checker is often selected to work automatically when you are creating a document. In this case the word processor underlines words and phrases with either red or green lines. Red indicates a spelling mistake while green shows a grammatical error.

Spell checkers have limitations. They can only detect spelling mistakes. If you have used the wrong word but spelt it correctly then it will not be identified (e.g. see and sea; fill and full, and so and sow). It is therefore important not to rely only on the spelling checker but also to proofread your documents.

Retrieving a file

Once you have saved a file, you can use the application you used to create it to retrieve it in order to print extra copies or change its contents.

Exercise 13

Retrieving a file

1. Open Microsoft® Word by clicking on Start, highlighting All Programs and single clicking on Microsoft® Word. The application will open. Maximise the window using the control buttons in the top right hand corner of the window if the display does not fill the screen. Insert your floppy disk into the drive.

2. Select File menu and Open option. This will reveal the Open window. Choose 3½ Floppy (A:) disk by using the down arrow button at the end of the Look in box. This should reveal the files stored on your floppy disk (Figure 1.28).

3. Highlight the file you want to retrieve by single clicking on it. Click on the Open button and you will see the contents of the file appear in the Microsoft® Word working area.

4. Close the application by selecting the File menu and the Exit option.

5. Repeat this exercise until you are confident that you can retrieve files.

Figure 1.28 Open window

Exercise 14

Introducing editing

1. Load Microsoft® Word by selecting the Start button, highlighting the All Programs option and clicking on the Microsoft® Word item or by double clicking on the Microsoft® Word icon on the desktop.

2. Using the keyboard, type:

   Titan is the largest satellite of Saturn and was discovered by Christiaan Huygens in 1655. It is a large moon with a radius of 2575 km and is the largest moon in the solar system. Titan has a nitrogen and methane-rich atmosphere. This makes observing the surface of the satellite difficult. The Voyager spacecrafts used a variety of methods to investigate Titan. These suggest that Titan has an atmospheric pressure greater than the Earth and possibly has methane clouds which rain ethane.

3. Observe that the text starts a new line when it needs to without your doing anything. This is called word wrapping. If you have been trained as a typist it can often be difficult to stop yourself trying to create a new line.

continued

4. Move your mouse pointer to the start of the text on the T of Titan. Click there and you will see that the cursor (flashing line) has moved to the start of the text. If you enter text now it will appear at the cursor. This is the way you insert text into a document. If you press the Enter key you will create a new line. Press the Enter key twice and using the up arrow key on the keyboard move up the two lines you have just created. Enter the word Titan and you will have added a heading to your passage. The Enter key is sometimes known as the Return key.

The text will look similar to Figure 1.29. Do not worry if in your work area you are not able to get the same number of words per line as in the example. This is a result of the settings within the word processor which you can change later.

5. When entering text you will sometimes make a mistake. It is therefore important to always proofread any text that you enter in order to remove errors.

Figure 1.29 Text

6. There are two main ways to remove or delete text. Using the above example, the cursor should be flashing at the end of Titan. If you press the Backspace key then the cursor moves left and deletes the last character. If you continue to tap the key, you can delete your entry.

7. The other way to remove text is to use the Delete key which is located in the bottom-right corner of the keyboard near the number pad. The Delete key works by removing the characters to the right of the cursor.

8. Enter Titan again to replace your heading.

9. We will now save this passage on to a floppy disk as the file Titan. This procedure is the same as in Exercise 12 (i.e. insert a floppy disk into drive A: and select the `File` menu and click on the `Save` option to open the Save As window).

10. You can close Microsoft® Word now by clicking on the `File` menu item and selecting the option `Exit`. An alternative way is to click on the Close button on the top right-hand corner of the application window.

Manipulating text

In Exercise 14 you typed a short passage and saved it to your floppy disk. Microsoft® Word and other word processors provide you with tools to insert, delete, move and replace text. There are three tools called Cut, Copy and Paste which are especially useful. They are available on the

Figure 1.30 Standard toolbar

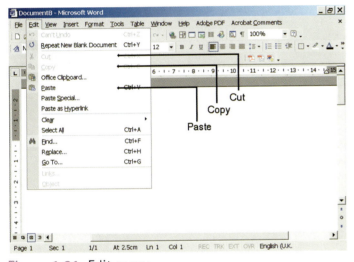

Figure 1.31 Edit menu

standard toolbar (Figure 1.30) and on the Edit menu (Figure 1.31). You can choose either option.

The three tools operate in similar ways:

The first step is to highlight the text you want to manipulate. To do this, you move your pointer to the start of the text you want to work on and click, holding down the mouse button and moving the pointer over the words that you want to manipulate. You will see them highlighted (i.e. the background colour changes). When you have highlighted all the words you need, release the mouse button. If you have made an error simply click the mouse away from the highlighted area and the highlighting will disappear so you can try again.

An alternative way of highlighting a line or a paragraph is to move the pointer into the page margin next to a line of text and it will change into an arrow shape. If you click the mouse when the pointer is arrow-shaped then the whole line will be highlighted. If you hold down the left button when the pointer is arrow-shaped then as you move the pointer you will continue to highlight the text. In this way you can highlight a whole passage.

If you click on the Copy tool or the menu option, the text you have highlighted will be copied to a special area of the computer's memory – the Clipboard. You can now paste it in another part of the passage. This process does not change the original text. You add the copied text by pointing to where you want to place it and clicking there. The cursor is now at the new location. If you then click on the Paste tool or the menu option, the highlighted text is inserted into the new location. You can see that the Copy and Paste tools work together. You cannot paste until you have copied.

The Cut tool or the menu option works in the same way but with the difference that when you select Cut, the highlighted text is removed.

An alternative to Cut is to highlight the text, release the left mouse button then hold it down again. You can then drag the words to a new location using the mouse pointer.

A common error when moving text is to leave behind a full stop or comma. It is always important to check that you have copied or cut the text you intended and have not left behind any parts of it.

The standard toolbar contains two important tools for when you make an error – Undo and Redo (Figure 1.30). If you make a mistake you can reverse it by clicking on Undo. If you make an error when using undo then you can turn the clock back with Redo. We will practise these functions in the next exercise along with Cut, Copy and Paste.

Printing

Printing documents is an important function of a word processor. However, it is important to always proofread your documents to ensure they are free of mistakes before printing them. Microsoft® Word offers a range of functions linked to printing, including an option to preview your text as a printed document without wasting any paper. Within the File menu, Print Preview opens up the window shown in Figure 1.32. This allows you to check if the document is presented in the way that you want it to be. When you have completed the preview, click on the Close button to return to the document.

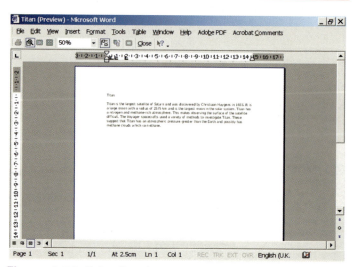

Figure 1.32 Print Preview

When you are ready to print, click on the File menu then choose the Print option to open the Print window (Figure 1.33).

You must first select the printer on which your document is to be printed. This is shown in the Printer area at the top of the window in the box entitled Name. The Microsoft® Windows® operating system allows you to link several printers to a single stand-alone computer. The list of printers is shown when you click on the down arrow next to the Name box. You select your printer by clicking on it.

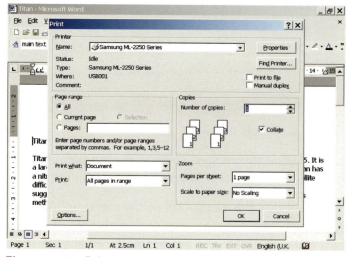

Figure 1.33 Print

You can choose what you want to print.

- All – whole document
- Current page – only the page on which your cursor is flashing
- Pages – you enter the page range you want to print (e.g. 23–34)
- Number of copies – how many copies you want to print

When you are ready you click on the OK button to start the printer.

Exercise 15

Manipulating and printing text

1 In Exercise 14 you saved a file called Titan. We are now going to load this file into Microsoft® Word.

2 Load Microsoft® Word either by selecting the **Start** button, highlighting the **All Programs** option and clicking on the **Microsoft® Word** item or by clicking on the **Microsoft® Word** icon on the desktop.

3 You can load a file by single clicking on the **File** menu item to open up the menu which has an option called **Open**. Click on **Open** and a window called Open will appear (Figure 1.28). An alternative approach is to click on the open icon on the standard toolbar (Figure 1.30).

4 The **Look in** box tells you what drive the window is looking at. You need to aim it at the 3½ Floppy (A:). You do this by clicking on the small button with the down arrow at the end of the **Look in** box. A menu will appear. Click on the 3½ Floppy (A:) option and the details of the Titan file will appear in the main working area. To open the file, click once on the file to highlight it and then on the open button on the right-hand side of the window. An alternative way is to double click on the Titan file. In either case the text of the file should now appear in the working area of Microsoft® Word.

5 Enter the following text as new paragraphs below the previous text.

The Voyager spacecraft were not simply on a mission to survey Titan. They were taking advantage of the outer planets (e.g. Jupiter, Saturn, Neptune and Uranus) being aligned in the 1970s so that it was possible to visit several in one space trip. Two Voyager spacecraft were launched a few weeks apart in 1977.

The Voyager-1 was to fly past Jupiter, Saturn and their moons while Voyager 2 was to visit Jupiter, Saturn, Uranus and Neptune and their moons. Both spacecraft had two cameras and took thousands of digital photographs of the outer planets and their satellites. The pictures were sent to Earth as radio signals containing the digital information.

6 Practise using the **Undo** and **Redo** icons so that you become familiar with how they work.

7 Practise using the Delete and Backspace keys. Remember that the Delete key removes text to the right while the Backspace key removes text to the left.

8 When you are confident about Undo, Redo, Delete and Backspace then attempt these tasks:

   a) Highlight

The Voyager spacecraft were not simply on a mission to survey Titan.

This is achieved by positioning the mouse pointer immediately in front of the 'The' and holding down the left mouse button then moving the pointer over the sentence until it is all highlighted (i.e. background changes colour). You will see the sentence gradually highlight as you move over the text. Remember, do not forget to highlight the full stop.

continued

b) Copy

With the sentence highlighted then click on the Copy icon. (If you place your mouse pointer over the copy icon you will see it animate and a small label will appear telling you it is the copy icon. This works with all the icons to help you identify their different functions.) You can also copy the text using the Edit menu which includes the Cut, Copy and Paste functions. When you click on Copy nothing will change and the sentence will remain highlighted.

c) Paste

To paste the text you have copied (i.e. the sentence highlighted) you need to move the mouse pointer to where you want to copy the text to. In this case move your pointer to the end of the passage and click once and you will see the cursor flashing in the new position and the highlighting will disappear. Now click on the Paste icon and you will see the sentence appear at the end of the passage (Figure 1.34).

9 If you click on the Undo icon the pasted text will be removed and you can practise pasting again. Continue copying and pasting until you feel confident.

10 Now try the Cut function.

a) Highlight the sentence below:

The pictures were sent to Earth as radio signals containing the digital information.

Figure 1.34 Paste

b) Cut

Click on the Cut icon and the sentence will disappear. You have not lost the text. It is simply saved to a special area of the memory called the Clipboard. Copied text is also saved here. Normally you can only paste the last item you have cut or copied. The clipboard does hold up to twelve items but to paste them you need to use the clipboard toolbar (select the Edit menu and then click on Office Clipboard to reveal the Clipboard window). Figure 1.35 shows the contents of the clipboard).

c) Paste

Position your cursor at the location you would like to

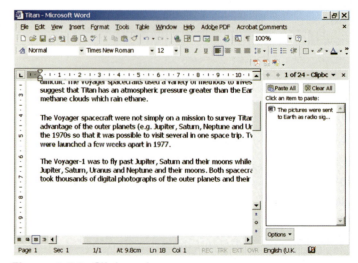

Figure 1.35 Clipboard

continued

paste the cut text to by clicking once. If you click on the Paste icon then the text will now appear at the new position.

An alternative to using Cut is to employ the drag and drop technique. If you highlight the text you want to move and then click on it and hold down the mouse button you can drag the text to a new position. The pointer changes during the move to provide a guide bar to accurately position the text.

11 Practise using the Copy, Cut and Paste functions. If you use Undo, Redo, Delete and Backspace functions you will be able to return to the original passage.

12 Practise using the drag and drop technique. If you use the Undo function you will be able to return to the original passage.

13 When you have finished save your text to the floppy disk. The file should be called New Titan.

14 Print your text after proofreading it and checking its appearance using the Print Preview option in the File menu.

15 You can close Microsoft® Word now by clicking on the File menu item and selecting the option Exit. An alternative way is to click on the Close button on the top right-hand corner of the application window.

Tables

Microsoft® Word can help you to insert tables of information into your document. The Table functions are located in the Table menu. If you highlight the Insert option then a menu is revealed which includes the Table option. If you select the Table option then the Insert Table window appears. This allows you to chose the number of rows and columns your table will contain. Figure 1.36 shows the Insert Table window.

Alternatively you can select the Insert Table icon on the Standard toolbar. This opens a grid of rows and columns. You need to highlight the number of rows and columns that you want in your table by moving your pointer over the cells.

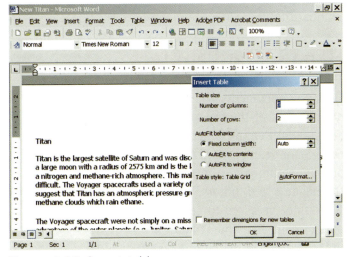

Figure 1.36 Insert table

Borders and shading

Microsoft® Word provides you with functions to enclose your documents or parts of them in a wide variety of borders. You can also shade your text to make it stand out. These functions are designed to help you produce quality documents but overuse of them can lead to the opposite effect. Shading is effective if the contrast between the text and background colours is sharp but if the colours chosen do not sufficiently contrast then the text can be difficult to read. Readability depends to a large extent on the degree of contrast between the colours.

The Borders and Shading option can be found in the Format menu and when it is selected the Borders and Shading window is opened (Figure 1.37). Across the top are three tabs – Borders , Page Border and Shading . The first tab provides a variety of ways of enclosing text while the third offers ways of shading text (Figure 1.38).

Alternatively you can select the Tables and Borders icon on the Standard toolbar.

Figure 1.37 Borders and shading

Figure 1.38 Shading

Headers and footers

On many documents you will have noticed that at the top and bottom are standard words which appear on every page (e.g. authors name, date and page numbers). These are called the headers and footers. You will sometimes be asked to add them as part of your assessment tasks in order to identify the work as your own.

If you select the View menu and the Header and Footer option then an

Figure 1.39 Header and Footer

area enclosed in a dashed line will appear at the top and bottom of your page with a toolbar containing a range of tools (Figure 1.39). Your page of text has a faded appearance. You can enter text from the keyboard into the dashed area or use the tools to insert items (e.g. date and filenames).

The tool Insert AutoText provides a range of items that you can enter into the header or footer such as Author, Page and Date.

Bullets and numbering

Microsoft® Word provides a variety of ways of producing lists. You can have many different sorts of bullets and numbers using the Bullets and Numbering option within the Format menu. This displays the Bullets and Numbering window (Figure 1.40) which has four tabs across the top – Bulleted, Numbered, Outline Numbered and List Styles. The first offers you a choice of different bullets and if you select the Pictures button in the bottom right corner then more graphic bullets are offered. The second tab offers a selection of numbers including alphabetical and employing brackets. The third tab provides access to more complex numbering and bullet systems and the fourth offers a range of list styles.

Alternatively you can choose the Numbering and Bullets icons on the Formatting toolbar.

Figure 1.40 Bullets and Numbering

Word count

When writing, you will often want to achieve a specific length of document. If you are studying then assignments are often limited to a precise length (e.g. no more than 1000 words). Microsoft® Word lets you count the words within a document by selecting the Tools menu and the Word Count option. This opens the Word Count window. Figure 1.41 shows the number of pages, words, characters and lines for the whole document or a highlighted section. If you highlight a section, the word count will focus only on that area.

Figure 1.41 Word count

Exercise 16

Tables, bullets, borders and shading

1. In Exercise 15 you saved a file called New Titan. We are now going to load this file into Microsoft® Word.

2. Load Microsoft® Word either by selecting the Start button, highlighting the All Programs option and clicking on the Microsoft® Word item or by clicking on the Microsoft® Word icon on the desktop.

3. You can load a file by single clicking on the File menu item to open up the menu which has an option called Open. Click on Open and a window called Open will appear (Figure 1.28). An alternative approach is to click on the open icon on the standard toolbar (Figure 1.30).

4. The Look in box tells you what drive the window is looking at. You need to aim it at the floppy disk. You do this by clicking on the small button with the down arrow at the end of the Look in box. A menu will appear. Click on 3½ Floppy (A:) and the details of the New Titan file will appear in the main working area. To open the file, click once on the file to highlight it and then on the open button on the right-hand side of the window. An alternative way is to double click on the New Titan file. In either case the text of the file will now appear in the working area of Microsoft® Word.

5. Enter the introductory text and table below at the end of the passage (select the Table menu, highlight the Insert option and click on the Table option).

   The four main moons of Saturn are shown below.

Moons	Size (radius)
Titan	2600
Rhea	760
Iapetus	730
Dione	560

6. Highlight the table and select the Format menu and the Borders and Shading option to display the window. Select the triple line style. Notice that the preview changes to show you what effect it will have on the table. Figure 1.42 shows the table with triple line style applied.

7. Explore some other borders for the table. Try highlighting a paragraph and enclosing it in a border.

8. Highlight the title Titan and select the Borders and Shading window then the Shading tab. Choose a colour to shade the title. I selected red. Now highlight the second paragraph and shade it another colour. I selected yellow.

9. An alternative way of displaying the information about the four largest moons of Saturn is a list. Highlight the table and select the Table menu, highlight the Delete option and

continued

click on Table. The table will be removed. Place your cursor one line below – The four main moons of Saturn are shown. Now select the Format menu and the Bullets and Numbering option to open the window. Choose the Bulleted tab and any of the bullets that you prefer. After the bullet enter the name of the moon and then press return. A new bullet will appear on the line below. Figure 1.43 shows the results of the bullets.

10 Now save your file with the name New Titan Extra.

11 The next step is to give the new document a header and footer. Select the View file and the Header and Footer option. The header dashed area and the toolbar will appear. Click on the Insert AutoText down arrow and a list of options will appear. Select the Author, Page, Date item. You should see that they appear in the header (Figure 1.44). Now scroll down the page and you will see a dashed area at the bottom for the footer. Click inside the area and select Insert AutoText and choose Filename: New Titan Extra.

12 The next step is to use the Word Count function to measure how many words are in your passage. Finally check your document for errors by proofreading it.

Figure 1.42 Triple line style

Figure 1.43 Bullets

Figure 1.44 Headers and Footers

continued

13 When you have finished, save your file on to the floppy disk and print your document (remember to use `Print Preview` to check before printing).

14 You can close Microsoft® Word now by clicking on the `File` menu item and selecting the option `Exit`. An alternative way is to click on the `Close` button on the top right-hand corner of the application window.

Replacing words and phrases

Obviously you can replace a word or phrase by simply deleting what you wish to replace and entering the new word or phrase. However, Microsoft® Word provides an automatic way to find and replace a word or a phrase. This is available within the `Edit` menu (Figure 1.31) as the `Replace` option. If you select this option by clicking on it then the window shown in Figure 1.45 will appear.

Type the text you want to replace in the `Find what` box and the replacement text in the `Replace with` box. The function will search for the text and either automatically replace it throughout the document (`Replace All`) or allow you to select which ones to change (`Replace`). You can just search for the text in the `Find what` box by clicking on the `Find Next` button.

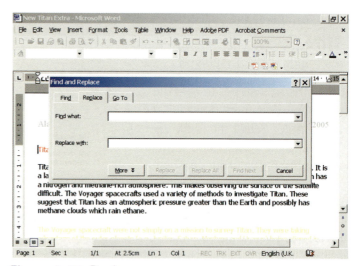

Figure 1.45 Replace

Appearance and layout

Word processors (e.g. Microsoft® Word) have many functions that allow you to change the layout and presentation of text. These include altering the margins, changing the line spacing, aligning (justifying) the text and emphasising words, phrases or whole passages. When you enter a passage of text there is no need to get the appearance right first time since these functions let you change it until you are satisfied.

Many organisations have a house style or a standard way of presenting their letters, documents and reports. This can take many forms but often it involves the use of a limited number of fonts and character sizes, leaving a space after each comma, two spaces after a full stop and using only main headings and one layer of sub-headings. This is intended to provide a common look and feel to all documents from an organisation. If you begin working for a new organisation it is important to know if they employ a house style.

Margins

The margins of a word processor document are controlled by the Page Setup item under the File menu. If you click on File and then on Page Setup, the window shown in Figure 1.46 will be opened.

Figure 1.46 shows you that you can change all four margins (i.e. Top, Bottom, Left and Right). You change the settings for each margin by clicking on the up or down arrow buttons. As you change the margin you can see the overall effect on your document by watching the Preview area. The changes take effect as soon as you click the OK button. If you make a mistake you can always use the Undo icon to reverse the changes.

The Page Setup window also provides access to functions that allow you to select the orientation of the the page. Figure 1.46 shows the choice between landscape and portrait orientation of the page. You select the orientation by clicking on your choice.

Figure 1.46 Page Setup

Line spacing

Word processors let you adjust the line spacing of your document, for example you could double space either a single paragraph or a whole document. The line spacing functions are provided within the Paragraph option of the Format menu. When you click on the Paragraph option, the window shown in Figure 1.47 will appear. Towards the middle of the window you will see the Line spacing box which, if you click on the down arrow at the end of the box, will display a range of options. These are selected by clicking on the one you want. When you enter text it will follow the new line spacing. To change existing text you need to first highlight the material you want to alter.

Figure 1.47 Paragraph

Tabs and indents

When you are writing you may want to indent text (e.g. at the start of a new paragraph) to provide emphasis or provide a visual clue for your readers. The Paragraph window (Figure 1.47) provides you with the means of controlling indents.

The Tab key on the keyboard allows you to indent text. The size of a tab (i.e. single press of the key – called a tab stop) is set by the Tabs option within the Format menu which opens the tab window. This controls size and justification of tabs. Figure 1.48 shows the Tab window.

Figure 1.48 Tabs

Inserting a new paragraph

To add a new paragraph break you need to position the cursor by clicking with the mouse pointer at the desired position and then press the Enter key twice. The first key press moves the start of the new paragraph to the next line while the second press inserts a blank line between the paragraphs.

Emphasise text

Microsoft® Word provides you with a range of tools to emphasise your words. These include:

- changing the font and character size of your text
- emboldening your words
- underlining your words
- changing your text into italics

These functions are available on the Formatting toolbar (Figure 1.49) and also in the Format menu (Figure 1.50) within the Font item. If you select one of the toolbar options it will change to indicate that it is active and that everything you now enter is in the emphasised form (e.g. underlined). You need to click on the option a second time to deselect it. It can also be used to change existing text. The normal process of changing text, from a single character to a

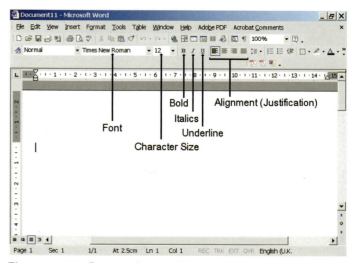

Figure 1.49 Formatting toolbar

whole document, is to highlight your selection and then choose the function's icon or menu option.

Alignment

There are four ways of aligning a document. These are:

- Left – the left text edge is parallel with the margin and the right is ragged
- Right – the right text edge is parallel with the margin and the left is ragged
- Centred – text is aligned down the centre of the page with both edges ragged
- Justified – both left and right text edges are parallel with the margins

Figure 1.50 Format menu

Alignment functions are provided in the Paragraph option (Figure 1.47) of the Format menu (Figure 1.50) and on the Formatting toolbar (Figure 1.49). If you select one of the toolbar options it will change to indicate it is active and then everything you now enter will be in new line alignment (e.g. centred). You need to click on the option a second time to deselect it. The process can be used to change existing text by highlighting the section and selecting the desired alignment icon or menu option.

Exercise 17

Appearance and layout

1 Load Microsoft® Word either by selecting the Start button, highlighting the All Programs option and clicking on the Microsoft® Word item or by double clicking on the Microsoft® Word icon on the desktop.

2 Enter the passage below in Times New Roman and character size 12.

(Hint – select the font and character size from the Formatting toolbar before entering text.)

Invasion of Russia

In 1812 Napoleon invaded Russia with one of the largest armies that had ever been assembled. Over 600,000 men had been brought together from all parts of Europe that formed the French Empire. Italians, Dutch, Belgians, Germans and Frenchmen marched across the frontier and the vast majority never returned. It was 700 miles to Moscow and the army had to march across a desolate landscape of forest and marsh where villages were days apart.

continued

> In past campaigns French armies had relied upon living off the countries they had attacked. Russia was not a rich land and a large force would not be able to subsist from pillage. The French knew that they could not use their old tactics so they had gathered stores to transport into Russia. Each soldier was heavily loaded with flour, bread, rice and biscuits to last many days. The army staff had planned to transport huge quantities of supplies to last through the normal fast and furious French assault to knock out the Russian armies.
>
> Napoleon's army entered Moscow less than three months later having fought several major and minor battles but it had not destroyed the Russian army. In past campaigns the occupation of the capital city had followed the destruction of the opposing army. It was not long before the French army had to retreat through winter weather with a supply system that had completely failed.

3 Save the passage on your floppy disk with the filename Invasion (there is a `Save` icon on the Standard toolbar – a picture of a floppy disk – or select the `File` menu and the `Save` option). It is good practice to save your text as soon as you can and then to update the file as you make changes. When you select `Save` later you will not be shown the Save As window since the application assumes that you simply want to update your original file. If you want to save the altered text as a different file you need to select the `Save As` option in `File` menu. The procedure is then the same as you earlier undertook for saving a new file.

The `Save As` option also serves the purpose of allowing you to change the file name of your document. This is useful if you want to create a master document for a whole series of publications or if you want to keep copies of the document at the different stages of its development.

4 Select the `File` menu and the `Page Setup` option to change the margins of your documents so that:

- left and right are 3 cm
- top and bottom are 3.5 cm

5 Change the line spacing to 1.5 by highlighting the text and selecting the `Format` menu and the `Paragraph` option.

6 Change the title Invasion of Russia so that it is in the Arial font and in character size 14 and embolden the text (i.e. highlight the text, choose the Arial font, the character size and bold option on the Formatting toolbar).

7 Change the alignment of the title to centred (i.e. highlight the title and select the `Center` icon on the Formatting toolbar).

8 Change the alignment of the rest of the passage to justified. Highlight the text and select the `Justify` icon on the Formatting Toolbar.

9 Insert a new paragraph at

> Each soldier was heavily loaded with flour, bread, rice and biscuits to last many days.

> **continued**
>
> Position your cursor before 'Each' and press Enter twice to break the text and insert a blank line between the paragraphs.
>
> 10 Remember to save your finished text and print the document (select the File menu, Print Preview and the Print icon). Check that the text is correct and correct any errors.
>
> 11 Close Microsoft® Word by selecting the File menu and the Exit option or use the Close button on the top right-hand corner of the window).

Templates

Many organisations base their correspondence and other documents on templates. These are standard documents in which the structure and layout is determined centrally. Users enter the content of the document but the rest is predetermined. This is to allow the organisation to present a consistent look and feel to the wider world. It allows the quality of documents to be more easily maintained.

Templates can be created to meet any document need such as:

- Letters
- Faxes
- Reports
- Minutes of meetings

To create a template you need to select the File menu and the New option to reveal the New Document area to the right of the work area. Select the General Templates item in the New from template section. This will open the Templates window. This has many tabs across the top. If you choose Letters & Faxes then a range of templates provided by Microsoft® Word are displayed (Figure 1.51). You can also create your own by selecting a document, clicking on the Template button in the area Create New in the bottom right-hand corner of the window and on the OK button. You can amend the templates provided by Microsoft® Word or create new ones.

Figure 1.51 Template

Changing a password

Computer security is extremely important for both office and home users. In the office, making sure systems are secure through the use of passwords is important for protecting data from unauthorised access. At home, although you may not have data that you wish to keep secret, good security protects against misuse, be it accidental or malicious. Viruses are a continuous threat to all computers so that it is vital to ensure access to them is controlled. It requires a major effort to remove a virus infection and can result in a considerable loss in data, waste a large amount of your time and require technical assistance to remove. It is now established practice to maintain virus protection systems and an important part of this is to regulate access through passwords.

Microsoft® Windows® and many other suppliers offer a wide range of security systems. Whatever security software you use it is important to understand the need to use original passwords and to change them regularly. Try not to use your name or anything obvious. Good practice is to pick a word at random from a dictionary and add some numbers either within or at the end of the word, or to use a completely random series of numbers and letters.

To change your Windows® password you need to access the Control Panel. This involves clicking on the Start button and clicking on Control Panel to reveal the Control Panel window. In this window there is an icon called User Accounts (shown as two people). When you click on this icon it will open the User Accounts window (Figure 1.52). This allows you to:

- Change an account
- Create a new account
- Change the way users log on and off

Each user has their own account. If you click on Create a New Account

Figure 1.52 User accounts

Figure 1.53 Alice's account

Figure 1.54 Create password

then you can add a new user to the computer system by following the sequence of choices. Alice is a new user and if you click on her name then her User Account appears (Figure 1.53) which allows you to create her password (Figure 1.54).

Other Control Panel options

The Control Panel provides ways of changing system settings. You can adjust:

- the sound volume of your system by selecting the Sounds and Audio Devices icon to display the Sounds and Audio Devices Properties window
- the date and time of the system by selecting the Date and Time icon to reveal the Date and Time Properties window

You can alter various other settings such as adjusting the display, mouse, keyboard and printers.

Screen prints

Windows provides you with a standard function to capture an image of the screen display (i.e. a screen print). This is available from the keyboard by pressing the PrtScr key. You can then open a blank document and use the Paste option to insert the image into a document. As part of the New CLAiT assessment you will occasionally be asked to use screen print to provide evidence of your work. It is therefore worth practising.

Safe working practice

There are a number of straightforward actions you can take to reduce the risk of injuring yourself when you are using a computer. One of the key problems is Repetitive Strain Injury (RSI) in which, by using the computer incorrectly, you place a strain on your body (e.g. hands, wrists and arms) which may result in permanent harm.

Some straightforward good practices include:

Space

It is important to give yourself plenty of space. You must have plenty of room for your legs and body. There should be enough space around the computer for your papers and books so that you can reach them without stretching. You can use a paper stand to hold your papers to help you copy text without turning. You should be comfortable. Even a tiny need to twist or turn your body can be harmful over a long period.

Breaks

It is good practice to take regular breaks away from the computer.

Chairs

Your chair should be adjustable so that you can alter the height and backrest. It should support your lower back. Your feet should either be placed squarely on the floor or on a foot rest with your knees slightly higher than the chair to ensure good circulation of blood. Again it is important to be comfortable.

Your eyes should be aligned slightly below the top of the monitor and you should be positioned about 45 cm from the display.

Reduce strain

When you are using the computer you must avoid placing any strain on hands and wrists by:

- keeping your wrists straight while typing (e.g. by using a rest)
- not resting on your wrists
- typing gently without excessive force
- taking frequent breaks and avoiding typing for long periods

Light

Computer monitors are very susceptible to reflection. It is therefore important to position your screen so it does not reflect light from the sun or the room lights. You will probably need to experiment. Monitors and other types of screen are normally designed to allow you to change their angle and their brightness and contrast.

Cables

Because computers often have a large number of cables near them to link them to other equipment, there is always a risk of tripping over them. It is good practice to inspect the general area around your computer to identify and remove any risks.

Shortcuts

You may have observed that when you are using Microsoft® Windows® or an application some of the menu options have a letter underlined. This is a keyboard shortcut. They provide you with an alternative way of selecting the option other than clicking on the option with the mouse pointer. You press the Alt key and, holding it down, press the letter that is underlined (e.g. **File**). This has the same effect as clicking on the option. It is useful if you are entering text as you can therefore select the option without taking your hands away from the keyboard.

Help

Microsoft® Windows® has a help function, accessed by selecting the **Start** button and clicking on the **Help and Support** option. The Help and Support Center window will

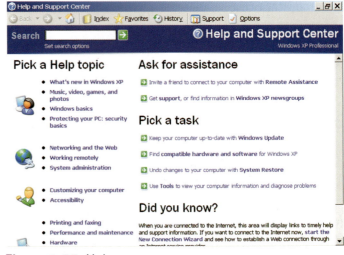

Figure 1.55 Help

appear (Figure 1.55). This provides help with many topics (e.g. What's new in Windows® XP) and ways of gaining assistance. You may wish to explore the topics. Click on the options which will reveal sub-topics and so on. You can return to the original display by clicking on the <mark>Back</mark> button in the left-hand top corner.

More practice

Activity 1

1. Load Microsoft® Word either by selecting the <mark>Start</mark> button, highlighting the <mark>All Programs</mark> option and clicking on the <mark>Microsoft® Word</mark> item or by clicking on the <mark>Microsoft® Word</mark> icon on the desktop.

2. Enter the passage below in Tahoma font and character size 10 by selecting the font and character size from the Formatting toolbar before entering text.

3. Set the margins as follows (<mark>File</mark> menu, <mark>Page Setup</mark> and <mark>Margins</mark> tab):

    Left and right – 4 cm
    Top and bottom – 3 cm

    The page orientation should be portrait.

    For many people guinea pigs are the perfect pet. They are small friendly animals who rarely bite and are easy to keep healthy. Guinea pigs are rodents and are not from Guinea so the name is a little misleading. They actually originate from Peru. There are several different breeds including Selfs which are smooth haired animals, Himalayans, Abyssinians and Crested.

    Guinea pigs are herbivores. They need to be given fresh vegetables every day since they cannot make their own vitamin C. Their teeth grow all the time so they need to be given food which they need to grind so that their teeth do not get too long. Dry food is available which has been enriched with vitamin C. Guinea pigs are enthusiastic about their food and will tell you when they are hungry. They will talk to you when you are late just to remind you they like their food on time.

    Guinea pigs can be kept indoors or outdoors. If they are in an outside hutch they need to be secured against both the cold and the local cats. A frosty night can leave pigs very distressed while they have few defences against cats. Indoor animals need the opportunity to exercise in the open air in a run or other secure enclosure. All guinea pigs love eating grass.

4. Create a header by selecting the <mark>View</mark> menu and the <mark>Header and Footer</mark> option. Enter your own name as the header and add a date to the footer and the file name Guinea Pig.

5. Once you have entered the text, carefully check it for mistakes and use the spell checker (<mark>Tools</mark> menu and <mark>Spelling and Grammar</mark> option) to ensure it is free from spelling mistakes. Save the passage on your floppy disk as a file called Guinea Pig by selecting the <mark>File</mark> Menu and then <mark>Save</mark>.

6. Insert a title 'Guinea Pig – Cavies' separated by one blank line from the rest of the passage in Arial font and character size 14. (Use the mouse to move the cursor, select the font and character size from Formatting toolbar before entering the title.)

7 Underline the title by highlighting the text and selecting the `Underline` icon from the Formatting toolbar.

8 Insert a new paragraph so that it becomes the third one.

> These little animals enjoy each other's company so should be kept together. Female pigs are called sows and males are boars. The young animals are born with their eyes open and will be running around their hutch soon after birth. They are suckled by their mothers but will soon eat vegetables and can be separated from them within a few weeks.

9 Change the line spacing to double (by highlighting the passage, selecting the `Format` menu and the `Paragraph` option).

10 Change the alignment of the passage to Left (by highlighting the text and selecting the `Align Left` icon on the Formatting toolbar).

11 Replace 'guinea pigs' with 'guinea pigs (cavies)' throughout the passage – you should find six occurences (use the `Edit` menu and the `Replace` option). Proofread your final document to ensure it is free from mistakes.

12 Save your changed file (`File` menu and `Save` option or `Save` icon on the Standard toolbar).

13 Print your document by selecting the `File` menu, the `Print Preview` and `Print` options (or the print icon from within `Print Preview`).

14 Close Microsoft® Word (by selecting the `File` menu and the `Exit` option or click on the close button).

Activity 2

1 Create a folder called Hobbies on your floppy disk by clicking My Computer, choosing 3½ Floppy (A:), selecting the `File` menu, `New` and `Folder` options. Enter the name Hobbies to replace the New Folder title.

2 Create a sub-folder called Pets in the folder Hobbies by opening the folder and selecting `File` menu, `New` and `Folder` options. Enter the name Pets to replace New Folder title.

3 Create another sub-folder called Extra in the folder Hobbies.

4 Rename the folder Hobbies as your name (i.e. Alan Clarke) by highlighting the folder, selecting File menu and the Rename option.

5 Copy the file Guinea Pig from Activity 1 into the sub-folder Pets (highlight the file and `Copy` and `Paste`).

6 Delete the sub-folder Extra (highlight the file and select the `Delete` option from the `File` menu).

7 Take a screen print of the folder with your name (i.e. Alan Clarke) by pressing the Shift and PrtSc keys.

8 Take a screen print of the file Guinea Pig in the sub-folder Pets.

9 Paste your screen prints into a Microsoft® Word document.

10 Add a header and footer to your document and enter your name and date in the footer.

11 Save the document with the file name Screen Print to your floppy disk.

12 Print the document.

13 Close your files.

The screen print method is sometimes required as part of the assessment process to provide evidence that you have completed the tasks.

Activity 3

1. Load Microsoft® Word by selecting the **Start** button, highlighting the **All Programs** option and clicking on the **Microsoft® Word** item or by clicking on the **Microsoft® Word** icon on the desktop.
2. Enter the table below in Times New Roman font and character size 12 by selecting the font and character size from the Formatting toolbar before entering text.
3. Set the margins as follows (**File** menu, **Page Setup** and **Margins** tab):

    Left and right – 2 cm
    Top and bottom – 4 cm

    The page orientation should be portrait.

Event	Team A Points	Team B Points
100 metres	10	2
200 metres	6	6
110 hurdles	0	12
400 metres	4	8
800 metres	2	10

4. Once you have entered the text, carefully check it for mistakes and use the spell checker (**Tools** menu and **Spelling and Grammar** option) to ensure it is free from spelling mistakes.
5. Embolden the titles Event, Team A Points and Team B Points.
6. Centre the headings Team A Points and Team B Points.
7. All the remaining text and numbers should be left aligned.
8. Save the table on your floppy disk as a file called Results by selecting the **File** menu and **Save**.
9. Print your table by selecting the **File** menu, the **Print Preview** and **Print** options (or the **Print** icon from within **Print Preview**).
10. Close Microsoft® Word (by selecting the **File** menu and the **Exit** option or click on the **Close** button).

SUMMARY

1 **What is a computer?** A computer consists of two main components: hardware and software.

2 **Hardware:** The physical elements of the equipment that you can see when you look at a computer. These include a monitor, main box (containing Central Processing Unit), printer, keyboard and mouse.

3 **Software:** The instructions that controls the hardware. Software is divided into two main types: operating systems and applications.

4 **Serial, parallel and USB ports:** Ports are the means of connecting peripheral equipment to the main computer.

5 **DVD and CD-RW drives:** These are different types of drives which allow disks to be used with a computer. DVDs allow the computer to read very large amounts of information which are stored on the disc. DVDs are often used to hold the contents of an entire movie. CD-RW drives allow you to save information onto a special type of CD-ROM and to read the information stored on the disc.

6 **Memory stick:** A portable device that allows you to store files and folders by plugging it into a computer's USB port. They are also called flash and pen drives and even a dongle.

7 **Mouse:** The mouse enables you to carry out a series of actions including single clicking with left and right mouse buttons, double clicking and dragging and dropping.

8 **Keyboard:** The keyboard allows you to enter text and numbers into computer applications.

9 **Window controls:** In the top right-hand corner of the window are three control buttons. These are minimise, maximise and close.

10 **Storing files:** Information is stored on disks (i.e. floppy and hard disks) in the form of files which are placed in folders to help organise them. Files have different formats depending on the nature of the information they store (e.g. documents and images).

11 **Windows Explorer:** Explorer provides the functions to search the disks for files and folders. Other functions include deleting and renaming files.

12 **Search:** Click on the Start button and Search option to reveal the Search Results window.

13 **Accessories:** Windows® contains several applications which come bundled with the operating system. These include WordPad (word-processing), Paint and Calculator.

14 **Load Microsoft® Word:** Open Microsoft® Word either by clicking on the Start button, highlighting All Programs and single clicking on Microsoft® Word option or double clicking on the Microsoft® Word icon on the Windows® desktop.

15 **Insert text:** You must position the cursor where you need to insert the text. Move your mouse pointer to the new position and click there. The cursor will appear as a flashing line and you can now enter your text.

16 **Save**: Select the <mark>File</mark> menu and the <mark>Save</mark> option. The Save As window (dialog box) opens. Select location (<mark>Look in</mark> box) and name your file (<mark>File name</mark> box) then click on the <mark>Save</mark> button.

17 **Save As**: Select the <mark>File</mark> menu and the <mark>Save As</mark> option. The Save As window opens. Select location (<mark>Save in</mark> box) and name your file (<mark>File name</mark> box) then click on the <mark>Save</mark> button.

18 **Save a file on a floppy disk**: Insert a floppy disk into drive A: and click on the <mark>File</mark> menu and the <mark>Save</mark> option to reveal the Save As window. Select the drive (3½ Floppy (A:)) and enter a file name.

    Having saved a file once, you can update it by clicking on the <mark>File</mark> menu and <mark>Save</mark> without the <mark>Save As</mark> window appearing again. It simply overwrites the original file.

    An alternative is to click on the <mark>Save</mark> icon on the Standard toolbar to update the file.

19 **Close**: Click on the <mark>File</mark> menu item and the <mark>Exit</mark> option or click on the close button in the top right-hand corner of the application window.

20 **Delete text**: You have two different keys which both work from the position of your cursor.

    Backspace key – this removes text, character by character to the left of the cursor position

    Delete key – this removes text, character by character to the right of the cursor position

    There is also Undo and Redo. Undo removes the last action you have undertaken while Redo carries out actions removed by Undo.

21 **Move text**: Highlight the text you want to move. Select either the Copy or Cut icons on the Standard toolbar or alternatively the <mark>Edit</mark> menu and the <mark>Cut</mark> or <mark>Copy</mark> options. Reposition the cursor at the place you want to move the text to and then select the <mark>Paste</mark> icon on the Standard toolbar or the <mark>Edit</mark> Menu and the <mark>Paste</mark> option.

22 **Drag and drop**: Highlight the text. Click on it and hold down the mouse button. Drag the text to the new position using the mouse. The pointer changes during the move to provide a guide bar to position the text accurately.

23 **Tables**: Use the <mark>Table</mark> menu, highlight the <mark>Insert</mark> option and <mark>Table</mark> option to open the Insert Table window.

24 **Borders and shading**: Select the <mark>Format</mark> menu and the <mark>Borders and Shading</mark> option to open the window with three tabs (<mark>Borders</mark>, <mark>Page Border</mark> and <mark>Shading</mark>) across the top.

25 **Headers and footers**: Use the <mark>View</mark> menu and the <mark>Header and Footer</mark> option.

26 **Bullets and numbering**: Use the <mark>Format</mark> menu and the <mark>Bullets and Numbering</mark> option.

27 **Word count**: Use the <mark>Tools</mark> menu and the <mark>Word Count</mark> option.

28 **Replace text**: Use the <mark>Edit</mark> menu and the <mark>Replace</mark> option to open the Replace window. Enter the text you want to replace in the <mark>Find</mark> what box and the replacement text in the <mark>Replace with</mark> box.

29. **Change margins**: Use the `File` menu and the `Page Setup` item to open the window which controls the four margins (i.e. left, right, top and bottom).

30. **Orientation**: Select the `File` menu and `Page Setup` option. This presents you with the choice between landscape and portrait orientation of the page.

31. **Line spacing**: Use the `Format` menu and the `Paragraph` option. The Paragraph window will open with the `Line spacing` function box.

32. **Alignment**: Select the `Format` menu and the `Paragraph` option or the Formatting toolbar.

    Select one of the toolbar options (Align Left, Align Right, Centered or Justify). It will change to show it is active and then everything you now enter will be in the new alignment. You need to click on the option a second time to deselect it.

    To change existing text, highlight it and then select the alignment icon or the menu option.

33. **Printing**: Select the `File` menu, click on the `Print` option and the OK button.

34. **Retrieve**: Select the `File` menu and the `Open` option. This will reveal the Open window. Choose the disk by using the down arrow button at the end of the `Look in` box and select the file to be retrieved.

35. **Change password**: Select the `Start` button and click on `Control Panel` to reveal the Control Panel window. Double click on the `Users and Passwords` icon.

36. **Safe working practice**: The straightforward issues to reduce the risk of harm are sufficient space, regular breaks, eliminating strain and reducing light reflections.

37. **Shortcuts**: Press the Alt key and, holding it down, press the letter that is underlined (e.g. `Edit`).

38. **Print screen**: Press the Alt and PrtSc keys. Paste the image of the screen into a Word document by opening a new document and selecting the `Edit` menu and `Paste` option.

39. **Help**: Select the `Start` button and click on the `Help and Support` option.

40. **Spell and grammar checker**: Select the `Tools` menu and `Spelling and Grammar` option. This opens the Spelling and Grammar window.

    The Spell Checker can be set work automatically so that spelling mistakes are undelined in red while green shows a grammatical error. It is always important to proofread text and not to rely only on the spell checker to identify mistakes.

Chapter 2

Unit 2

Creating spreadsheets and graphs

> This chapter will help you to use spreadsheets and charts and graphs applications. You will be able to:
>
> - identify and use a spreadsheet, including charts and graphs, correctly
> - use an input device to enter and edit data accurately
> - insert, replicate and format arithmetical formulas
> - use common numerical formatting and alignment
> - manage and print spreadsheets, charts and graphs
> - develop pie charts, line graphs and bar/column charts
> - select and present single and comparative sets of data
> - set numerical parameters and format data

Assessment

This unit does not assume any previous experience of spreadsheets. However, it may be useful to have studied Unit 1: File management and e-document production. You will be assessed through a practical realistic assignment which is designed to allow you to demonstrate your knowledge and skills against each objective. Your tutor can provide you with more guidance.

Spreadsheet applications

Figures 2.1 and 2.2 show Microsoft® Excel® XP. Figure 2.1 shows Microsoft® Excel® with the New Workbook task pane open. The task pane is intended to help you undertake some frequent tasks in this case to open an existing workbook (spreadsheet) or start a new one. If you prefer to have the task pane closed you need to select the Close button in the top right-hand corner of the task pane or select the View menu and the Task Pane option to remove the tick icon next to the option. To open the task pane then repeat the operation (i.e. View menu and Task Pane option to insert the tick).

Figure 2.2 shows that Microsoft® Excel® XP is similar to other Microsoft® Office applications in that it comprises a menu and toolbars (e.g. Standard toolbar), work area and a status bar at the bottom of the display. On the top right-hand corner are the three control buttons – Minimise,

Maximise and Close which are displayed in all Microsoft® application windows. However, there are some differences which are:

1. The work area is divided into a grid of rows and columns to form many individual cells. The active cell illustrated in Figure 2.2 is in row 1 and column A and is known as A1. When you are developing formulas it is important to identify particular cells and this is done by stating the column and row intersection.
2. At the bottom of the work area are tabs indicating Sheet 1, Sheet 2 and Sheet 3. These show which worksheet is being used and Microsoft® Excel® allows you to group sheets together to form a workbook. Figure 2.2 shows that Sheet 1 is being displayed.
3. Beneath the formatting toolbar is a row called the Formula Bar which shows A1 at the left-hand end followed by a grey area with the f_x symbol. A1 indicates the active cell and therefore changes as this moves. After the f_x symbol, any formulas which are in the active cell are displayed. We will discuss formulas later in this chapter.

There are several ways of loading an application such as Microsoft® Excel®. The two most common are using:

- the Start button
- the Microsoft® Excel® icon on the Microsoft® Windows® desktop

In the bottom left-hand corner of the Microsoft® Windows® desktop is a button called Start. This allows you to access various applications and standard features of the operating system. If you single click on Start, a menu will pop up. If you place the mouse pointer over the All Programs item it will become highlighted (i.e. the background will change colour) and a new menu will appear alongside. If you click on the item shown as Microsoft® Excel® then the application will load. In a similar way if you double click on the Microsoft® Excel® icon shown on the desktop then Excel® will similarly load.

The exercises included in the chapter are intended to help you understand how to use spreadsheets, graphs and charts. They are simplified examples that are not intended to be tutorials on accountancy but explanations of Microsoft® Excel®.

Figure 2.1 Microsoft® Excel® XP with task pane open

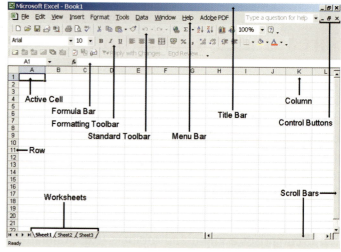

Figure 2.2 Microsoft® Excel® XP features

Exercise 18

Load and use Microsoft® Excel®

1 Load Microsoft® Excel® using either the **All Programs** menu or the **Microsoft® Excel** icon on the desktop.

2 Enter the table of information below to form your first spreadsheet. It shows a simple breakdown of the costs of operating the Acme Newsagent. Position your pointer in cell C3 and you will see the cell is highlighted by its borders becoming emboldened. Now enter Acme Newsagent. Repeat this entering Newspapers in B8, Groceries in B9, Stationery in B10, Wages in B11, Total in B12, Costs in C6, Overheads in D6 and Total Costs in E6. Now add the numeric cost data to form the column of figures in column C in rows 8, 9, 10 and 11.

Acme Newsagent			
	Costs	Overheads	Total Costs
Newspapers	12000		
Groceries	10000		
Stationery	8000		
Wages	6000		
Total			

3 To select an individual cell you need to click within it and it will be highlighted. However, you can also select a whole row or column. To select a row or column click in the letter (e.g. A) or number (e.g. 1) which is at the end of the row or the top of the column, respectively. The row or column will then be highlighted. To remove the highlighting you need to click in another part of the sheet.

4 If you make a mistake when entering text or numbers then you can delete the characters using the Backspace key. However, if you have moved to a new cell then you can either overwrite your original entry by clicking on the cell with the error and entering the correct text or numbers or edit the text as it appears on the formula bar. If you highlight the cell which contains the error you will see its contents appear in the formula bar and you use your mouse pointer to position your cursor in order to amend the text.

5 This table is perhaps a little crowded so you need to separate the rows with a blank row. Microsoft® Excel® allows you to insert new rows and columns. To insert a row, click on Groceries to tell Microsoft® Excel® where you want to insert the row (it is inserted above the row the cursor is in) and on the **Insert** menu (Figure 2.3) click the **Rows** item. A new row will be inserted between Groceries and Newspapers.

6 Now add a row between Groceries and Stationery, between Stationery and Wages, and, finally, between Wages and Total.

continued

7 Insert a column of information by highlighting column F and and then select the Insert menu (Figure 2.3) and then the Columns item. A new column will be created. Enter headings 'Income' in cell G6, and 'Total Profit' in cell H6 and the information shown in Figure 2.4. The menus in all Microsoft® Office applications are sometimes presented in a shortened form ending with two arrows. If you click on the arrows the reminder of the menu options are displayed.

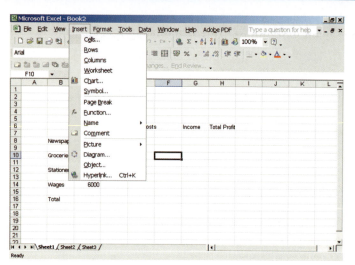

Figure 2.3 Insert menu

8 Save the spreadsheet you have created on to a floppy disk. This procedure is the same in all Microsoft® Windows® applications – you save a spreadsheet, database or graphic image in exactly the same way. Insert a floppy disk into drive A: and click on the File menu item and a menu will open showing a list of options. Select Save and a window will open.

Figure 2.4 Spreadsheet

9 Click in the box File name and enter A:\Acme Newsagent. Now click on the Save button on the right of the window. You have now saved the table as a file called Acme Newsagent. You may hear drive A: work during this process.

10 It is possible to save the spreadsheet again under a different file name so that you have two identical files. Because they have different file names, they are treated as individual files. In order to do this you need to select the File menu and the option Save As.

11 You can close Microsoft® Excel® by clicking on the File menu item. A menu will appear with a list of options. At the bottom of the list is the option Exit. If you click on Exit then Microsoft® Excel® will close. An alternative way is to click on the Close button in the top right-hand corner of the application window.

New

On occasions you will want to start a new spreadsheet once you have completed the one you have been working on. This is achieved by selecting the File menu and the New option. This opens the New Workbook task pane (Figure 2.1) which is divided into a number of sections. These provide access to many standard templates for spreadsheets. Select the Blank Workbook option. A new blank spreadsheet will appear.

Delete, clear and hide

Microsoft® Excel® provides three useful options linked to deleting the contents of cells, rows and columns. These are:

- Delete (Figure 2.5)
- Clear (Figure 2.5)
- Hide (Figure 2.6)

The first step in using the options above is to identify the row, column, cell or area of the spreadsheet by highlighting or placing the mouse pointer in the cell or row or column. The Edit menu provides access to the Delete and Clear options. If Delete is selected, then a small Delete window appears providing different options for removing the item. Delete permanently removes the item and adjusts the spreadsheet layout. If Clear is selected, then another menu of options appears (e.g. if All is chosen the contents of the selected area are removed but not the spreadsheet structure/layout).

Figure 2.5 Edit menu

The difference between Delete and Clear is that Delete removes the contents and the spreadsheet structure, while Clear simply removes the contents. Clear also provides some extra options such as removing the formatting of an entry while leaving contents behind. You would probably use Clear to amend an area in the heart of a spreadsheet and Delete if you wanted to start again.

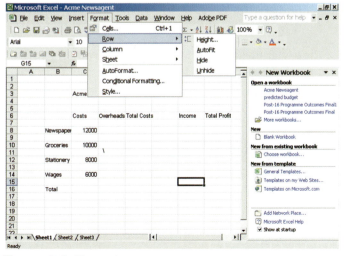

Figure 2.6 Format menu

The Hide function is accessed by selecting the Format menu, then the options Row, Column or Sheet (Figure 2.6). Again you identify the area you want to hide by highlighting or placing the mouse pointer in the particular row or column. By selecting Hide, that area of the spreadsheet will disappear. It can be returned by selecting the Unhide option. Hide does not delete the items, it only hides them from view: useful if you do not want to disclose confidential information.

Exercise 19

Delete, clear and hide

1. Load Microsoft® Excel® using either the All Programs menu or the Microsoft® Excel® icon on the desktop.

2. Enter the table of information below to form your first spreadsheet. It shows a family budget:

	January	February	March
Food and drink	300	320	270
Clothes	80	75	145
Travel	160	400	140
Leisure	60	110	95
Services	25	42	67
Council Tax	105	105	105

3. Save the spreadsheet you have created on to a floppy disk. Insert a floppy disk into drive A: and click on the File menu item and a menu will open showing a list of options. Select Save and a window will open.

4. Click in the box File name and Enter A:\Budget. Now click on the Save button on the right of the window. You have now saved the table as a file called Budget. You may hear drive A: work during this process.

5. If you make a wrong choice while working with the spreadsheet you can retrace your steps by using the Undo option in the Edit menu. This is also useful when you want to explore the effects of different options without making any permanent changes.

6. Explore the three options Delete, Clear and Hide. Highlight the February column (i.e. from the February title to 105) and then select the Delete option on the Edit menu. This opens a another menu with four options – Shift cells left is the default setting. Don't change the default just click on OK and notice what happens. You should observe that the column is deleted and the gap between January and March closes (i.e. the structure of the spreadsheet is removed).

7. Now select the Edit menu and Undo Delete and the column will reappear.

continued

8. Highlight the February column again and select the Edit menu and highlight Clear to reveal a menu with four options. Click on All. Observe what happens. The content disappears but the gap between January and March does not close (i.e. the structure is not removed).

9. Now select the Edit menu and Undo Clear and the content will reappear.

10. Select the Highlight February cell and select the Format menu and highlight the Column option to reveal a menu of five choices. Select the Hide option. Observe what happens. The column disappears and a line of highlighting is left between January and March.

11. Now select the Format menu and highlight the Column option to reveal the menu of options. Select the Unhide option and you will see the column reappear.

12. Explore the three options using Undo or Unhide to return to the original spreadsheet until you understand the different effects of Delete, Clear and Hide.

13. You can close Microsoft® Excel® now by clicking on the File menu item and a menu will appear with a list of options. At the bottom of the list is the option Exit. If you click on Exit then Microsoft® Excel® will close. An alternative way is to click on the Close button on the top right-hand corner of the application window

Spreadsheet formulas

Figure 2.7 shows a spreadsheet of the costs and income of the Acme Newsagent. This spreadsheet employs a number of formulas to:

- add up columns and rows of figures
- calculate overheads
- calculate the total profit of the business

Formulas are used by spreadsheets to calculate numerical values. They allow you to add up columns of figures to produce a total, subtract the contents of different cells, multiply, divide and undertake more complex calculations. One of the most important features of a spreadsheet is that you can build formulas within the sheet to calculate almost anything.

The mathematical operators used in Microsoft® Excel® are:

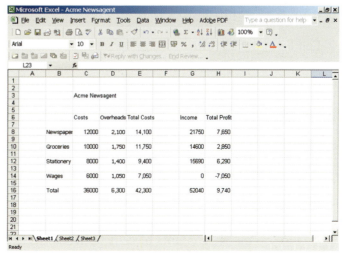

Figure 2.7 Acme Newsagent spreadsheet

- \+ add
- \- subtract
- * multiply
- / divide

Brackets are also important because they tell Microsoft® Excel® to calculate anything in the brackets first before going on with the remaining parts of the calculation.

Formulas are based on giving each cell a reference (e.g. A1, D12, M7, etc.) made up of the column letter and the row number.

Example

B8   Column B and Row 8

In Figure 2.7 you can see the column letters and row numbers. Cell C8 (Column C and Row 8) contains the number 12 000. To calculate overheads (i.e. contents of D8) of the newspapers this number needs to be multiplied by 0.175 which represents the current rate of overheads (17.5% or 0.175). The formula is C8*0.175 (i.e. contents of cell C8 multiplied by the overhead rate). By using a formula referring to the cell's unique address C8 then each time the number placed in the cell changes the new value of overheads is automatically calculated.

Example

C8 = 12000   D8 = 2100 (Overheads)
C8 = 8000   D8 = 1400 (Overheads)
C8 = 4000   D8 = 700 (Overheads)

It is possible to have formula based on the actual number so that our example overhead formula could be 12000 * 0.175. This would give the correct value but each time the cost of newspapers changed you would also need to change the formula.

Figure 2.7 shows four examples of formulas. These are:

1. Cell D8   =C8*0.175

   Overheads on newspapers are the cost of the newspapers (Cell C8) multiplied by 0.175 which produces 17.5% of the cost (the current rate of overheads). To avoid confusion with the letter x, spreadsheets use the symbol * as the multiplication sign.

2. Cell E8   =C8+D8

   To produce the total cost of newspapers requires the cost of the papers (C8) to be added to the Overheads (D8).

3. Cell H8   =G8-E8

   Total profit is income minus cost, so the profit on newspaper sales is the total income from the newspapers (cell G8) less their total cost (cell E8).

4. Cell C16   =SUM(C8:C14)

   To total or add up a column or row of figures, the Microsoft® Excel® spreadsheet provides a standard function called SUM. This function means that all the contents of cells between C8 to C14 are added together (i.e. C8+C9+C10+C11+C12+C13+C14).

These four examples show that a spreadsheet is able to add, subtract and multiply the contents of any cell or combination of cells.

It is also possible to divide the contents of any cell. If we want to know what the profit was likely to be in a quarter (three months) we could divide the total profit (cell H16) by 4 (H16/4). The use of brackets tells Microsoft® Excel® to calculate anything inside them first. This is important since it changes the result.

Example

If C8 = 5 and D8 = 8   then C8+D8/2 = 9   but (C8+D8)/2 = 6.5

Replication

Formulas can be copied to new locations in a similar way to other Microsoft® Office applications. However, there is an important difference in that in most cases when you copy a formula to a new location it changes to allow for the new position in the spreadsheet. However, before you replicate a formula check that it is correct or you will be spreading an error across the spreadsheet.

Example

Formula to total three cells A1+A2+A3 and is in cell A5.

Copy the formula to B5 and the formula will change to B1+B2+B3 so that it carries out the same function but in the context of the new row.

Copying in a spreadsheet is called replication to show this change in formulas. In order to replicate data or a formula then highlight the area or cell to be copied and then use the Edit menu and the Copy option. Use the Paste option to copy the data or formula to the new location.

Exercise 20

Formulas

1. In Exercise 18 you saved a file called Acme Newsagent and we are now going to load this file into Microsoft® Excel®.

2. Using either the Start and All Programs menu or the Microsoft® Excel® icon methods, load Microsoft® Excel®.

3. You can load a file by single clicking on the File menu item to open up the menu which has an option called Open. Click on Open and a window called Open will appear.

4. The Look in box tells you which drive the window is looking at. You need to aim it at drive A:. You do this by clicking on the small button with the down arrow at the end of the Look in box. A menu will appear. Click on 3½ Floppy (A:) and the details of Acme Newsagent will appear in the main working area. To open the file, click on the file once to highlight it and then on the Open button on the right-hand side of the window. An alternative way is to double click on the Acme Newsagent file. In either case the content of the file should now appear in the working area of Microsoft® Excel®.

continued

5 The first step is to enter a formula to calculate the Overheads on the Costs. Overheads are 17.5% of the costs so if you multiply costs by 0.175 you will calculate the Overheads. Enter =C8*0.175 into cell D8. To enter the other Overheads amounts you can use a technique called replication. Highlight cell D8 by single clicking on the cell and clicking on the copy icon on the Standard toolbar or the **Edit** menu and the **Copy** option. Now click on the cell you want to copy the formula to (e.g. D10) by highlighting the cell and clicking on paste on the Standard toolbar or the Paste option in the **Edit** menu. The formula is copied into the new cell but will change to adapt to its new location so it will now read =C10*0.175. Paste the formula into D12 (=C12*0.175) and D14 (=C14*0.175).

6 The second step is to enter the formula to total the costs and overheads. Microsoft® Excel® provides a standard function called SUM, available on the Standard toolbar (Figure 2.8). You highlight both cells C8 and D8 by clicking on C8 and holding down the left mouse button then dragging the pointer over D8 and E8 and releasing. The three cells should now be highlighted. By clicking on the SUM icon

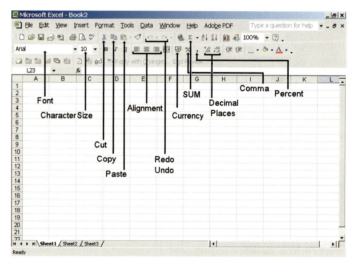

Figure 2.8 **Standard and formatting toolbars**

on the toolbar you will see the formula appear in E8 (=SUM(C8:D8)). Repeat this action for rows 10, 12 and 14. This will produce formulas in E10 (=SUM(C10:D10)), E12 (=SUM(C12:D12)) and E14 (=SUM(C14:D14)).

7 Now enter the formula to calculate Total profits. This is equal to Income minus Total Costs. In cell H8 enter =G8-E8 and then replicate the formula in H10, H12 and H14. If you make a mistake you can delete all the formula by highlighting the area (i.e H10 to H14) and selecting the Delete key or the **Edit** menu and the **Delete** option. It does not matter that you are deleting some blank cells. It will not have any effect.

8 Now total each column using the SUM function (i.e. highlight C8 to C16 and click on the SUM button to enter the formula in cell C16 =SUM(C8:C15)). Replicate the formula in D16, E16, G16 and H16.

9 Save the new file on your floppy disk as file A:\Acme Newsagent Formula. Select the **File** menu and the **Save As** option which will reveal the Save As window and you can save the file under the new name. If you select the **Save** option you will overwrite your original file. The **Save As** function allows you to save files under different names.

10 Close Microsoft® Excel® by selecting the **File** menu and the **Exit** option or click on the **Close** button on the top right-hand corner of the application window.

Presentation

Microsoft® Excel® provides the normal presentation options that are available in many Microsoft® Office applications. You can therefore:

- change or select fonts (Figure 2.8) and character size (Figure 2.8) using options on the Formatting toolbar
- embolden, italicise and underline text using options on the Formatting toolbar
- align (justify) text (align left, align right and centre text – Figure 2.8) using options on the Formatting toolbar
- change the format of numerical data (Figure 2.8) using options on the Formatting toolbar
- change the width and depth of rows and columns (Format menu – Figure 2.6)

These presentation options work in a similar way to other Microsoft® Office products. You can either select the option (e.g. font) before you enter text or numbers or change the option later. You change the formatting by highlighting the area that needs to be changed (e.g. cell, row or column) and then selecting the desired option.

Spreadsheets have extra formatting options to allow numerical information to be presented in a variety of ways. These include (Figure 2.8 – Formatting toolbar):

- Currency – to display numerical information with a £ sign in a currency format
- Percent – to display data in percentage style
- Comma – formats numbers with commas in appropriate places
- Decimal places – increase and decrease the number of decimal points shown

Figure 2.9 Right click menu

An alternative approach to changing the formatting is to use a pop-up menu that appears if you right click on the item or highlighted area you want to change. This opens a menu (Figure 2.9) with the option Format Cells which, if selected, opens a window of format options (Figure 2.10). This allows you, among other options, to change the format of numbers (i.e. decimal points, currency, etc.) by selecting the Number tab or using the Font tab to select fonts, character size, bold, italics and underline.

Figure 2.10 Format cells

Calculation

When you change data in a spreadsheet it will recalculate other values that are dependent upon the item. This may be carried out automatically so it can be confusing if you are unaware that it has happened.

The calculation takes account of the true value of the item, not simply what is displayed. If the display has removed or limited the number of decimal places then the values displayed will reflect the formatting. However, the calculation will be based on the actual value with all decimal places. The example below shows that this can be confusing faced with a spreadsheet calculation that adds 20 to 34 to produce 55. This looks wrong if you have forgotten that actual values typed in were 20.2 and 34.4 and that by selecting no decimal places you rounded up the result (i.e. 54.6 becomes 55 when rounded up).

Example

Actual value

20.2 plus 34.4 = 54.6

Excel® spreadsheet format without any decimal places

20 plus 34 = 55 (the decimal value is rounded up to the next whole number)

Exercise 21

Formatting

1. In Exercise 20 you saved a file called Acme Newsagent Formula and we are now going to load this file into Microsoft® Excel®.

2. Using either Start and the All Programs menu or the Microsoft® Excel® icon load Microsoft® Excel®.

3. You can load a file by single clicking on the File menu item to open up the menu which has an option called Open. Click on Open and a window called Open will appear.

4. The Look in box tells you what drive the window is looking at. You need to aim it at drive A:. You do this by clicking on the small button with the down arrow at the end of the Look in box and a menu will appear. Click on 3½ Floppy (A:) and the details of Acme Newsagent Formula will appear in the main working area. To open the file, click on the file once to highlight it and then on the Open button on the right-hand side of the window. An alternative way is to double click on the Acme Newsagent Formula file. In either case the content of the file should now appear in the working area of Microsoft® Excel®.

5. The title of the worksheet is not prominent. Enhance Acme Newsagents by selecting a new font and a new character size. Highlight the title then click on the arrow button on the Font box (Formatting toolbar) and a list of fonts will appear. You select one by single clicking on the item. Explore the fonts until you find one that you like. Now select the character size by using the down arrow next to the size box (the title must still be highlighted). Another list will appear from which you can choose a size. Pick one that emphasises the importance of the title.

continued

6. The headings of the rows and columns need to be emboldened. Highlight the row or column and click on the Bold icon on toolbar. Now centre the row headings by highlighting them and selecting the Center alignment icon.

7. Some of the headings are too wide for their columns. The columns can be adjusted by placing the mouse pointer over the row or column headings edge on the line that divides the row or column. The mouse pointer will change shape (i.e. double headed cross arrows) and if you hold down the left mouse button you can drag the column wider or narrower. Use the same technique to adjust the height of the rows. An alternative approach is to use the Format menu (Figure 2.6)

8. Adjust the column widths so that the headings fit the columns better.

9. In a spreadsheet it is important to be able to format the numerical data. In the Acme Newsagents example we are dealing with money so the data should be formatted as currency. This is achieved by highlighting the data and clicking on the Currency icon on the toolbar. Observe the change – a pound (£) sign will be added and a decimal point and two zeros added to show pence. If the result is too wide for the column then a series of hash marks (i.e. ####) will be shown.

10. The example worksheet does not have any data which include pence so we could remove the decimal point. Highlight the numerical data and click on the Decrease Decimal icon (Formatting toolbar – Figure 2.8). Click twice on the icon to remove the two digits after the point. Experiment with adding decimal places using the Increase Decimal icon, but finish with a display without decimal places (i.e. no pence). Figure 2.11 shows the final spreadsheet.

11. Save the new file on your floppy disk as file A:\Acme Newsagent Presentation. Select the File menu and the Save As option which will reveal the Save As window and you can save the file under a new name. If you select the Save option you will overwrite your original file. The Save As function allows you to save files under different names.

12. Close Microsoft® Excel® by selecting File menu and the Exit option or click on the Close button in the top right-hand corner of the application window.

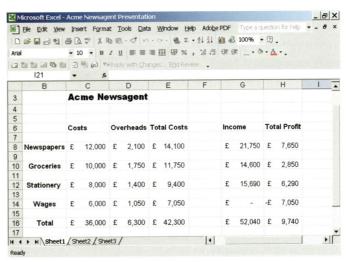

Figure 2.11 Acme Newsagent spreadsheet

Page setup

Microsoft® Excel® provides a range of functions to allow you to select the overall appearance of the page presenting the worksheet. These let you select the orientation of the page. There are two options: portrait or landscape. Figure 2.12 compares the two orientations and illustrates that you can set the four page margins at the top, bottom, right and left of the page.

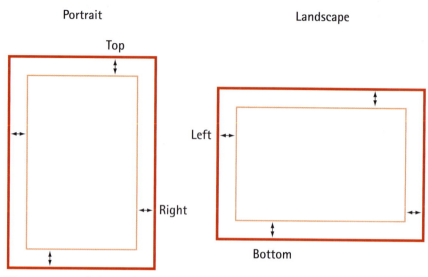

Figure 2.12 Orientation

To select orientation and margins you need to choose the File menu and Page Setup to reveal the Page Setup window (Figure 2.13). This has four tabs across the top. They are:

- Page
- Margins
- Header/Footer
- Sheet

Each tab provides access to a number of options. The Page tab (Figure 2.13) offers you the means to:

Figure 2.13 Page Setup – Page tab

- choose orientation (i.e. landscape and portrait)
- scale the sheet to fit the paper
- select the paper size
- print the sheet
- preview what the sheet will look like when printed

The Margins tab (Figure 2.14) offers you the means to:

- set all four page margins (i.e. left, right, top and bottom)

Figure 2.14 Page Setup – Margins tab

- set the size of the header and footer
- centre the sheet
- print the sheet
- preview what the sheet will look like when printed

The Header/Footer tab (Figure 2.15) offers you the means to:

- enter a header
- enter a footer
- enter custom headers and footers (i.e. date, filename and page number)
- print the sheet
- preview what the sheet will look like when printed

The Sheet tab (Figure 2.16) offers you the means to:

- choose how the sheet is printed including if the gridlines and row and column headings appear
- print the sheet
- preview what the sheet will look like when printed

Figure 2.15 Page Setup – Header/Footer tab

Figure 2.16 Page Setup – Sheet tab

Find and replace

You will occasionally need to change an entry in a spreadsheet. You can obviously do this by deleting what you wish to replace and entering a new item. However, Microsoft® Excel® provides an automatic way to find and replace an entry. This is available within the Edit Menu as the Replace option. This is very useful if you need to make several identical changes since it removes the risk of making a mistake in entering the replacement. A related function is the Find option in the Edit menu which will locate an entry. This is useful in large or complex spreadsheets.

Exercise 22

Presentation

1 Load Microsoft® Excel® using either the All Programs menu or the Microsoft® Excel® icon on the desktop.

2 Set the page orientation to landscape using the File menu and Page Setup option.

continued

3 Enter the table of information below to form your first spreadsheet. It shows the operating costs of three different cars.

	January	February	March	April	May	June	Total
Model A	88	93	90	89	92	96	
Model B	102	108	101	99	105	111	
Model C	65	71	70	64	67	64	
Total							

4 Create a header using the **File** menu and **Page Setup** option. Use Custom header button to enter your name and insert an automatic date.

5 Save the new file on your floppy disk as file A:\Operating Costs. Select the **File** menu and the **Save** option which will reveal the Save As window and you can save the file.

6 Use the SUM function to calculate the total for January column.

7 Replicate the formula to display the total for all the months (i.e. February to June).

8 Use the SUM function to calculate the total for the Model A row (i.e. January to June).

9 Replicate the formula to display the total for all the remaining Models (i.e. Models B and C).

10 Insert the rows Model D and E between Model C and Total. Enter the information below:

	January	February	March	April	May	June
Model D	128	132	138	126	129	135
Model E	35	39	31	37	41	33

11 Insert a new column, Price, before January.

	Price
Model A	12235
Model B	14679
Model C	8980
Model D	17568
Model E	6950

12 Replicate the total formula to rows Model D and E and Column Price.

13 Develop a formula to calculate the mean price of the five car models (i.e. divide total of the prices by 5). Figure 2.17 displays the spreadsheet.

continued

14 Save the file on your floppy disk as file A:\Operating Costs.

15 Close Microsoft® Excel® by selecting the File menu and the Exit option or click on the Close button in the top right-hand corner of the application window.

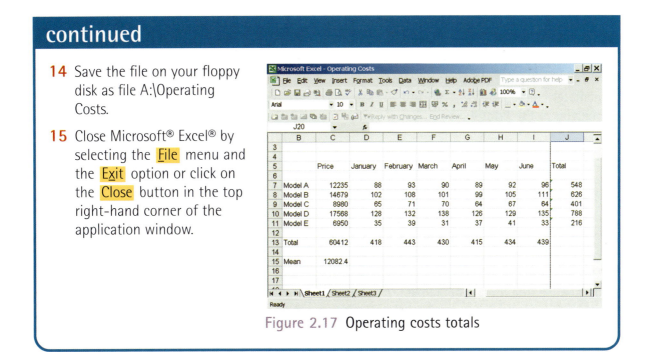

Figure 2.17 Operating costs totals

Borders and shading

Borders and shading can be added to spreadsheets to improve their appearance and highlight key aspects. This is important if you are preparing numerical information for your manager or a client. People often judge quality on appearance so even if you have developed a sophisticated mathematical model, if it is poorly presented it may be regarded with suspicion.

Microsoft® Excel® offers the borders function on the formatting toolbar which if selected opens a small window with a variety of options. These are shown in Figure 2.18. You can choose to enclose a whole sheet, draw an individual line or provide borders around each cell. This allows you to select the areas of the sheet you want to emphasise.

On the Formatting toolbar next to the Borders icon is the Fill Color function with which you can add colour shading to the sheet. When you chose Fill Color it will reveal a pallete of colours. Both Borders and Fill Color operate by highlighting the area you want to format and then choosing the type of border or colour you want. If you highlight a row and select red then you will see that the row gains a red background colour.

Printing

It is important to be able to print out a sheet or workbook. Microsoft® Excel® offers a range of functions linked to printing. These include previewing your sheet as a printed

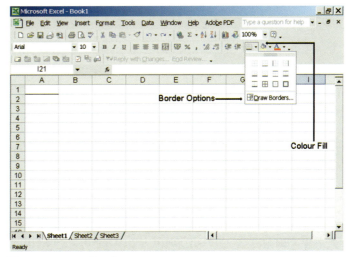

Figure 2.18 Borders

document. Within the File Menu, Print Preview opens up a window shown in Figure 2.19. This lets you check if the printed sheet is presented in the way that you want it to be. When you have completed the preview, click on the Close button to return to Microsoft® Excel®. If you want to print the spreadsheet immediately there is a Print button to link you to the Print window.

Usually, the default is to print in portrait mode, that is, with the narrow edge of the paper at the top so that when you preview your sheet you may discover that it flows over two pages. If you would prefer it to be presented on a single page, you need to change the default to landscape (i.e. the long edge across the top). This can be carried out from the Print Preview window by selecting the Setup button, which opens the Page Setup window. Select Landscape by clicking on the Landscape radio button and then clicking on the OK button to confirm the change. When you print now it will be in landscape mode. The example shown in Figure 2.19 would be printed in Portrait since we did not change the default.

When you are ready to print then click on the File menu and the Print option. The window shown in Figure 2.20 appears. You are presented with a number of options which people initially may find puzzling.

Figure 2.19 Print preview

Figure 2.20 Print

1. You must first select the printer on which your spreadsheet is to be printed. This is shown in the Printer area at the top of the window in the box entitled Name. Microsoft® Windows® operating system allows you to link many different printers to a single stand-alone computer. The list of printers is shown when you click on the down arrow next to the Name box. Select your printer by clicking on it. The printer shown is the default printer.

2. You need to decide how much of the document you want to print (Print range). The choices are:
   - All – whole document (the default setting)
   - Pages – you enter the page range you want to print (e.g. 23–34)

3. You can select what to print (Print what). The choices are:
   - Selection (a highlighted area of the sheet)

- **Active sheet(s)** (whole sheet) (the default setting)
- **Entire workbook** (multiple related sheets)

4 You can select how many copies to print with the **Number of copies** scrollbar.

When you are ready, click the **OK** button to start the printer. If you change none of the settings, the default ones will be used.

When printing a spreadsheet, it is important to decide whether you want to include the gridlines or not. This has to be set in the **Page Setup** option of the **File** menu within the **Sheet** tab. The **Gridlines** checkbox must be clicked, which will put a tick in the box. Gridlines will be inserted in the spreadsheet printout. Another important option is to print the sheet showing the heading. This can be achieved through the **Page Setup** option within the **Sheet** tab. The **Row and column headings** checkbox must be clicked, which will put a tick in the box (Figure 2.16).

In some cases you will want to print the formulas rather than their results. Select the **Tools** menu and the **Options** item. This opens the Options window. Click on the **View** tab and look for the Window options section and the **Formulas** checkbox. You need to click in this box. A tick will appear and then you can click on the **OK** button to confirm the change. You should notice that you can also select options for printing rows and column headings and gridlines. This is an alternative way to using the Page Setup function.

To return to printing with the actual numbers or without gridlines you will have to repeat the operation and click once more in the **Formulas** and **Gridline** boxes. This will remove the ticks. Confirm the change by clicking on the OK button.

When you choose to print the formulas, your spreadsheet format will change to accommodate their different lengths. It will change back when you deselect this option.

As part of your assessment you will need to be able to print a spreadsheet showing the formulas.

Exercise 23

Borders, shading and printing

1 In Exercise 22 you saved a file called Operating Costs and you are now going to load this file into Microsoft® Excel®.

2 Using either **Start** and the **All Programs** menu or the **Microsoft® Excel®** icon on the desktop load Microsoft® Excel®.

3 You can load a file by single clicking on the **File** menu item and then the **Open** option to display the Open window.

4 The **Look in** box tells you what drive the window is looking at. You need to aim it at drive A:. You do this by clicking on the small button with the down arrow at the end of the **Look in** box and a menu will appear. Click on 3½ Floppy (A:) and the details of Operating Costs will appear in the main working area. To open the file, click on the file once to highlight it and then on the Open button on the right-hand side of the window.

continued

An alternative way is to double click on the Operating Costs file. In either case the contents of the file should now appear in the Microsoft® Excel® working area.

5. Insert a new row to form a new top line of the sheet and then insert a new column to the left of the Model column. This is to allow you to enclose the whole area in a border.

6. Highlight the whole area containing the data you have entered. Select the **Borders** function and explore the different options. Use the **Undo** function (**Edit** menu) to return your sheet to its original state. When you are confident that you understand the different options highlight the whole area and choose the option that provides a border around each cell (Figure 2.21).

7. Highlight the top row of the sheet (i.e. Price to Total) and select the **Fill Color** function and choose the colour red. The top row should now have a red background colour (Figure 2.21).

8. Create a header (i.e. select the **File** menu and **Page Setup** at the **Header/Footer** tab entering your name and automatic date).

9. Save the file on your floppy disk as file A:\Operating Costs Borders. Select the **File** menu then the **Save As** option which will reveal the Save As window and you can save the file.

10. Print the sheet in landscape orientation showing the data with gridlines but without row and column headings (i.e. Select **File** menu and **Page Setup** with **Sheet** tab (alternatively select **Tools** menu and **Options**). Ensure that the sheet prints onto a single page.

11. Print the sheet in landscape orientation showing the formulas (select **Tools** menu and **Options** item) with gridlines and row and

Figure 2.21 Borders and Shading

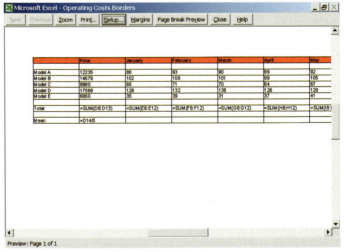

Figure 2.22 Displaying Formulas

> **continued**
>
> column headings (i.e. select File menu and Page Setup with Sheet tab). Ensure that the sheet prints on to a single page.
>
> 12 Figure 2.22 displays the formulas in Print Preview.
>
> 13 Close Microsoft® Excel® by selecting File menu and the Exit option or click on the Close button on the top right-hand corner of the application window.

Graphs and chart applications

When presenting numerical information, it is sometimes difficult even for highly numerate people to understand the relationship between the different elements. However, if you can convert the information into visual images then it is far easier to see the trends and relationships. There are several forms of visual representations such as pie charts, line graphs and bar or column charts. Microsoft® Excel® has a number of functions to turn numerical information into graphs and charts. There are other applications which allow you to model live data, that is, systems which take data as it is created (e.g. output from a processing plant) and show it in the form of a chart or a graph. These charts and graphs continuously change because the data they are modelling is altering all the time. This type of continuous output is often printed on a special printer called a plotter. Microsoft® Excel® graphs and charts are, in comparison, static representations of data.

Nevertheless, if the spreadsheet information changes then you can produce new graphs and charts. These allow you to monitor the information visually and are useful if you produce a monthly spreadsheet of sales figures, salary costs or staff absences. Charts and graphs also provide opportunities to compare numerical information.

Spreadsheets allow you to create models of information so that you can see the consequences of changes (e.g. price rises, decreased costs, changes in interest rates and pay increases). These changes can also be converted into graphs and charts to help you analyse the changes and their effect on other factors. A visual presentation of data (i.e. a graph or chart) may enable you to identify effects which are not easy to see in a table of numbers.

Figure 2.17 shows a comparison of the running costs of five models of cars. Although the table helps you to see the relationships, visual representation adds another dimension, assisting people to identify connections between the models that may not be otherwise obvious.

Pie charts

A pie chart is used to represent numbers as slices of a circle so that the size of each slice is

Figure 2.23 Price comparison

proportional to the whole. In Figure 2.23, the pie chart shows the comparison of the price of the five models.

Line graphs

A line graph helps you to compare different factors. The graph in Figure 2.24 compares the running costs of the five models over six months.

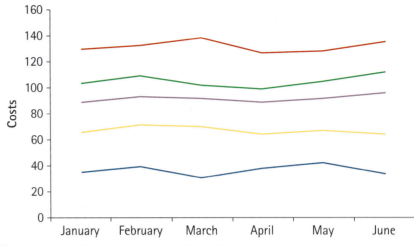

Figure 2.24 Running costs – Line chart

Column charts

A column chart represents numbers as columns of different height. Figure 2.25 shows the column chart for the running costs of the five models.

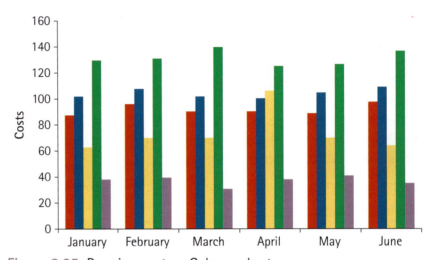

Figure 2.25 Running costs – Column chart

Bar chart

A bar chart is similar to a column chart except that the data is represented as bars rather than columns. Figure 2.26 shows a bar chart comparing the running costs of the five models.

Comparison

Figures 2.23, 2.24, 2.25 and 2.26 are based on the same numerical information (Figure 2.16) in the form of pie, line, column and bar charts. You should

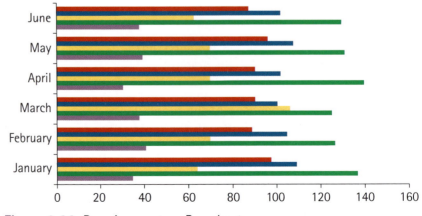

Figure 2.26 Running costs – Bar chart

review and compare the different visual presentations. How effective do you feel the displays are in showing the information? You need to consider what purpose the different forms of charts and graphs serve.

Creating a chart

Microsoft® Excel® contains a range of functions to present numerical information in the form of graphs and charts. These are available within the Chart function of the Insert menu. Alternatively you can select the Chart icon on the Standard toolbar (Figure 2.27).

The first step is to insert data into the spreadsheet in the normal way. Highlight the data and select the Insert menu and then Chart or alternatively the Chart icon. This opens up the Chart Wizard (Figure 2.28). On the left-hand edge is a list of Chart types from which you choose the type of chart or graph you wish to use. This is done by clicking once on the one you select. On the right-hand side of the window the charts will change to show you examples of your chosen chart. Again you need to select the example you want to use. This is achieved by a single click. A description of the chart is given below the examples. If you want to see what your actual chart will look like then you click on the Press and Hold to View sample button holding the left mouse button down. When you release the mouse button then the chart will disappear.

At the top of the Chart Wizard window you will see that it states that it is step 1 of 4. Figure 2.28 shows step 1 of the process. You move between the steps by clicking on the Next button. The second step is shown in Figure 2.29 which illustrates a column chart. The data range is shown in this display as =Sheet1!$E$8:$J$12. This may look confusing but if you ignore the $ signs it reads Sheet 1 E8:J12, that is,

Figure 2.27 Chart function

Figure 2.28 Chart Wizard – Step 1

Figure 2.29 Chart Wizard – Step 2

the data is drawn from sheet 1 and the area E8 to J12.

It is vital to check that the Wizard has used the correct data range. It does not always get the range right and therefore your chart will be wrong. You should check the data range is correct each time you create a graph or chart. Each exercise will ask you to check your data range. In the middle of the window is an area called Series in. This offers two options, Rows and Columns. If you change the option you will see the chart change. It is worth considering the two options to identify which one serves your purpose best.

When the Next button is clicked again the display will change to step 3 (Figure 2.30). This dialog box allows you to label your chart. You can enter an overall title for the chart or graph, label the axes of the graphs and add a legend. The options available in step 3 will depend on the chart or graph you have selected. For example, a pie chart does not have axes so there is no point in providing options to label them. The legend is essentially an explanation of the colour coding of the chart. In this case it is needed since five colours are employed. You can use Step 3 to remove the legend.

Click the Next button again to display step 4 (Figure 2.31). This dialog box determines whether the chart is placed on a new sheet or as an additional object in an existing sheet (e.g. a chart placed alongside the data). A chart placed on a separate sheet allows you more freedom to present your chart or graph in the way you want while placing a chart alongside its related data helps to illustrate inter-

Figure 2.30 Chart Wizard – Step 3

Figure 2.31 Chart Wizard – Step 4

Figure 2.32 Column chart

relationships. The exercises will ask you to create your graphs or charts on a separate sheet. However you may wish to experiment with the other option. Once you have made this decision you can complete the process by clicking on the Finish button. At each step you can return to the previous step by clicking on the Back button. This allows you to correct errors.

On clicking the Finish button the chart or graph appears. Figure 2.32 displays the Column chart overlaying the related data. It can be dragged around using the mouse so that the data and the chart can be seen side by side.

To create the titles and labels for your charts and graphs requires that you understand the terms. Figure 2.33 displays the main titles and labels. The only one missing is the data label since it was not appropriate for this particular chart. You can add data labels to your charts. In Figure 2.33 you could show the value (i.e. the X-axis value, e.g. 100) against the actual column.

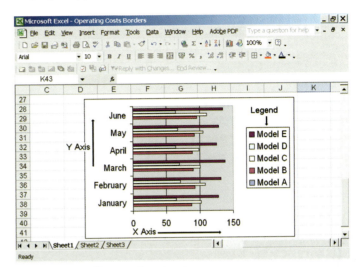

Figure 2.33 Parts of a chart

Editing a chart or graph

Once you have finished a chart or graph you can move it around the display, adjust its size and change the layout. This is done by single clicking on the chart. The chart's surrounding rectangle (enclosure) changes to show small black squares in each corner and the middle of the lines (Figure 2.32). These are called handles. If the pointer is clicked within the chart's enclosure and the mouse button held down and dragged then the whole chart can be moved to a new location. If the same approach is used with individual objects within the chart they too will be enclosed in a rectangle (Figure 2.34). You must click on the chart object itself, not on the surrounding white space. The objects can then be dragged to a new position within the chart's overall enclosure.

The mouse pointer changes shape when dragging the chart enclosure to new positions and when the mouse is being used to change the shape and size of the chart. If you place the mouse over the small black squares (handles) either in the middle of the lines or on the corners then they change to double-headed arrows and by holding down the mouse pointer you can drag the side or corner of the enclosure to expand the chart or push the line in to reduce the chart's size.

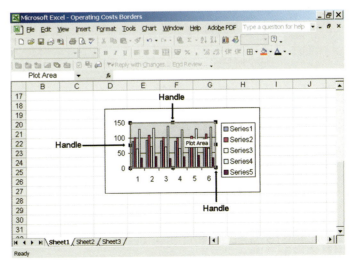

Figure 2.34 Editing a chart

Once you have created a chart you can still make changes and amend it by right clicking on the enclosure. This reveals a menu of options, shown in Figure 2.35. This is the Format Chart Area menu which allows you to access the options available during the Chart Wizard process and edit the chart or graph.

If you right click on the individual chart objects different menus of options appear such as Format Legend, Format Plot Area, Format Data Series and Format Axis.

Figure 2.35 Format Chart Area menu

Exercise 24

Creating a column chart

1. Load Microsoft® Excel® using either Start and the All Programs menu or the Microsoft® Excel® icon on the desktop.

2. Enter the table of information below. It shows a simple breakdown of the sales of motor cars over a six month period.

January	35,000
February	47,500
March	21,000
April	32,900
May	16,000
June	34,780

Start your sheet in cell A1 (with January) with the sales information in B1 (35,000) so that the table covers the area A1 to B6.

3. Highlight the table (i.e. A1 to B6) by clicking once in A1 and holding down the mouse button, dragging the pointer to B6. The whole table will be highlighted and you can then release the button.

4. Select the Chart Wizard (i.e. Insert menu and Chart option). Explore the options of Column, Bar, Line and Pie charts by clicking on each in turn and then considering the different options and their descriptions.

continued

5. Finally select Column Chart type and the default sub-type, which is in the top left-hand corner. Using the Press and Hold to View sample button review the chart. Remember that you must hold down the left mouse button to see the chart. If you release it, the image will disappear.

6. Select the Next button to move to Step 2 and review the data range to ensure it is correct. Click on the Next button again to move to Step 3.

7. In Step 3 select the Title tab and enter:

    Chart title – Car Sales

    Category (X) axis – Months

    Value (Y) axis – Income (pounds)

8. In Step 3 of the Wizard select the Legend tab and remove the tick from the Show legend radio button. In this case there is no need for a legend since there is only one set of data.

9. Click on the Next button to move to Step 4. Select As new sheet and enter the Car Sales Column Chart. When you are ready, click on the Finish button. The chart will appear on a separate sheet from the data it relates to (Figure 2.36).

Figure 2.36 Car Sales Column chart

10. Save the spreadsheet you have created on to a floppy disk. This procedure is the same in all Microsoft® Windows® applications so you can save a spreadsheet, database or graphic image in exactly the same way. Insert a floppy disk into drive A: and click on File menu item and a menu will open showing a list of options. Select Save and a window will open.

11. Click in the box File name and Enter A:\Car Sales Column Chart. Now click on the Save button on the right of the window. You have now saved your chart as a file called Car Sales Column Chart. You may hear drive A: work during this process.

12. You can now close Microsoft® Excel®. Click on the File menu item and a menu will appear with a list of options. At the bottom of the list is the option Exit. If you click on Exit then Microsoft® Excel® will close. An alternative way is to click on the Close button on the top right-hand corner of the application window.

Exercise 25

Creating a line chart/graph

1. Load Microsoft® Excel® using either **Start** and the **All Programs** menu or the **Microsoft® Excel®** icon on the desktop.

2. Enter the table of information below. It shows a breakdown of the travel expenses claimed by an employee of a large company.

	Mileage	Subsistence	Other
April	230	85	56
May	450	120	32
June	80	16	6
July	167	45	14
August	144	23	7

   Start your sheet in cell C8 (with April) with the final item of Other (i.e. 7) in F12 so that the table covers the area C7 to F12.

3. Highlight the months and mileage part of the table entered (i.e. C8 to D12) by clicking once in C8 and holding down the mouse button, dragging the pointer to D12.

April	230
May	450
June	80
July	167
August	144

4. Select the Chart Wizard (i.e. **Insert** menu and **Chart** option). Explore the Column, Bar, Line and Pie charts by clicking on each in turn and then considering the different options and their descriptions.

5. Finally select **Line Chart/Graphs** type and the default example. Using the **Press and Hold to View** sample button review the chart. Remember that you must hold down the left mouse button to see the chart. If you release it the image will disappear.

6. Select the **Next** button to move to Step 2 and review the data range to ensure it is correct. Then click on the **Next** button again to move to Step 3.

7. In Step 3 select the Title tab and enter:

   Chart title – Expenses

   Category (X) axis – Months

continued

Value (Y) axis – Claim (pounds)

8. In Step 3 select the Legend tab and remove the tick from the Show legend radio button. In this case there is no need for a legend since there is only one set of data. Select the Gridlines tab and tick the Category (X) axis Major gridlines box and the Value (Y) Axis Major gridlines box. Watch the addition of gridlines.

9. Select the Next button to move to Step 4. Select As new sheet and enter Expenses Graph. When you are ready click on the Finish button. The chart will appear on a separate sheet from the data it relates to (Figure 2.37).

10. Save the spreadsheet you have created on to a floppy disk. This procedure is the same in all Microsoft® Windows® applications. You can save a spreadsheet, database or graphic image in exactly the same way. Insert a floppy disk into drive A: and click on the File menu item. A menu will open showing a list of options. Select Save and a window will open.

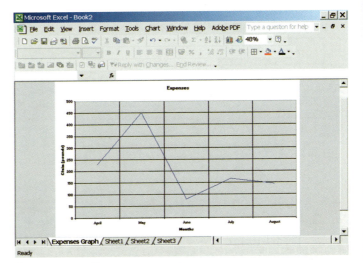

Figure 2.37 Expenses graph

11. Click in the box File name and Enter A:\Expenses Graph. Now click on the Save button on the right of the window. You have now saved your graph as a file called Expenses Graph. You may hear drive A: work during this process.

12. You can now close Microsoft® Excel®. Click on the File menu item and a menu will appear with a list of options. At the bottom of the list is the option Exit. If you click on Exit then Microsoft® Excel® will close. An alternative way is to click on the Close button on the top right-hand corner of the application window.

Exercise 26

Creating line graphs/charts – non-continuous data

1. In Exercise 25 you created a line chart for the mileage expenses for a company. This exercise offers you the opportunity to repeat the exercise and create two additional line charts for subsistence and other expenses. This involves selecting data that is not continuous.

continued

2. Load Microsoft® Excel® using either the Start and All Programs menu or the Microsoft® Excel® icon on the desktop.

3. Highlight the months and subsistence parts of the table by first clicking once in C8 and holding down the mouse button, dragging the pointer to C12 and releasing. Now hold down the Ctrl key and click in the E8 cell and holding down the mouse button, drag the pointer to E12. You should now have:

April	85
May	120
June	16
July	45
August	23

4. Select the Chart Wizard (i.e. Insert menu and Chart option). Select the Line Chart/Graph type and the default example. Using the Press and Hold to View sample button review the chart. Remember that you must hold down the left mouse button to see the chart. If you release it the image will disappear.

5. Select the Next button to move to Step 2 and review the data range to ensure it is correct. Then click on the Next button again to move to Step 3.

6. In Step 3 select the Title tab and enter:

    Chart title – Expenses Subsistence

    Category (X) axis – Months

    Value (Y) axis – Claim (pounds)

7. In Step 3 select Legend and remove the tick from the Show legend radio button. In this case there is no need for a legend since there is only one set of data. Select the Gridlines tab and tick the Category (X) axis Major gridlines box and the Value (Y) Axis Major gridlines box. Watch the addition of gridlines.

8. Select the Next button to move to Step 4. Select As new sheet and enter Subsistence Expenses. When you are ready click on the Finish button. The chart will appear on a separate sheet from the data that relates to it.

9. Save the spreadsheet on the floppy disk with the file name Expenses Graph.

10. Now repeat the process but produce a line chart of the months and other expenses data. This will allow you to practice working with non-continuous data.

11. Highlight the months and other parts of the table by first clicking once in C8 and holding down the mouse button, dragging the pointer to C12 and releasing. Now hold down the Ctrl key and click in the F8 cell and holding down the mouse button, drag the pointer to F12. You should now have:

continued

April	56
May	32
June	6
July	14
August	7

12 Create a new line chart for this data.

13 When you have completed both charts close Microsoft® Excel® by selecting the File menu and Exit option. Alternatively click on the Close button in the top right hand corner of the application.

Exercise 27

Creating a pie chart

1 Load Microsoft® Excel® using either Start and the All Programs menu or the Microsoft® Excel® icon on the desktop.

2 Enter the table of information below. It shows the number of books borrowed, by type, from a small branch library.

Library Books	
Romance	126
Historical	34
Crime	87
Contemporary	12
Factual	95

Start your sheet in cell D4 (with Romance) with the final item of expenditure (i.e. 95) in E8 so that the table covers the area D4 to E8.

3 Highlight the library data (i.e. D4 to E8) by clicking once in D4 and holding down the mouse button, dragging the pointer to E8.

4 Select the Chart Wizard (i.e. Insert menu and Chart option). Explore the options of Column, Bar, Line and Pie charts by clicking on each in turn and then considering the different options and their descriptions.

continued

5. Finally select Pie Chart type and the default example which is in the top left-hand corner. Using the Press and Hold to View sample button review the chart (remember that you must hold down the left mouse button to see the chart. If you release it the image will disappear).

6. Select the Next button to move to Step 2 and review the data range to ensure it is correct and then click on the Next button again to move to Step 3.

7. In Step 3 select the Title tab and enter:

    Chart title – Library Books

8. In Step 3 select the Legend tab and change the placement of the legend to the left by clicking on the appropriate radio button.

9. In Step 3 select the Data Labels tab and select Value by clicking the tick box. This will display the value of each sector on the Pie chart.

10. Select the Next button to move to Step 4. Select As new sheet. The chart will appear on a separate sheet (Figure 2.38). This chart has a legend which is appropriate since it is important to know what each colour relates to. In this pie chart we have also added data labels (i.e. the value of each segment).

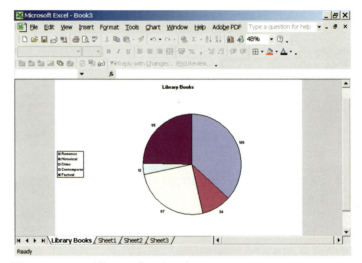

Figure 2.38 Library Books chart

11. Save the spreadsheet you have created on to a floppy disk. This procedure is the same in all Microsoft® Windows® applications. You save a spreadsheet, database or graphic image in exactly the same way. Insert a floppy disk into drive A: and click on the File menu item and a menu will open showing a list of options. Select Save and a window will open.

12. Click in the box File name and enter A:\Library Books. Now click on the Save button on the right of the window. You have now saved your chart as a file called Library Books. You may hear drive A: work during this process.

13. You can close Microsoft® Excel®. Click on the File menu item and a menu will appear with a list of options. At the bottom of the list is the option Exit. If you click on Exit then Microsoft® Excel® will close. An alternative way is to click on the Close button in the top right-hand corner of the application window.

Comparative charts and graphs

Displaying a single set of data can be important but charts and graphs are very useful when comparing several sets of information. In Exercise 25 you created a line graph (Figure 2.37) showing the relationship between months and mileage claimed. The spreadsheet (Expenses Graph) included data on subsistence and other claims. It is possible to produce a chart comparing these different elements.

Exercise 28

Comparison

1 Load Microsoft® Excel® using either Start and the All Programs menu or the Microsoft® Excel® icon on the desktop.

2 Load Expenses Graph by single clicking on the File menu to show the Open option. Click on Open and a window called Open will appear.

   The Look in box tells you which drive the window is looking at. You need to aim it at drive A:. You do this by clicking on the small button with the down arrow at the end of the Look in box. A menu will appear. Click on 3½ Floppy (A:) and the Expenses Graph will appear in the main working area. To open the file, click on it once to highlight it and then on the Open button on the right-hand side of the window. An alternative way is to double click on the Expenses Graph file. In either case the spreadsheet and chart will appear in the working area of Microsoft® Excel®.

3 The spreadsheet is on Sheet1 so click on the tab to locate it. Highlight the whole table of data (i.e. C7 to F12). This includes the row and column headings.

4 Select the Chart Wizard (i.e. Insert menu and Chart option). Select the Bar Chart type and the default example which is in the top left-hand corner. Using the Press and Hold to View sample button review the chart (remember that you must hold down the left mouse button to see the chart. If you release it the image will disappear).

5 Select the Next button to move to Step 2 and review the data range to ensure it is correct. Then click on the Next button again to move to Step 3.

6 In Step 3 select the Title tab and enter:

   Chart title – Comparing Expenses

   Category (X) axis – Months

   Value (Y) axis – Amount (pounds)

7 In Step 3 select Legend and explore the placement of the legend (top, bottom and right) by clicking on the appropriate radio buttons.

8 Select the Next button to move to Step 4. Select As new sheet and enter Comparing Expenses. When you are ready click on the Finish button. The chart will appear on a separate sheet from the data it relates to (Figure 2.39). The three coloured bars represent the different parts of the expenses claim.

continued

9. Save the spreadsheet you have created on to a floppy disk. This procedure is the same in all Microsoft® Windows® applications. You save a spreadsheet, database or graphic image in exactly the same way. Insert a floppy disk into drive A: and click on the File menu item and a menu will open showing a list of options. Select Save As and a window will open.

10. Click in the box File name and enter A:\Comparing Expenses. Now click on the Save button on the right of the window. You have now saved your chart as a file called Comparing Expenses. You may hear drive A: work during this process.

11. Now repeat the process (remember that the data is on Sheet 1) but select a line graph instead of a bar chart. Call the new graph Comparing Expenses2. Figure 2.40 shows the line graph. Compare the bar chart with it and decide which you feel provides the more useful image. Try to identify which one helps you compare the three sets of data.

12. Save the spreadsheet you have created on to a floppy disk. This procedure is the same in all Microsoft® Windows® applications. You save a spreadsheet, database or graphic image in exactly the same way. Insert a floppy disk into drive A: and click on the File menu item and a menu will open showing a list of options. Select Save As and a window will open.

13. Click in the box File name and enter A:\Comparing Expenses2. Now click on the Save button on the right of the window. You have now saved your chart as a file called Comparing Expenses2. You may hear drive A: work during this process.

14. You can close Microsoft® Excel® now. Click on the menu item and a menu will appear with a list of options. At the bottom of the list is the option Exit. If you click on Exit then Microsoft® Excel® will close. An alternative way is to click on the Close button on the top right-hand corner of the application window.

Figure 2.39 Comparing Expenses – Bar chart

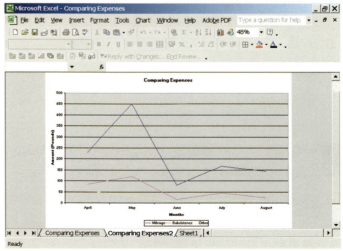

Figure 2.40 Comparing Expenses2

Axes and upper and lower limits

With any chart and graph it is important to be able to set the axes because these provide you with the scale against which to judge the display. Microsoft® Excel® provides functions to edit the scale. If you click on the corner of your axes then a handle will appear. Double clicking on the value axis (notice a small label appears to help you identify the axis) will open up the Format Axis window (Figure 2.41).

To change the scale you enter new values in the boxes within the Scale tab. The range is set by changing the Minimum and Maximum values.

Figure 2.41 Set axes

Editing line graphs

Line graphs rely on the colour and thickness of the lines to distinguish them from the background. This is especially important when they are printed. The lines can be edited in a similar way to changing the scale of the axes. Double click on the line and the Format Data Series window will appear. Alternatively single click on the line to reveal the handles and then right click to reveal a menu with the option Format Data Series which, if selected, will display the Format Data Series window (Figure 2.42). To change the colour, thickness or style of the line you need to select from the options revealed by clicking on the down arrow alongside the options.

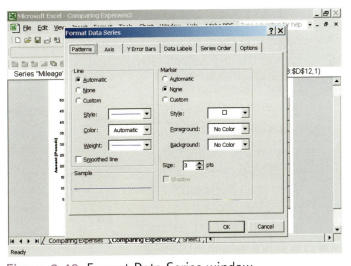

Figure 2.42 Format Data Series window

Exercise 29

Edit graph

1 Load Microsoft® Excel® using either Start and the All Programs menu or the Microsoft® Excel® icon on the desktop.

continued

2. Load Comparing Expenses by single clicking on the **File** menu to show the **Open** option. Click on **Open** and a window called Open will appear.

3. The **Look in** box tells you which drive the window is looking at. You need to aim it at drive A:. You do this by clicking on the small button with the down arrow at the end of the **Look in** box. A menu will appear. Click on 3½ Floppy (A:) and Comparing Expenses will appear in the main working area. To open the file, click on it once to highlight it and then on the **Open** button on the right-hand side of the window. An alternative way is to double click on the Comparing Expenses file. In both cases the spreadsheet and graph will appear in the working area of Microsoft® Excel®.

4. The graph is on Comparing Expenses2 tab so click on it to display it.

5. Change each of the lines to improve their visibility. Double click on each line to open the Format Data Series window and explore the Style, Color and Weight options within the **Patterns** tab. Chose the options that you prefer.

6. Change the scale of the Y-axis to 0 to 500 and the major unit to 100 by clicking on the axis to reveal the handles and then right click to show a short menu with the **Format Axis** option. When this is chosen it will open the Format Axis window. Alternatively double clicking the axis will open the Format Axis window. Change the values in the option boxes and confirm the changes by clicking on the **OK** button.

7. Change the character size of the title, Y-axis, X-axis labels and legend lables by double clicking on them to reveal appropriate menus and tabs.

   Figure 2.43 shows the outcomes of these changes.

8. Save the spreadsheet you have created on a floppy disk. This procedure is the same in all Microsoft® Windows® applications. You save a spreadsheet, database or graphic image in exactly the same way. Insert a floppy disk into drive A: and click on the **File** menu item and a menu will open showing a list of options. Select **Save As** and a window will open.

   Figure 2.43 Comparing Expenses changes

9. Click in the box **File name** and enter A:\Comparing Expenses ammended. Now click on the **Save** button on the right of the window. You have now saved your chart as a file called Comparing Expenses amended. You may hear drive A: work during this process.

10. You can close Microsoft® Excel® now. Click on the **File** menu item and a menu will appear with a list of options. At the bottom of the list is the option **Exit**. If you click on **Exit** then Microsoft® Excel® will close. An alternative way is to click on the **Close** button on the top right-hand corner of the application window.

Printing a chart

Charts are visual representations of data so it is appropriate to print them in order that they can be distributed. Colour is also employed to distinguish between the different components; it is useful to provide coloured printouts whenever possible. If you do not have access to a colour printer then it is important to check that the colours you are using are clear when reproduced using different shades of grey. You can do this by using the Print Preview option in the File menu. If your computer is connected to a colour printer the preview will be in colour but if your printer is black and white only, then the preview will use different shades of grey.

To print a chart you need to select the File menu and then the Print option. Figure 2.44 shows the Print dialog box. The dialog box is divided into different areas. Printer shows the printer that your computer is connected to, Print range allows you to select All or a page range, Copies allows you to print multiple copies of the chart and Print what allows you to select which sheet to print (i.e. active sheet or the whole workbook). The Preview button allows you a final check to see if your chart is correct.

When your chart has been included in the sheet with the data (i.e. selected as Object within sheet at Step 4 in Chart Wizard) you can print the chart with the sheet data. This is obviously useful since you show the visual representation alongside the numerical information. However, there are also occasions when you need to print the chart separately. In order to print the chart or graph you need to highlight it and then select the File menu and Print option. The Print window will show in the Print what area with the Selection option selected (i.e. button filled). Alternatively you can choose the File menu and Print Preview option to review the Chart or Graph. The chart or graph can be printed directly by selecting the Print button to open the Print window. Figure 2.45 shows the Print Preview of the Comparing Expenses bar chart when the computer is linked to a colour printer.

Figure 2.44 Print

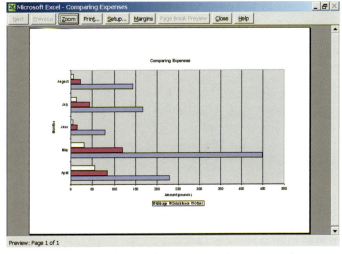

Figure 2.45 Printing a chart or graph separately

Exercise 30

Printing

1. Load Microsoft® Excel® using either Start and the All Programs menu or the Microsoft® Excel® icon on the desktop.

2. Load Car Sales Column Chart by single clicking on the File menu to show the Open option. Click on Open and a window called Open will appear.

3. The Look in box tells you which drive the window is looking at. You need to aim it at drive A:. You do this by clicking on the small button with the down arrow at the end of the Look in box. A menu will appear. Click on 3½ Floppy (A:) and Car Sales Column Chart will appear in the main working area. To open the file, click on it once to highlight it and then on the Open button on the right-hand side of the window. An alternative way is to double click on the Car Sales Column Chart file. In either case the spreadsheet and graph will appear in the working area of Excel.

4. The graph is on the Car Sales Column Chart tab so click on it to display it.

5. Change the Y-axis scale to 0 to 60000 by double clicking on it to open the Format Axis window and entering the new scale.

6. Add the data value to each column by double clicking on the bars to open the Format Data Series window and selecting the Data Labels tab and the Value radio button. Click on the OK Button to include the changes.

7. Save the revised chart as the file Car Sales Column Chart Revised by selecting the File menu and the Save As option on your floppy disk.

8. Using Print Preview look at the chart to check what Car Sales Column Chart Revised will look like when printed (Figure 2.46).

9. Print the chart on a single sheet by selecting the Print button to open the Print window. Click the OK button to print the chart.

10. You can close Microsoft® Excel® now. Click on the File menu item and a menu will appear with a list of options. At the bottom of the list is the option Exit. If you click on Exit then Microsoft® Excel® will close. An alternative way is to click on the Close button on the top right-hand corner of the application window.

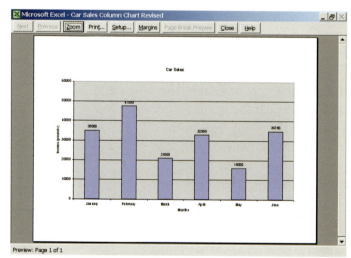

Figure 2.46 Print Preview

More practice

Activity 1

1. Load Microsoft® Excel® using either **Start** and the **All Programs** menu or the **Microsoft® Excel®** icon on the desktop.
2. Enter the table of information below to form a spreadsheet with two decimal places for cost and price. It shows a production plan of an engineering company called Tames Engineering. (Do not enter the information under potential profit. This shows how to calculate the formula).

	Volume	Cost	Price	Potential Profit
Nuts	6,000,000	0.03	0.04	(Price minus Cost) x Volume
Bolts	2,300,000	0.07	0.09	(Price minus Cost) x Volume
Bar	2,560,000	3.45	4.95	(Price minus Cost) x Volume
Sheet	2, 76,000	12.87	15.32	(Price minus Cost) x Volume
Plate	2, 17,000	36.80	39.50	(Price minus Cost) x Volume
Total				

3. Insert formulas to calculate potential profit, total volume and total potential profit (remember to replicate your formulas). You need to check if your formulas are correct. Once they are, you can change your numerical data many times with confidence that the calculations will be accurate.
4. Create a header and enter your name and an automatic date.
5. Improve the appearance of the sheet by:
    - Adding a title – Tames Engineering in Tahoma, size 14 and bold
    - Centring all the column headings and changing their font size to 14 and making them bold
    - Changing the column widths of Volume and Potential Profit so that they fit
    - Embolden all the row headings and change their fonts to 14.
6. Change the format of the Cost, Price and Potential Profit columns to currency.
7. Reduce decimal places in the Potential Profit column to nil.
8. Print your spreadsheet, showing gridlines and both formulas and actual values.
9. Investigate the effect on Potential Profit if you reduce prices to 0.035, 0.08, 4.70, 14.85 and 38.50, respectively. A key advantage of spreadsheets is that they allow you to model what will happen if you make changes to increase output or prices, or if costs change.
10. Print your spreadsheet showing gridlines and actual values.
11. Investigate what happens to the spreadsheet if you set the cost column to show only one decimal place. What you should observe is that the cost of Nuts appears to be 0.0 while the profit remains the same. This is because the formulas operate on the

real value not on what is presented. Change the cost column back to two decimal places.

12 Save the spreadsheet you have created with the file name Tames Engineering.

13 Close the file and exit Microsoft® Excel®.

Activity 2

1 Load Microsoft® Excel® using either Start and the All Programs menu or the Microsoft® Excel® icon on the desktop.

2 Enter the table of information below to form a spreadsheet with two decimal places. It shows the sales forecast of a printer, Jones Printing.

	April	May	June	Total	Price	Cash Flow
Books	6,000	7,500	5,600		1.84	(Total multiplied by Price)
Journals	11,000	9,890	7,600		0.37	(Total multiplied by Price)
Stationery	4,300	7,600	5,500		0.11	(Total multiplied by Price)
Catalogues	5,600	2,300	4,500		0.45	(Total multiplied by Price)
Total						

3 Insert formulas in Total (April+May+June) and Cash Flow (Total multiplied by Price) rows as well as totals for April, May, June, Total and Cash Flow columns (remember to replicate your formulas). You need to check that your formulas are correct. Once they are, you can change your numerical data many times with the confidence that the calculations will be accurate.

4 Create a header and enter your name and an automatic date.

5 Improve the appearance of the sheet by:
   - Adding a title Jones Printing in Arial, size 16 and bold
   - Changing all the column headings to centred Times New Roman, changing their font size to 14 and making them bold
   - Emboldening all the row headings and changing their fonts to Times New Roman, character size 14
   - Changing the column width of Cash Flow and the row headings so that they fit

6 Change the format of Price and Cash Flow columns to currency.

7 Print your spreadsheet showing gridlines and both formulas and actual values.

8 Investigate the effect on Cash Flow of increasing volumes during June to 6,000, 8,000, 6,000 and 5,000, respectively. A key advantage of spreadsheets is that they allow you to model what would happen if you made changes.

9 Print your spreadsheet showing gridlines and actual values.

10 Save the spreadsheet you have created on a floppy disk with the file name Jones Printing.

11 Close the file and exit Microsoft® Excel®.

Activity 3

1. Load Microsoft® Excel® using either Start and the All Programs menu or the Microsoft® Excel® icon on the desktop.
2. Open the spreadsheet file called Jones Printing that contains information about the sales of products.
3. Create a line graph showing the sales of the products during April, May and June.
4. Display the months along the X-axis.
5. Give the graph the title Jones Printing.
6. Call the X-axis Months.
7. Call the Y-axis Sales.
8. Use a legend to identify each line. Make sure each line is easily identified. Select the position of the legend.
9. Create the graph on a full page on a sheet separate from the source data. Figure 2.47 shows the result.
10. Create a header and enter your name and automatic date.
11. Save your graph as a file called Jones Printing Sales Graph
12. Print a copy of your graph
13. Close your file and exit Microsoft® Excel®.

Figure 2.47 Jones Printing sales graph

Activity 4
Graphs and charts

1. Load Microsoft® Excel® using either Start and the All Programs menu or the Microsoft® Excel® icon on the desktop.
2. Enter the table of information below to form a spreadsheet. It shows the opinions of people by age.

Opinion polls by age					
	18 to 25	26 to 35	36 to 50	51 to 65	over 65
Sample A	11	23	35	6	7
Sample B	17	45	12	3	1
Sample C	4	15	22	32	21
Sample D	27	39	31	24	16
Sample E	3	11	17	9	3

3 Create a header and enter your name and an automatic date.

4 Create a column chart to compare the results of the opinion poll. Display the age ranges along the X-axis.

5 Give the chart the title Opinion Poll, call the X-axis Samples and the Y-axis Number.

6 Use a legend to identify the colours of each sample. Position legend so that it is visible.

7 Create the chart on a full page on a sheet that is separate from the source data. Figure 2.48 shows the result.

8 Save the file with the name Opinion Poll Chart.

9 Print a copy of the chart.

10 Close your file and exit Microsoft® Excel®.

Figure 2.48 Opinion Poll chart

Activity 5

It is most important to practise creating charts and graphs. The following examples are provided to help you refine your skills. In each case, create the sheet and produce an appropriate chart or graph. Explore editing the chart by moving it, altering its shape and changing the axis scales. Finally print the chart.

Example 1	Population
Town A	23,000
Town B	46,000
Town C	106,000
Town D	213,000
Town E	11,000

Example 2	Household Expenditure
Family 1	9,700
Family 2	11,870
Family 3	29,450
Family 4	17,600
Family 5	5,600
Family 6	31,700
Family 7	12,150

Example 3 Comparisons – Internet users					
	1997	1998	1999	2000	2001
Education	1.2	1.4	1.9	2.7	3.5
Business	2.1	3.15	4.65	7.2	11.7
Home	0.2	0.3	0.45	0.7	1.35

Example 4 Comparisons – Rainfall					
	January	February	March	April	May
Area 1	12	15	17	11	9
Area 2	4	3	5	8	14
Area 3	7.5	9	8	7	6
Area 4	22	17	19	20	21
Area 5	16	18	23	15	18

In this chapter you have created a variety of spreadsheets, graphs and charts. They are a useful resource to provide you with many opportunities to practise your skills.

SUMMARY

1. **Load Microsoft® Excel®**: Select the Start button, highlight the All Programs menu and click on the Microsoft® Excel® item or double click on the Microsoft® Excel® icon on the desktop.

2. **Close Microsoft® Excel®**: Select the File menu item and the Exit option or click on the Close button on the top right-hand corner of the application window.

3. **New**: Select the File menu and the New option. This opens the New Workbook task pane which is divided into a number of sections. These provide access to many standard templates for spreadsheets. Select the Blank Workbook option. A new blank spreadsheet will appear.

4. **Enter text or numerical data**: Click on the chosen cell and enter text or numbers from the keyboard.

5. **Open Task Pane**: Select the View menu and the Task Pane option. To close the Task Pane repeat this operation or click on the Close icon in top right-hand corner of task pane.

6. **Delete, close and hide**: Select the Edit menu and either the Delete or Clear options. Each will provide you with a range of choices. Select the Format menu and one of the options Row, Column or Sheet and the Hide option. The Unhide option is also available.

7. **Undo**: Select the Edit menu and the Undo option.

8. **Insert rows and columns**: Select where the row or column should be inserted and then the `Insert` menu and either the `Rows` or `Columns` item.

9. **Delete rows or columns**: Select the row or column to be deleted by clicking in headings and then chose `Edit` menu and the `Delete` option.

10. **Cell references**: Each cell has a unique reference which is made up of the column letter and row number (e.g. A7, P16 and F12).

11. **Enter formulas**: Formulas are used to calculate numerical values (e.g. total columns of figures).

    Formulas start with = sign (e.g. =F5-F9)

    Mathematical operators
    + add
    - subtract
    * multiply
    / divide

    A standard function (SUM) adds together the contents of a highlighted row or column of numbers (e.g. SUM(C3:C6) =C3+C4+C5+C6).

    Brackets – operations inside brackets are carried out first.

12. **Change presentation**: Highlight the item and select the font, character size, embolden, italics, underline and align text icons from the Formatting toolbar.

    Numerical formatting is again based on highlighting the item or area and then selecting the icon from the Formatting toolbar:

    - Currency – to display numerical information with a £ sign in a currency format
    - Percent – to display data in percentage style
    - Comma – formats numbers with commas in appropriate places
    - Decimal points – increase and decrease the number of decimal points shown
    - Change the width and depth of a row

    Place the mouse pointer over the row or column heading edge until the pointer changes shape. Hold down the left mouse button and drag the edge to widen or narrow the row or column.

    or

    Right click on the chosen item or highlighted area to reveal a pop-up menu. Select the `Format Cells` option to open a Format Cells window.

13. **Page Layout**: Select the `File` menu and the `Page Setup` option.

14. **Headers and Footers**: Select the `File` menu and the `Page Setup` option to open the Page Setup window. Choose the `Header/Footer` tab.

15. **Borders**: Select the Borders icon on the Formatting toolbar.

16 **Preview printing**: Select the `File` Menu and the `Print Preview` option.

17 **Printing**: Either select the Print button within the `Print Preview` window or Select the `File` menu, the `Print` option and the `OK` button.

18 **Print gridlines**: Either select the `File` menu, the `Page Setup` option, the `Sheet` tab, click in the `Gridlines` box and the `OK` button or Select the `Tools` menu, the `Options` item, the `View` tab, click in the `Gridlines` box and the `OK` button.

19 **Print Formulas**: Select the `Tools` menu, the `Options` item, the `View` tab, click in the `Formulas` box and the `OK` button.

20 **Print Row and Column headings**: Either select the `File` menu, the `Page Setup` option, the `Sheet` tab, click in the `Row and column` headings box and the `OK` button or Select the `Tools` menu, the `Options` item, the `View` tab, click in the `Row and column` headings box and the `OK` button.

21 **Open the Chart Wizard**: Insert data into the spreadsheet. Highlight the data then select the `Insert` menu and the `Chart` option.

22 **Column, bar, line and pie charts**: At the left-hand edge of the Chart Wizard is a list of `Chart` types. Click once on the type of chart. On the right-hand side of the window are displayed examples of your chart. Select the example with a single click and a description of the chart is given below the examples.

23 **Preview charts**: Click on the Press and Hold to `View` sample button holding the left mouse button down. If you release the mouse button then the chart will disappear.

24 **Data range**: The second step of the Chart Wizard shows the data range in the form of =Sheet1!$B$8:$C$14. Removing the $ signs, the data range is Sheet1 B8:C14.

It is crucial to check that the chart or graph is based on the correct data range.

25 **Titles, legends and labels**: Step 3 of the Chart Wizard provides options depending on the type of chart being developed.

26 **Correct errors**: Use the `Back` button to move back through the Chart Wizard steps.

27 **New sheet**: Step 4 of the Chart Wizard provides you with the options to present your graph or chart on a new sheet or as an additional object in an existing sheet (e.g. the one containing the data it relates to).

28 **Change display**: Single clicking on the chart will reveal handles which allow you to move and change the size of the chart using the mouse.

29 **Edit chart**: Right click in the chart. The `Format Plot Area` menu will appear allowing you to access the options available during the Chart Wizard process and make any changes.

30 **Alter axes**: Double clicking on the value axis (a small label appears to help you identify the axis) will open up the Format Axis window. The `Scale` tab allows you to change the scale of the chart axes.

31 **Save a file on a floppy disk**: Insert a floppy disk into drive A: then click on the **File** Menu and **Save** . Select drive (Floppy (A:)) and enter the file name.

Having saved a file once, you can update it by clicking on the **File** menu and **Save** without the **Save As** window appearing again. It simply overwrites the original file.

32 **Find and Replace**: Select the **Edit** menu and then **Replace or Find** .

Chapter 3

Unit 3

Database manipulation

This chapter will help you to:
- identify and use database software correctly
- use an input device to enter data in an existing database and present and print database files
- create simple queries/searches on one or two criteria and sort data
- produce appropriate predefined reports from databases using shortcuts
- present data in full, sorted alphabetically and numerically

Assessment

This unit does not assume any previous experience of using a computer. You may find it useful to have completed Unit 1: File management and e-document production. You will be assessed through a practical realistic assignment which is designed to allow you to demonstrate your knowledge and skills against each objective. Your tutor can provide you with more guidance.

New CLAiT syllabus

New CLAiT does not require you to create a database table. You must only be able to add and edit its contents and query them. This chapter nevertheless offers you the opportunity to create small straightforward databases and then to practise adding and editing their contents. This is useful if you are planning to extend your studies to CLAiT Plus, which does require students to develop a database or if you are studying on your own without any access to a database.

If you do not want to create a database (i.e. undertake the extra tasks) then the databases are available from the supporting website (www.hodderclait.co.uk) and you are free to download them. We suggest that you download and save them on to a floppy disk.

Exercises which are not part of the New CLAiT requirements are marked as OPTIONAL.

Database applications

Microsoft® Access is a database creation application. You can use it to design databases for your own personal use (e.g. records of your video collection) or for an enterprise (e.g. customer information). In this chapter you will learn how to create a table of information in which information can be entered, stored and presented. A database can have one or many tables depending on the complexity of the system. In our exercises, we will concentrate on a single table, which is the basic building block of more extensive databases.

Figure 3.1 shows the opening display of Microsoft® Access. The application window resembles other Microsoft® Office applications in that it is divided into:

- menu and toolbars at the top of the display
- a working area in which to develop the database
- a status bar at the bottom of the window
- a New File task pane on the right side of the display

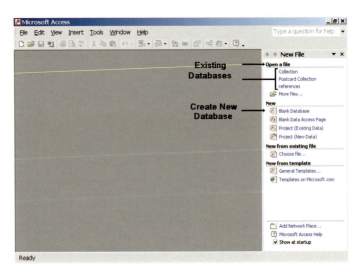

Figure 3.1 Microsoft Access

The New File task pane offers a range of options including:

- Open a file section
- a Blank Database option

The Open a file section shows a list of files that represent existing databases that you have recently opened. You can open them now by clicking on them. The Blank Database option opens a new database for you to create.

Spreadsheets versus databases

While both spreadsheets and databases create tables of information and so appear very similar, there are considerable differences between them.

A database can be designed so that:

- data can be continuously changed in an efficient and effective way without the operator needing to know about the structure of the database
- data held in the database can be presented in many different ways to meet a wide range of information needs
- data held in a database can be searched to locate any combination of data that it contains and the results of the search can be presented in a wide variety of ways

Microsoft® Access provides:

- Forms – these offer different ways of entering, editing and viewing information
- Queries – these allow you to answer any questions you may have about the data contained in the database
- Reports – these enable you to present information combining data from several tables or from a single one

Tables

The key feature of a database is a table. Figure 3.2 shows a Microsoft® Access table. Tables are groups of records. A record is a group of related fields, a field being a single item of the record, e.g. name, organisation and telephone numbers.

In Microsoft® Access there are various different types of field which include: text, number, yes/no (i.e. can only contain a yes or a no), memo (i.e. a longer piece of text), date/time, currency (i.e. money), autonumber (i.e. automatically numbers the records in a table) and hyperlink (i.e. links to a website). The number fields can be used as part of your calculations.

When you are creating a database table, you need to define the type of each field within the records. In Figure 3.2 first name, last name, organisation, works telephone and email are all text fields whereas Order Value is a currency field. The table illustrated is called Contact Example.

Figure 3.2 Microsoft Access table

Creating a new database – optional

The first step in creating a database is to consider the information you may want it to contain. The example below shows the information that you might want to include in a staff holiday record table.

Example
Name – individual's name (i.e. text field)
Team – which team the individual works in (i.e. text field)
Staff Number – pay number (i.e. number field)
Holiday – number of days holiday entitlement (i.e. number field)
Taken – number of days taken (i.e. number field)

Name	Team	Staff Number	Holiday	Taken
Singh	Personnel	23	25	12
Brown	Computers	35	30	15
Jones	Production	41	25	10
Carr	Sales	44	35	25
Patel	Computers	17	25	18
Scott	Personnel	14	30	20
Jenks	Production	51	30	14

This table of information consists of seven records with each record composed of five fields.

Optional Exercise 31

Creating a database table

1 Load Microsoft® Access by selecting Start, highlighting the All Programs menu and clicking on the Microsoft® Access item or click on the Microsoft® Access icon on the desktop.

2 Microsoft® Access will load (Figure 3.1). Select the Blank Database option within the New File task pane. The File New Database window opens to enable you to save your new database (Figure 3.3).

Figure 3.3 File New Database

You need to select a drive or folder in which to store your new database as a file. If you click on the arrow button next to the Look in box, you can select 3½ Floppy(A:). Next you need to give the file a name. Insert the name Holidays in the File name box and click on the Create button (Figure 3.3). You will have saved your blank database as a file called Holidays on your floppy disk. The Holidays database window is now shown (Figure 3.4).

3 The Holidays database window shows three options with the Tables object on the left-hand side selected:

- Create table in Design view
- Create table by using wizard
- Create table by entering data

Double click on Create table in Design view and the table window opens (Figure 3.5).

Figure 3.4 Holidays database window

4 You need to insert your field names and their types. If you enter Name in the Field Name box and click in the corresponding Data Type box, a small down arrow will appear revealing a list of types. Select Text. Click in the next Field Name box then enter Team. Complete the table, as shown in Figure 3.5.

continued

5 When you enter a type, observe that, in the Field Properties pane at the bottom of the window, the Field Size shows a value (e.g. 50) with a text type and Long Integer with a number type. The value 50 indicates the number of characters that the field can store while a Long Integer is a whole number (i.e. no decimal places). If you wanted to show real numbers (i.e. with decimal places) then you would need to click in the Long Integer box to produce a down arrow which, when clicked, gives you other options. In this case all our numbers are whole.

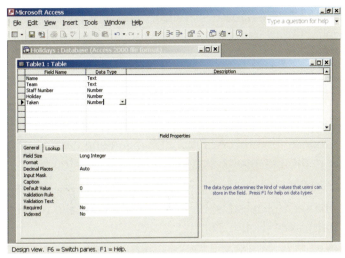

Figure 3.5 Design View

6 Close the window and you will be prompted to save your table. Indicate that you want to save the table and the Save As window will now appear allowing you to name your table. Call it Records and click on the OK button.

7 A warning message will now appear asking you to define a primary key. In this case you do not need to define one so click on the No button. A primary key is a unique number which allows different tables to relate to each other.

8 You can now see the Holidays database window but with an extra item added – Records (Figure 3.6).

9 Double clicking on Records allows you to begin entering the data. We will return to this table to enter the data later. Close the window by clicking on the Close button in the top right-hand corner of the Holidays database window.

10 Close Microsoft® Access by clicking on Close button in top right-hand corner of the main application window or select the File and the Exit option, unless you wish to carry on immediately with the next exercise.

Figure 3.6 Record table

Exercise 32

The Holidays database is available on the supporting website (www.hodderclait.co.uk) if you would like to undertake this exercise without completing Exercise 30 (i.e. creating a database table).

Entering data

1 Insert your floppy disk into your drive. Load Microsoft® Access by selecting Start, highlighting the All Programs menu and clicking on the Microsoft® Access item or click on the Microsoft® Access icon on the desktop.

2 Microsoft® Access will load (Figure 3.1). In the New File task pane, Open a file section will be the Holidays file. Double click this item and the Holidays database window will be displayed (Figure 3.6).

3 Double click on Records and a blank table will appear. Using the example, complete the records, moving between the fields by clicking in each box. Alternatively use the arrow keys, Tab key or Enter key to move between fields.

4 When you have completed the table check each entry against the original data. It is vital that the data in a database is correct since you will use this data later and often base decisions on it. If you find an error, click into the field box to move the cursor into the box, and delete the mistake and insert the correct entry. Figure 3.7 shows the completed table.

5 If you move your mouse pointer between row or column headings you will see it change shape into an arrow (pointing to the right in the row heading and down in the column heading). If the pointer goes over the edge of a heading it changes into cross arrows. By holding down the left mouse button you can drag the column wider or row higher when the arrow's pointer is shaped as cross arrows.

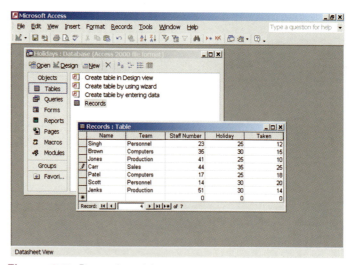

Figure 3.7 Records table

The down or right pointing single arrow will select (highlight) the row or column if clicked.

6 You now need to save the completed table. This is straightforward since it is saved automatically by closing the window. Click on the Close button in the top right-hand corner of the window.

7 Close Microsoft® Access by selecting the File menu and the Exit option.

Editing data

Microsoft® Access has several tools to assist you with adding, deleting, amending and inserting records. You can insert new records (i.e. rows) and fields (i.e. columns). If you left click with the pointer shaped as an arrow the row or column is highlighted (i.e. the pointer is over the column or row heading). By then clicking the right mouse button, a menu appears. Figure 3.8 illustrates the menu that appears when a row (i.e. a record) is highlighted. OCR New CLAiT requires that you are able to add and delete a record (i.e. a row).

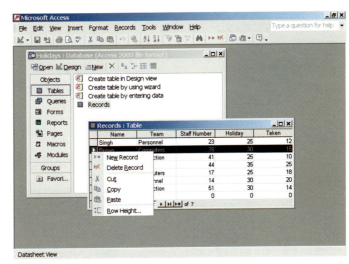

Figure 3.8 Right button menu

To alter a single field, click into the field and delete the entry before entering the new content. If you have a large database and a number of changes to make then it is more efficient to use the Replace or Find functions in Microsoft® Access rather than change each one separately. In the example we have been working on you might want to change a team's name (e.g. from Personnel to Human Resources). You could do this by going through all the records and manually changing them one by one. This is both time consuming and also likely to produce errors. The more efficient way is to select the Edit menu and the Replace option to open the Find and Replace window.

Exercise 33

Editing data

1. Insert your floppy disk into your drive. Load Microsoft® Access by selecting Start, highlighting the All Programs menu and clicking on the Microsoft® Access item or click on the Microsoft® Access icon on the desktop.

2. Microsoft® Access will load (Figure 3.1). In the New File Task Pane, Open a file section will be the Holidays file. Double click this item and the Holidays database window will be displayed (Figure 3.6).

3. Double click on Records and the holiday data will appear.

4. The records need to be amended.

   Carr has been transferred to Production. Change the Team field by clicking in the field, delete Sales using the Delete key and enter Production.

   Jenks has left the company so this record needs to be deleted. Position the mouse pointer over the row heading and when the pointer has changed into an arrow, click on the right mouse button. The menu (Figure 3.8) will appear. By clicking on Delete Record you will

continued

remove the Jenks record. You may see a message appear asking if you are certain that you want to delete a record. Click on Yes to remove the record.

A new person has joined the company so you need to insert a record for Simba. The record is:

– Simba, Sales, 178, 25, 0

If you click in the bottom empty line of the table in the Name field you can begin to enter the new record. You move between fields by clicking or pressing the Tab or Enter keys.

5 When you have finished entering the new record and amending the others, carefully check the table. It is vital that databases contain no errors or the information you extract from it will be flawed. Figure 3.9 shows you the final table.

6 You now need to save your changes. Close the table by clicking on the Close button in the top right-hand corner of the table window. Your changes will be saved automatically.

Figure 3.9 Amended table

7 Close Microsoft® Access by selecting the File menu and the Exit option.

Printing

An important aspect of all computer applications is the ability to print information. Microsoft® Access provides you with the functionality to print a table. This is available from the File menu and the Print option, which reveals the Print window and you can print using the default settings by clicking on the OK button.

The Page Setup option in the File menu opens the Page Setup window which has two tabs: Margins and Page. Within Margins, you can

Figure 3.10 Print Preview Holidays

adjust the four margins and print using the `Print Headings` option. Within Page you can choose the orientation of the page (i.e. either portrait or landscape).

`Print Preview` in the `File` menu allows you to check the appearance of the printed document before you print it. Figure 3.10 shows the Print Preview window of the Holiday table. If you are content with the appearance, you can print it immediately by clicking on the `Print` icon and then on the `OK` button on the Print window which will then appear. Notice that the mouse pointer has changed into a magnifying glass which allows you to make the image larger or smaller.

Sorting, searching and querying

With a database, you can store a large amount of data and access it in any way you need to. Microsoft® Access lets you sort, query (i.e. question) and search the data to give you information.

Sorting lets you reorder the data and present it in a new sequence. You can sort the records into alphabetical, numerical or date order. This is useful if you want a list of the holidays information presented in the order of Staff Number, alphabetically by the name of the employee or the date of starting work. You can sort in ascending or descending order.

A, B, C and D – ascending or D, C, B and A – descending
or
1, 2, 3 and 4 – ascending or 4, 3, 2 and 1 – descending

Searching is the term used for finding a particular piece of data within the database. By selecting the `Edit` menu and the `Find` option, you reveal the Find and Replace window which enables you to search the table for a particular field of data. This is useful if, say, you want to find those employees who had not taken any holiday, those who had 25 days holiday entitlement and so on.

Exercise 34

Simple sorting (alphabetically and numerically)

1. Insert your floppy disk into your drive. Load Microsoft® Access by selecting `Start`, highlighting the `All Programs` menu and clicking on the `Microsoft® Access` item or click on the `Microsoft® Access` icon on the desktop.

2. Microsoft® Access will load (Figure 3.1). In the New File task pane, Open a file section will be the Holidays file. Double click this item and the Holidays database window will be displayed (Figure 3.6).

3. Double click on Records and the holiday data will appear.

4. Highlight the Taken column by placing your mouse pointer over the column heading until the mouse pointer changes to an arrow. Click on the left mouse button and the column will be highlighted.

continued

5 With the Taken column highlighted, you can sort the data in the column using the Ascending and Descending icons on the toolbar. Figure 3.11 shows the records sorted with the Taken column sorted ascending (i.e. low to high).

6 Explore sorting this table using these icons and print each option (e.g. numerical ascending and descending). Select the File Menu, the Print option and the OK button.

7 Experiment with alphabetical sorting using the Name column and again print each option. Figure 3.12 shows the Name column records sorted by ascending name.

8 Compare your printouts.

9 Close the table by clicking on the Close button in the top right-hand corner of the table window. You will be asked if you want to save the changes you have made (i.e. save the new format of your table). In this case click on the Yes button so that the new layout of the table is preserved.

10 Close Microsoft® Access by selecting the File menu and the Exit option unless you wish to continue with the next exercise which you will start at step 3.

Figure 3.11 Sorted records

Figure 3.12 Name sorted alphabetically

By using the Microsoft® Access functions, you can sort or search the database at any time but in each case you need to enter your requirements. These are useful for individual questions that you are unlikely to want to repeat. However, Microsoft® Access also provides a way of saving useful searches or sorts by using a Query.

Exercise 35

Creating a query

1 Insert your floppy disk into your drive. Load Microsoft® Access by selecting Start, highlighting the All Programs menu and clicking on the Microsoft® Access item or click on the Microsoft® Access icon on the desktop.

2 Microsoft® Access will load (Figure 3.1). In the New File task pane, Open a file section will be the Holidays file. Double click this item and the Holidays database window will be displayed (Figure 3.6).

3 Select the Queries button in the list of Objects on the left-hand side of the window. Figure 3.13 shows the new view. Double click on Create query in Design View. A new window will open with an overlaid window called Show Table (Figure 3.14). Click on the Add button in this window with the Records table highlighted. A small window will appear headed Records within the Query1 window.

4 Click on the Close button on the Show Table window to reveal Figure 3.15, the Query window.

5 In the Query window, a small box (Records) will have been added that shows the fields making up the Holidays table. The cursor will be flashing in the first Field box and a small down arrow will be shown at the end of the same box. Click on the down arrow and a list of the Records fields will appear. Select Name by clicking on it. Name will appear in the first box. Move to the next box (to the right) and repeat the operation selecting Team this time and so on, until all five fields have been chosen.

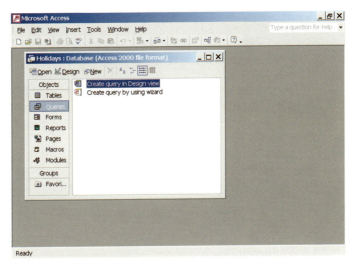

Figure 3.13 Queries

6 In the Table row you will see the name of the table, Records, appear.

7 The third row is called Sort. If you click in any of the boxes you will see a down arrow appear which if you

Figure 3.14 Show Table

continued

click on it reveals a list showing Ascending, Descending or Not Sorted. You can sort the table in this query in any way you choose. Let's create a new sort. Select the Holiday column Sort box and select Descending. The query will sort the data table into the number of days of holiday from highest to lowest.

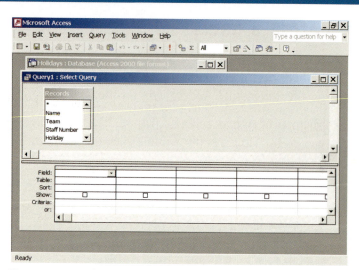

Figure 3.15 Query1: Select Query

8 We can now save this query by selecting the File menu and the Save As option. The Save As window will appear and you need to enter Holiday Entitlement in the box entitled Save Query then click on the OK button.

9 We could now close the query window by clicking on the Close button but instead we are going to create another query. First remove the sort from Holiday by clicking on the down arrow in the Holiday Sort field and selecting Not Sorted.

10 In the Show field you will have noticed that there is a tick in each field. This indicates that when the query is run, the contents of this field will be shown. If you click on the tick, it will disappear and then that field will not be shown. The tick is replaced by clicking again in the tick box.

11 The query you are going to create will show the holiday records of all people working in the Production team.

12 In the Criteria field on the Team column enter Production. When you click away from this field, you will see Production enclosed in inverted commas (i.e. "Production"). If you make a mistake when entering Production then the query will not find any information since it cannot match the fields – your entry must be exact.

13 Save this query by selecting the File menu and the Save As option. Then enter Production Holidays as the name of the query and click the OK button.

14 Again, you could close this window but we will extend

Figure 3.16 Production holidays 25 days Query

continued

this query by adding a second criterion. In the criteria field on Holiday enter 25. In this case the number is not enclosed in inverted commas. Your query will show all the Production employees who have 25 days holiday entitlement. Figure 3.16 shows the final query.

15 Save this query by selecting the **File** menu and the **Save As** option and entering Production Holidays 25 days as the name of the query. Then click on the **OK** button.

16 Close the window by selecting the **Close** button in the top right-hand corner of the window. You will now see Figure 3.17 which shows the three saved queries. To run a query double click it. Try the three queries to see if they are producing the results you desire. The results of the query are removed by clicking on the close button.

Figure 3.17 Three queries

17 If you find that the query is producing the wrong outcomes you can amend it by single clicking the query to highlight it and then by clicking on the **Design** button on the toolbar. This will open the query to allow you to make the required changes.

18 When each query is run, print the results by selecting the **File** menu, the **Print** option and the **OK** button.

19 Compare each printout and think about the queries you have created.

20 Close the Database window by selecting the close button and then close Microsoft® Access by selecting the **File** menu and the **Exit** option.

Search criteria

In the last exercise we used numerical criteria. It is possible to qualify the numerical criteria using the following symbols:

>   greater than
<   less than
>= greater than or equal to
<= less than or equal to
<> not equal to

These symbols are available on the keyboard.

> greater than (hold the Shift key down and then press full stop key)
< less than (hold the Shift key down and then press the comma key)
>= greater than or equal to (hold the Shift key down and then press the full stop key, release the keys and press the equals key)
<= less than or equal to (hold the Shift key down and then press the comma key, release the keys and press the equals key)
<> not equal to (hold the Shift key down, press the comma key and then the full stop key)

In your exercise you used the criteria of selecting records for Production employees with 25 days holiday entitlement. With these symbols you could vary these criteria to select employees with less than 25 (i.e. <25), more than 25 (i.e. >25), greater than or equal to 25 (i.e. >=25), less than or equal to 25 (i.e. <=25) and not equal to 25 (i.e. <>25).

Exercise 36

Using numerical criteria

1 Insert your floppy disk into your drive. Load Microsoft® Access by selecting Start, highlighting the All Programs menu and clicking on the Microsoft® Access item or click on the Microsoft® Access icon on the desktop.

2 Microsoft® Access will load (Figure 3.1). In the New File task pane, Open a file section will be the Holidays file. Double click this item and the Holidays database window will be displayed (Figure 3.6).

3 Select the Queries button in the list of Objects on the left-hand side of the window. Double click on Create query in Design View. A new window will open with an overlaid window called Show Table. Highlight Records and click on the Add button on Show Table.

4 Click on the Close button on Show Table window (Figure 3.14).

5 In the Query window a small box (Records) will have been added which shows the fields that make up the table. The cursor will be flashing in the first Field box and a small down arrow will be shown at the end of the same box. Click on the down arrow and a list of the table fields will appear. Select Name by clicking on it. Name will appear in the first box. Move to the next box and repeat the operation selecting Team this time and so on until all five fields have been chosen.

6 You are going to create a query that will identify the holidays for staff with a Staff Number less than 40 and who have taken more than 5 days holiday.

Figure 3.18 Two numerical criteria

continued

7. Click in the Staff Number criteria field and enter <40 and then click in the Taken criteria field and enter >5. Figure 3.18 shows the selections.

8. Save this query by selecting the File menu and the Save As option then enter Staff Numbers as the name of the query and click the OK button.

9. Close the window by clicking on the Close button in the top right-hand corner of the window.

10. Run the new query and check the results that it produces. Amend if necessary. Figure 3.19 shows the result of running the query.

11. Print the results of your query (select the File menu, the Print option and the OK button).

12. Close the Database window by selecting the Close button and then close Microsoft® Access by selecting File menu and the Exit option.

Figure 3.19 Staff Numbers query

Reports

If you need to print out the results of a query or to display records from tables, the report function lets you do this. On the left-hand side of the database window is the Reports button which will change the display to show two options:

- Create report in Design View
- Create report by using wizard

Clicking the second option (Create report by using wizard) (Figure 3.20) shows the first step of the Report Wizard. You can create a report based on either a database table of information or the results of a query. You can present the chosen information in both cases. The fields are shown in the left-hand column (Figure 3.20). The fields that you

Figure 3.20 Holidays database Reports Wizard – Step 1

want to appear in the report need to be selected by highlighting them and selecting the single arrow button pointing to the right. The item is transferred into the right-hand column. If you want all the fields in the report then click on the double arrow button. The process of selection can be reversed using the arrow button pointing to the left which removes the chosen fields.

Once you have selected your fields, click on the Next button and a new display appears providing you with the option to group your data. Figure 3.21 shows the grouping display.

Figure 3.21 Data grouping

Having made your selections, click again on the Next button which allows you to sort the data. This is followed by options to choose the layout and page orientation of the report, select the style of the report from a set of templates and finally to name the report so that you can find it again. The final options also allow you to preview the report.

If you make a mistake then you can retrace your steps by using the Back button or use the Modify the report's design option on the final display (Figure 3.25). Figures 3.22 to 3.25 show the Wizard steps.

Figure 3.22 Sort data

With any printed report it is important that the data is displayed in full with records and headings completely shown. Your readers can easily be confused by only a partial display and you will be judged on the quality of the output rather than the excellent design of your database.

Figure 3.23 Layout and orientation

Figure 3.24 Style

Figure 3.25 Preview Report

Exercise 37

Report

1. Insert your floppy disk into your drive. Load Microsoft® Access by selecting Start, highlighting the All Programs menu and clicking on the Microsoft® Access item or click on the Microsoft® Access icon on the desktop.

2. Microsoft® Access will load (Figure 3.1). In the New File task pane, Open a file section will be the Holidays file. Double click this item and the Holidays database window will be displayed (Figure 3.6).

3. Select the Report button in the list of Objects on the left-hand side of the window and the Create Report by using wizard option. This will open the Report Wizard window.

4. Select the query Staff Numbers and all the fields in the query by using the double arrow button. Check that all the fields have been transferred and then click on the Next button. There is no need to select any groupings so click on Next.

continued

5 Select the sort on Name so that the report is presented in descending order of staff names (i.e. Z to A) and then click on Next.

6 Select the Tabular layout and Landscape orientation and then click on Next.

7 Select the Formal style and then click on Next.

8 Give the report the title Report Staff Numbers, select the Preview the report radio button and then click on the Finish button. The report will be shown since you have selected preview. Figure 3.26 shows the resulting report. It is important to check that you have displayed the data in full with complete field headings.

9 Print the report (select the File menu, the Print option and the OK button), check the contents are correct and that the data is printed in full.

10 Close the Database window by selecting the Close button and then close Microsoft® Access by selecting the File menu and the Exit option.

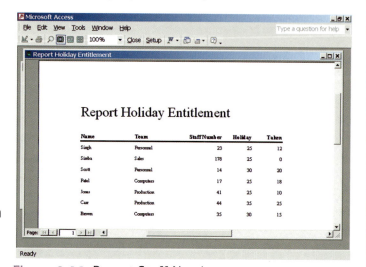

Figure 3.26 Report Staff Numbers

More practice

Activity 1

Creating a table – Optional

1 Load Microsoft® Access by selecting Start, highlighting the All Programs menu and clicking on the Microsoft® Access item or click on the Microsoft® Access icon on the desktop.

2 Microsoft® Access will load (Figure 3.1). Select the Blank Database option within the New File task pane. The File New Database window opens to enable you to save your new database (Figure 3.3).

You need to select a drive or folder in which to store your new database as a file. If you click on the arrow button next to the Look in box you can select 3½ Floppy (A:).

Next we need to give the file a name. Insert the name Customer Accounts in the File name box and click on the Create button. You will have saved your blank database as a file called Customer Accounts on your floppy disk.

3 The Customer Accounts database window shows three options with the Tables object on the left-hand side selected:
   – Create table in Design view
   – Create table by using wizard

- Create table by entering data

Double click on Create table in Design view and the table window will open.

4 You are going to create the table below:

Customer Accounts

Name – company name (Text)
Address – address of the company (Text)
Contact – name of company customer contact (Text)
Credit – credit limit of the company (Currency)
First Order – date of the first order from the company (Date/Time)
Size – size of the first order (Number)

Name	Address	Contact	Credit	First Order	Size
Deans	London	Anne	2500	01/10/90	500
Big Shop	Birmingham	Keith	1500	13/02/92	750
Mint	Sheffield	Jane	1000	26/06/96	250
Gordons	London	Stephanie	3000	19/08/95	250
Youngs	Manchester	David	2000	30/04/94	900
Palmers	Sheffield	Peter	3000	07/11/96	750

This table of information consists of six records with each record comprising six fields.

You need to insert your field names and their types. If you enter Name in the Field Name box and click in the corresponding Data Type box, a small down arrow will appear revealing a list of types. Select Text then click in the next Field Name box and enter Address. Complete the table – Contact, Credit, First Order and Size. Both Credit and Size are Currency type. First Order is Date/Time type.

5 When you enter a type you should observe that in Field Size a value (e.g. 50) will appear with a text type and Long Integer with a number type. The value 50 indicates the number of characters that the field can store while a Long Integer is a whole number (i.e. no decimal places).

6 Close the window and you will be prompted to save your table. Indicate that you want to save the table and the Save As window will now appear allowing you to name your table call it Accounts and click on the OK button.

7 A warning message will now appear asking you if you need a primary key. In this case you do not need to define one, so click on the No button. The table window reappears and you should close it by clicking on the Close button in the top right-hand corner of the table window. You can now see the Customer Accounts database window but with an extra item added – Accounts.

8 You can now enter the data by double clicking on Accounts. Enter the text to produce Figure 3.27.

9 When you have completed the table, check each entry against the original data. If you find an error, click in the field box to move the cursor into the box. Delete the mistake and insert the correct entry.

10 Explore sorting the information using the Ascending and Descending icons on the toolbar. Sort the Name, Credit and First Order Fields. This will show you how to sort alphabetically, numerically and by date.

Figure 3.27 Accounts table

11 Close the window. The completed table will be saved automatically.

12 Click on the Close button in the top right-hand corner of the window.

13 Close Microsoft® Access by selecting the File menu and the Exit option.

Activity 2

The database Customer Accounts is available on the supporting website (www.hodderclait.co.uk) if you would like to undertake this exercise without creating the database.

Queries

1 Insert your floppy disk into your drive. Load Microsoft® Access by selecting Start, highlighting the All Programs menu and clicking on the Microsoft® Access item or double click on the Microsoft® Access icon on the desktop.

2 Microsoft® Access will load (Figure 3.1). In the New File task pane, Open a file section will be the Customer Accounts file. Double click this item and the Customer Accounts database window will be displayed.

3 Select the Queries button in the list of Objects on the left-hand side of the window. Double click on Create query in Design view. A new window will open with an overlaid window called Show Table. Click on the Add button on Show Table and then on the Close button.

4 In the Query window a small box (Accounts) will have been added which shows the fields that make up the Accounts table. The cursor will be flashing in the first Field box and a small down arrow will be shown at the end of the same box. Click on the down arrow and a list of the Customer Account fields will appear. Select Name by clicking on it. Name will appear in the first box. Move to the next box and repeat the operation selecting Address this time. Repeat the process adding contact, credit and size fields.

5 You are going to create a query based on two criteria. These are:

Customers in London

Customers who have a Credit limit greater than or equal to £2500

6 Click in the criteria box of Address and enter London.

7 Click in the criteria box of Credit and enter >=2500

8 Save this query by selecting the File menu and the Save As option then enter Location and Credit as the name of the query and click on the OK button.

9 Close the window by selecting the Close button in the top right-hand corner of the window. You will now see that the Customer Accounts window shows the query. Double click on the query to see if it produces the desired results (Figure 3.28). The results of the query are removed by clicking on the Close button.

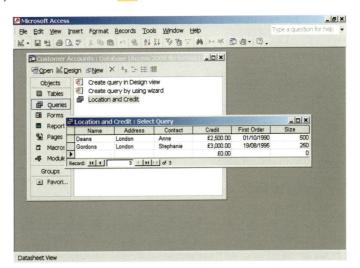

Figure 3.28 Location and Credit query results

10 If you find that the query is producing the wrong outcomes then you can amend it by single clicking the query to highlight it and then on the Design button on the toolbar. This will open the query to allow you to make the required changes.

11 When the query is run, print the results by selecting the File menu, the Print option and the OK button. Check that the data is displayed in full.

12 You are now going to design a query to identify all customers who first placed an order on or after 30/04/94. The Customer Accounts database window should be displayed.

13 Select the Queries button in the list of Objects on the left-hand side of the window. Double click on Create query in Design view. A new window will open with an overlaid window called Show Table. Click on the Add button on Show Table and then on the Close button.

14 In the Query window a small box (Accounts) will have been added which shows the fields that make up the Accounts table. The cursor will be flashing in the first Field box and a small down arrow will be shown at the end of the same box. Click on the down arrow and a list of the Customer Account fields will appear. Select First Order by clicking on it. First Order will appear in the first box. Move to the next box and repeat the operation selecting Name this time. You simply want to identify the names of the customers.

15 You are going to create a query based on one criterion:

Customers who have placed orders on or after 30/04/94

16 Click in the criteria box of First Name and enter >=30/04/94.

17 Save this query by selecting the File menu and the Save As option then enter First Order as the name of the query and click on the OK button.

18 Close the window by selecting the Close button in the top right-hand corner of the window. You will now see that the Customer Accounts window shows the new query.

Double click on the query First Order to see if it produces the desired results (Figure 3.29). The results of the query are removed by clicking on the Close button.

19 If you find that the query is producing the wrong outcomes then you can amend it by single clicking the query to highlight it and then on the Design button. This will open the query to allow you to make the required changes.

20 When the query is run, print the results by selecting the File menu, the Print option and the OK button. Check that the data is displayed in full.

21 Close the Database window by selecting the Close button and then close Microsoft® Access by selecting the File menu and the Exit option.

Figure 3.29 First Order results

Activity 3
Reports

1 Insert your floppy disk into your drive. Load Microsoft® Access by selecting Start, highlighting the All Programs menu and clicking on the Microsoft® Access item or double click on the Microsoft® Access icon on the desktop.

2 Microsoft® Access will load (Figure 3.1). In the New File task pane, Open a file section will be the Customer Accounts file. Double click this item and the Customer Accounts database window will be displayed.

3 Select the Report button in the list of Objects on the left-hand side of the window. Double click on Create report by using wizard. The Report Wizard window will open. Select the table: Accounts.

4 Select all the fields by clicking on the double arrow and transferring them to the right-hand column and then click on the Next button.

5 There is no need to group fields so click on the Next button.

6 Sort (i.e. A–Z) by Size and then click on the Next button.

7 Select the Tabular layout and the Landscape orientation and then click on Next button. Remember that you need to display the data in full.

Figure 3.30 Size report

8 Choose the **Compact** style and then click on the **Next** button.

9 Give your report the title Size and select **Preview**. Click on the **Finish** button.

10 The report will appear for you to check (Figure 3.30). It is important to check that the data is displayed in full.

11 When the report is run, print the results by selecting the **File** menu, the **Print** option and the **OK** button.

12 Close the Database window by selecting the **Close** button and then close Microsoft® Access by selecting the **File** menu and the **Exit** option.

Activity 4

The Collections database is available on the supporting website (www.hodderclait.co.uk) if you would like to undertake the adding, editing and query tasks. If you are interested in creating the Collecting database, consider the instructions below:

Create the Postcard Collecting database

Category – different groups of cards
Type – specific types of cards
Date – date first cards published
Condition – physical condition of card
Price – price paid for card
Value – current market price
Location – album card stored in

Add data to the database

Category values are Glamour, Message, Liverpool and Modern

Category	Type	Date	Condition	Price	Value	Location
Glamour	Barribal	12/03/88	Mint	£8	£10	A
Glamour	Nanni	23/01/79	Good	£4	£5	B
Glamour	Other	01/12/92	Poor	£1	£1	B
Message	Davies	24/08/94	Very Good	£1.50	£1.50	C
Message	Other	13/06/93	Good	£0.75	£1	C
Liverpool	Tunnel	07/09/92	Good	£2	£1.50	D
Liverpool	Centre	17/11/93	Poor	£3	£2	A
Liverpool	Suburbs	03/04/91	Poor	£5	£6	B
Liverpool	Other	29/01/90	Poor	£2	£1	C
Modern	Political	22/07/91	Mint	£0.75	£0.25	D
Modern	Royalty	11/05/90	Mint	£0.50	£0.50	E
Modern	Cricket	20/12/90	Very Good	£1	£1.25	F
Modern	Football	14/02/89	Very Good	£0.60	£1	G

The table is shown in Figure 3.31.

Figure 3.31 Postcard Collection

Activity 5

1 Open the Postcard Database.

2 Change the orientation of the page to portrait.

3 Print the Postcards Table showing all the information and field names.

4 Close the table and rename the table Postcards Your Name (e.g. Postcards Alan Clarke).

5 Open the Postcards Your Name table.

6 Change the condition of Liverpool Centre to Good from Poor.

7 Delete the Modern Cricket record.

8 Insert the following new records:

Message, American, 11/05/91, Very Good, £1, £1.50, C

Message, Europe, 16/11/97, Poor, £0.75, £0.90, C

Modern, Space, 23/09/99, Mint, £0.35, £0.50, F

Modern, Ships, 02/02/02, Mint, £0.50, £1.00, G

Carefully check that the information has been entered accurately. Correct any mistakes.

9 Save the table as Postcards Your Name. Figure 3.32 shows the table.

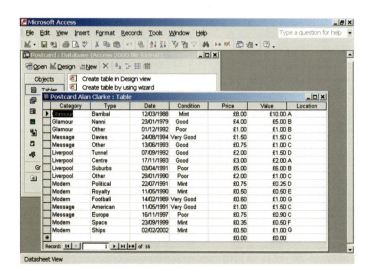

Figure 3.32 Postcards Alan Clarke

10 Change the page orientation to landscape and print all the table information with field headings. All the information should be visible.

11 Create the following Queries:

- Query to sort the records by ascending value
- Query to find records with a price less than £2
- Query to find all the records in location A with a value greater than £5

Check the accuracy of the queries.

Print each query result.

Save all the queries.

12 Create the following Reports (data should be displayed in full):

- Report to present postcards with a value greater than £5 showing the category, type and date purchased only
- Report to present all postcards in the table sorted in order of value (Figure 3.33)

13 Check the accuracy of the reports and that the data is displayed in full.

14 Print the reports.

15 Close the database.

Figure 3.33 Value report

Activity 6

The Trip database is available on the supporting website (www.hodderclait.co.uk) if you would like to undertake the adding, editing and query tasks. If you are interested in creating the Trip database, consider the instructions below:

Create the Trip database

Date – the date of the different bus trips
Name – people who have booked a place
Start – time of the start of journey
Return – time bus returns
Destination – final destination of bus trip
Cost – cost of trip

Add data to the database

Date	Name	Start	Return	Destination	Cost
03/05/05	William Hall	8.00	20.00	Harrogate	£25
03/05/05	Jane Hall	8.00	20.00	Harrogate	£25
18/05/05	Gordon King	7.30	22.00	Durham	£32
23/05/05	Lorna Alena	9.15	23.30	Lancaster	£27
12/06/05	Shubhanna Aris	6.00	22.30	Birmingham	£23
19/06/05	Eva Garcia	7.45	19.00	Northampton	£18
23/07/05	Harry Jones	8.30	21.00	Leicester	£15
07/08/05	Linda Brown	9.30	23.30	Warwick	£28

The Trip Customer table is shown in figure 3.34.

Figure 3.34 Trip Customer

Activity 7

1 Open the Trip Database.

2 Change the orientation of the page to portrait.

3 Print the Trip Customer table showing all the information and field names.

4 Close the table and rename the table Trip Customer Your Name (e.g. Trip Customer Alan Clarke)

5 Open the Trip Customer Your Name table.

6 Change the date of the trip to Warwick from 07/08/2005 to 09/09/2005.

7 Delete the trip to Northampton record.

8 Insert the following new records:

20/09/2005	Silvia Lewis	7.00	21.30	Shrewsbury	£35
25/09/2005	Jill Morris	8.15	20.00	Wolverhampton	£21
02/10/2005	Peter Jolly	9.30	21.00	Derby	£15
12/10/2005	Keith Smith	8.30	23.30	Burton	£20

Carefully check that the information has been entered accurately. Correct any mistakes.

9 Save the table as Trip Customer Your Name.

10 Change the page orientation to landscape and print all the table information with field headings. All the information should be visible.

11 Create the following Queries:

- Query to sort the records by ascending cost of trip
- Query to find records with trip costing more than £20

Check the accuracy of the queries.

Print each query result.

Save all the queries.

12 Create the following Reports (data should be displayed in full):

- Report to present the trip records sorted alphabetically by customer name
- Report to present records of trips costing more than £20

13 Check the accuracy of the reports and that the data is displayed in full.

14 Print the reports.

15 Close the database.

SUMMARY

1 **Load Microsoft® Access**: Use either the Start button and the All Programs menu or double click on the Microsoft® Access icon on the Windows® desktop.

2 **Close**: Click on the File menu and the Exit option or click on the Close button in the top right hand corner of the application or other window.

3 **Create a database – optional**: Load Microsoft® Access and select the Blank Database option within the New File task pane. The File New Database window opens to enable you to save your new database.

Select a drive or folder in which to store your new database as a file. If you click on the arrow button next to the Look in box you can select floppy disk.

Give the file a name. Insert the name in the File name box and click on the Create button. Your database is now saved.

The Database window is now revealed with three options with the `Table` object on the left-hand side selected:

- Create table in Design view
- Create table by using wizard
- Create table by entering data

Double click on `Create table in Design view` and the table window opens.

Insert your field names and their types.

You will be prompted to save your table when you close the window.

4. **Enter data**: Load Microsoft® Access. Double click on the database of your choice in the list displayed in task pane. The database window will appear.

   Double click on the table of your choice and the blank table will appear. Complete the records, moving between the fields by clicking in each box. Alternatively use the arrow keys, Tab key or Enter key to move between fields.

   Check each entry against the original data.

   To amend a single field, click on the field, delete its incorrect content and then re-enter the data.

5. **Delete a record**: Highlight the record by positioning the mouse pointer over the row heading until the pointer changes shape. Click the left mouse button. Right click in the highlighted row, the menu will appear and you select `Delete Record`.

6. **Add a record**: Click on the blank row at the bottom of the table and insert data, moving between fields using the Tab or Enter keys or by clicking in the next field.

7. **Create a query**: Select the `Queries` button in the list of Objects on the left-hand side of the database window. Double click on the `Create query in Design view` option. A new window will open with an overlaid window called Show Table. Click on the `Add` button on Show Table and then on the `Close` button.

   In the Query window a small box shows the fields that make up the table. The cursor will be flashing in the first Field box and a small down arrow will be shown at the end of the same box. Click on the down arrow and a list of the table fields will appear. Select the field which will then appear in the box. Move across the boxes, entering the chosen fields.

   Enter criteria in appropriate boxes.

   Sort data by clicking in the sort boxes. Select the down arrow and choose `Ascending`, `Descending` or `not sorted`.

8. **Save a query**: Save the query by selecting the `File` menu and the `Save As` option. Then enter the name of the query and click the `OK` button.

9. **Printing**: Select the `File` menu and the `Print` option. This reveals the `Print` window and you can print using the default settings by clicking on the `OK` button.

   or

Select the <mark>File</mark> menu and <mark>Print Preview</mark> to check the appearance of the printed document before you print it. Click on the <mark>Print</mark> icon and then on the <mark>OK</mark> button in the Print window.

10 **Report**: Select the <mark>Reports</mark> button in the list of Objects on the left-hand side of the database window. Double click on the <mark>Create report by using wizard</mark>. The window Report Wizard will appear. This will guide you through a series of choices about the content and presentation of your report. This includes saving the report so it can be used again.

Chapter 4

Unit 4

Producing an e-publication

This chapter will help you to use desktop publishing to:

- identify and use desktop publishing software correctly in accordance with laws and guidelines
- use basic file handling techniques for the software
- set up a standard page layout and text properties
- use basic tools and techniques appropriately
- import and place text and image files
- manipulate text and images to balance a page
- manage publications and print composite publications

Assessment

This unit does not assume any previous experience of using a computer though you may find it useful to have completed Unit 1: File management and e-document production. You will be assessed through a practical realistic assignment which is designed to allow you to demonstrate your knowledge and skills against each objective. Your tutor can provide you with more guidance.

Microsoft® Publisher

Microsoft® Publisher XP is a desktop publishing application with which you create publications. These can be for your own personal use (e.g. a village newsletter) or for your business (e.g. an advertising leaflet). In this chapter you will learn how to create a publication using images and text. Many people find it difficult to understand the difference between word processing and desktop publishing (DTP). Word processing is about producing a document while DTP provides tools to control the precise presentation of text and images. DTP is more a tool for laying out text and pictures. It gives you control over the flow of text and the positioning and size of images.

Figure 4.1 shows the opening display of Microsoft® Publisher XP. This consists of three areas:

- Menus and toolbars that are similar to other Microsoft® Office applications

- New Publication task pane on the right of the display
- Quick Publications on the left of the display

If you observe the New Publication task pane, the Quick Publications option is highlighted in the Start from a design section. If you highlight any of the other options (e.g. Newsletters, Web Sites and Word Documents) in the scroll box then the left display changes to present you with more choices related to the type of publication you have selected. These options provide you with a choice of types of publication relating to them, based on the standard design you have chosen. Microsoft® Publisher XP offers a wide range of standard publications on which to base your design.

Below the Start from a design section is the New section which has three options:

- Blank Publication – this assumes you want to start from scratch
- From existing publication
- From template

Finally at the bottom of the Task Pane is the section Open a publication.

If you select the Blank Publication option, the display changes to show the working area (Figure 4.2). A blank full page publication is displayed.

The application provides access to a range of tools through menus and toolbars. To the left of the window is the Objects toolbar offering a range of tools (e.g. to create WordArt, draw rectangles and access clip art). At the top of the window is a series of toolbars that let you print, save and format your publication. The Menu toolbar provides alternative routes to the same functions and other tools such as the selection of page sizes, margins and to check your spelling.

Figure 4.1 Microsoft® Publisher

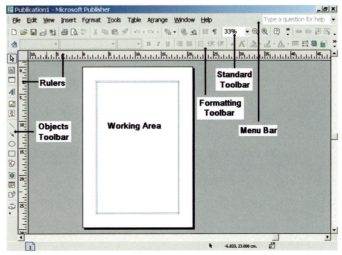

Figure 4.2 The Microsoft® Publisher window

Exercise 38

Exploring Microsoft® Publisher

1 Load Microsoft® Publisher by selecting the Start button, highlighting the All Programs option and clicking on the Microsoft® Publisher item or double click on the Microsoft® Publisher icon on the desktop. Observe that the Microsoft® Publisher opens as shown in Figure 4.1.

2 Explore the different designs and options. Under the Start from a design section is a box with a down arrow at the right hand end. If you click this button three options will be revealed:

- By Publication Type
- By Design Sets
- By Blank Publications

Select the different options and observe how the list of options in the section and also the choices on the right side of the display changes. By Blank Publications offers you a wide selection of different blank publications on which you can develop your design (e.g. web pages, poster, business card and postcard). You select an option by clicking on it. Click on the Full Page option in the task pane and it will be highlighted. On the right side of the display the full page option will be enclosed in a blue rectange to indicate it is also highlighted.

3 When you are ready, select the Blank Publications and Full Page options in the task pane. Double click on the Full Page design on the right side and Figure 4.3 will appear.

4 The blank full page will occupy the work area and to the left is the Publication Design task pane. You will see towards the right side of the standard toolbar a percentage (e.g. 33%). This tells you the relative size of the document. The working area is enclosed in a ruler. If you move the mouse pointer you will see that on both the top and left-hand rulers a thin line moves with respect to the mouse. This gives you guidance as to the position at which you are working on the document.

Figure 4.3 Blank publication

5 On the left-hand edge is a series of tools – the Objects toolbar (Figure 4.2).

6 Explore the menus – what functions does each contain? Try to locate Page Setup (which is on the File menu), Layout Guides (Arrange menu), Copy (Edit menu) and Picture (Insert menu).

> **continued**
>
> 7 Explore the Publication Design task pane. Click on each of the four options at the top of the task pane (i.e. `Quick Publication Options`, `Publication Designs`, `Color Schemes` and `Font Schemes`) and observe the changes. Consider some of the options revealed and the sub-options linked to them.
>
> 8 When you are familiar with the different choices then close the task pane by clicking on the `Close` button in the top right-hand corner of the pane. This will change the display so that it appears like Figure 4.2.
>
> 9 Close Microsoft® Publisher by clicking on the `Close` button in the top right-hand corner of the window or by selecting `File` menu and the `Exit` option. You may be asked if you want to save the changes that you have made. Select the `No` button.

Designing

Microsoft® Publisher provides the tools to produce professional publications but it leaves the design to you. The critical factors in designing a publication are:

- Limit the use of variables – few things are worse than overuse of the desktop publishing features (e.g. too many colours, fonts (sometimes called typefaces) character sizes, etc.). A useful rule is to use a feature for a distinct reason (e.g. using a different character size for each heading – main heading size 36, sub-headings 20 and ordinary text size 12).
- Consistency – in a way the design is a form of code that tells your readers how to understand the document so it is important that you follow a consistent design plan (e.g. the address is always in the bottom right-hand corner of a page).
- Attractive – initially your publications need to be visually attractive so that people will consider reading them. The use (not overuse) of pictures, colour and different fonts can provide an interesting publication. It is important for a document to be visually balanced.
- Appropriate – consider who your readers are and design for them.
- Readability – a good publication is one which is easy to read. Readability is a combination of many factors but some simple tips are to provide plenty of white space (e.g. overcrowding text makes it difficult to read, so do not reduce line spacing unless you have no other choice), pictures relating to the text increase the readers' interest and short sections are often easier to understand than long ones.
- Balance – a balance between text and images will make your publication attractive, pleasing on the eye and effective.

Standard page setup

The first task in designing a publication is to set the page size, orientation and margins.

Select `File` menu then the `Page Setup` option to reveal the Page Setup window (Figure 4.4) which provides you with options to choose the publication type, paper size and orientation (i.e. either portrait or landscape). When you select a type, you are able to see your choice in the

Preview area. Types are chosen by clicking on them. Click on the OK button to confirm your selections.

Extra options will appear with some publication types, such as envelope where you will see an additional box appear allowing you to select from a range of different sizes of envelope (e.g. C3 and DL).

To set the margins, select the Arrange menu then the Layout Guides option to reveal the Layout Guides window (Figure 4.5). This allows you to preview your choices. You can change each margin left, right, top and bottom by clicking on the up and down arrows.

Frames

Every item (e.g. images and text) that makes up a desktop publication is an individual object. Each object is enclosed in a frame which is invisible when printed unless you choose to create a border around it. Frames can be resized, rotated and moved using your mouse. They can be placed on top of each other so that a series of layers is created. Figure 4.6 shows a highlighted frame. The small empty circles, which form part of the enclosure and allow you to resize the frame, are called handles. At the top of the frame is a green circle which if you place the mouse pointer over changes it into a circle with arrows. This allows you to rotate the object with movements of the pointer.

Figure 4.6 shows the shape of the mouse pointer when you place it over the frame in order to move the whole frame (i.e. object) to a new position. If you place the pointer over one of the handles it will change to a double headed arrow with the label

Figure 4.4 Page setup

Figure 4.5 Layout guides

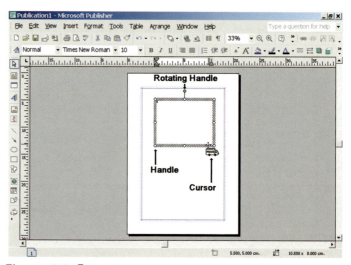
Figure 4.6 Frames

'Resize'. To move the object or resize it requires that you hold down the left mouse button and drag the object to a new location, or expand or contract its size.

Template

A template can save you a great deal of time and trouble. It is essentially a basic model of the publication which you use over and over again. Normally you will define the layout and format of the publication and then use this foundation to create new versions. This is useful if you are regularly publishing a document such as a monthly newsletter which you would like to have a standard appearance but with a variable content.

You create a template in the same way that you produce any other publication except that you save the layout and format before adding the detail content. The template is saved in the Microsoft® Publisher template format. When you next want to create a similar publication you load the template and immediately begin to add the detail. In this way you save time and also produce a consistent document. A company may create templates for all their standard documents such as sales leaflets, technical data sheets and briefing sheets. This allows them to present a desired image to their customers.

Master page

The master page concept is similar to that of a template. You create a standard page which is reused throughout a multiple page publication. This again provides a standard and consistent appearance to a document. There are no particular rules for layout of a master page since it depends on what you are designing. A textbook, for example, will need a different master to a sales brochure.

A master page allows you to increase your productivity while maintaining a high standard of presentation. In addition, readers like a consistent presentation since it aids readability and helps them locate information.

Exercise 39

Page setup

1 Load Microsoft® Publisher by selecting the Start button, highlighting the All Programs option and clicking on the Microsoft® Publisher item or by double clicking on the Microsoft® Publisher icon on the desktop.

2 Select the By Blank Publications option in the Start from a design section of the task pane. Double click on the Full Page option on the right of the display.

3 The Microsoft® Publisher work area will appear with the Publication Design task pane on the left of the display (Figure 4.3). It may show the Quick Wizard Publication on the left of the display. Close the task pane by clicking on the Close button on top right-hand corner of the pane. This will change the display to show a blank full page in the centre of the work area.

continued

4 Select the **File** menu, then the **Page Setup** option to reveal the Page Setup window. Explore the different layouts by considering their appearance in the Preview window before selecting the **Full Page** option. Options are chosen by clicking on them. Change the page orientation to landscape and observe its appearance in the Preview window. When you are ready, click on the **OK** button to confirm the changes.

5 Select the **Arrange** menu then the **Layout Guides** to reveal the Layout Guides window (Figure 4.5). Explore changing the margins by observing the selections in the Preview area. When you are confident that you understand the choices, set the right and left margins to 4 cm and the top and bottom to 3 cm. Click on the **OK** button to confirm your selections. You can change the size of the margins by simply clicking on the up and down arrows or in the left, right, top or bottom boxes and entering the size from the keyboard.

6 You have now created a basic layout for a publication which might be useful as a newsletter or a handout in a presentation. This is a good time to save your outline publication. You could consider it as a master document or template. Microsoft® Publisher provides several master documents for you to choose from but you can also create your own. A master is simply a framework which serves a particular purpose that you can use over and over again to produce a particular type of publication. If you regularly produce a newsletter, it aids productivity and ensures they all follow a consistent design.

7 Insert a floppy disk into the computer's drive. To save your outline publication, select the **File** menu then the **Save** option to reveal the Save As window. You need to choose the location in which to store your publication by clicking on the down arrow at the end of the **Look in** box. This will reveal a list. Click on the floppy disk option. You will then see this appear in the box. Now click in the **File name** box and enter from the keyboard the name 'Landscape Column' then click on the **Save** button. You will hear the drive working and the publication will be saved on the floppy disk as a file called Landscape Column.

8 It is good practice to save your work early and to update your saved file at regular intervals. This safeguards you against any problems with the application or computer. You will always have most of your work saved so that you can start again later without having to repeat all of it.

9 You have now established a basic layout. The next step is to consider where to place your text. Select the **Text Box** tool on the Objects toolbar. If you place the mouse pointer over a tool icon then a small label appears to tell you the name of the tool. When you have selected the **Text Box** the mouse pointer will change to a crosshair that allows you to accurately position your text. We are going to establish a text frame or area that will cover the top half of the page. You do this by positioning your pointer in the top left-hand corner of the column and then holding the mouse button down. Move the pointer down to form a rectangle at the top of the column. Your rectangle will be framed as shown in Figure 4.7. You can drag the rectangle to adjust the frame to your needs. Use the layout guides to help position the text frame.

continued

10 If you move your mouse pointer across the frame it will change to explain its purpose:

- Resize – double-headed arrow whenever you place the pointer on one of the small empty circles (called handles) at the corners or middle of the lines. This allows you to change the size of the text frame.

- Move – crossed, double-headed arrows whenever you place your pointer near the lines but away from the handles. This lets you move the whole frame.

Figure 4.7 Text frames

11 Experiment with changing the size of the rectangle and moving it. When you have finished, place the frame to cover the top half of the page. If you click away from the frame, the heavy lines and handles will disappear (i.e. it is no longer highlighted) to show you it is fixed. However, if you need to manipulate it, highlight it again by clicking on the rectangle. If you make a mistake and need to delete the frame, you must highlight it then press the Delete key or select the Edit menu, then the Delete Object option.

12 Microsoft® Publisher provides you with tools to manipulate the text frame precisely. With the text frame highlighted, select the Format menu, then the Text Box option to reveal the Format Text Box window (Figure 4.8).

13 With the Format Text Box window you can divide your text frame into columns, set the spacing between them and set the four margins for the text frame. These may seem unnecessary matters but desktop publishing is about providing you with the tools to produce accurate and detailed publications. Microsoft® Publisher lets you produce publications equivalent to those of professional printers.

14 Select the Text Box tab. Set all the margins of your text frame to 0.5 cm. Click on the Columns button and create three columns with a spacing of 0.3 cm. This is the space between the three columns.

15 You will notice that within your text box the cursor is

Figure 4.8 Format Text box

continued

flashing. This is the place where any text you enter will appear (Figure 4.9). Enter the heading Guinea pigs. You may see a message appear to tell you the text is too small to be visible and offering you the option of zooming in on the text by pressing the function key F9. The Zoom option is also available on the Standard toolbar.

Figure 4.9 Enter Text – Zoom image

16 You can resize the text by highlighting it (click on the start of the text and, holding the left mouse button down, move the pointer to the end of the text). Now select the Font Size icon on the format toolbar. The small down arrow button to the right of the box will reveal a list of sizes. In a similar way, the down arrow next to the Font box will list fonts that you can select. Fonts are also called typefaces.

For this publication you are creating the initial heading so it is important to select a font and character size that is eye catching. The list of fonts includes two different types called serif and sans serif. A serif type font has small flags on the ends of the characters while a sans serif type font does not. You might say that serif fonts have more fancy characters or that sans serif fonts have plain characters. You need to experiment with your choice of fonts to find the ones that you like.

Serif Font characters	Sans Serif Font characters
FT	FT

17 Select a character size of 20 by clicking on that number in the list and then select Arial font (or one of your own choice). Observe how your title now appears. You are going to create a heading that will fit the first column of the publication. While selecting your font, scroll down the list and you should notice many with similar names. These are likely to belong to the same family of fonts. Fonts are divided into families that vary in size from a single item to ones with many elements.

18 Save your publication by selecting the File menu and the Save option. The Save As window will not appear since the system assumes you are updating your previously saved file Landscape Column. If you wanted to create a new saved file you need to select the Save As option. This will reveal the Save As window and you can enter a new file name.

19 Close the application by clicking on the Close button on the top right-hand corner of the window or by selecting File and then the Exit option.

Manipulate fonts

An alternative way to manipulate the fonts and character sizes is available from the Format menu. Select the Font option, revealing the Font window (Figure 4.10). The Text frame and the selected words need to be highlighted for these options to be available. You can also embolden, underline and display your text in italics style from this window, although these options are, of course, also available on the Format toolbar.

Figure 4.10 Font window

Alignment

You can align your text using the icons on the Formatting toolbar. These allow you to align your text in four ways (Figure 4.11). These are:

- left – the left text edge is parallel with the margin and the right is ragged
- right – the right text edge is parallel with the margin and the left is ragged
- centred – text is aligned down the centre of the page with both edges ragged
- justified – both left and right text edges are parallel with the margins

Highlight the text and select the respective icons from the toolbar.

Left	Right	Centred	Double
AAAAA	AAAAA	AAAAA	AAAAA
AAA	AAA	AAA	A A A
AAAA	AAAA	AAAA	A A A A
AA	AA	AA	A A
AAAA	AAAA	AAAA	A A A A

Figure 4.11 Alignment

Inserting text and pictures

Although you can enter text into your publication from the keyboard, desktop publishing is primarily designed to allow you to manipulate objects to produce high quality presentations of information. One such object is text, which is best prepared using a word processor. This can either be in the form of text copied from other Microsoft® Office applications and pasted into the publication or by importing text files.

To insert text files you select the Insert menu and the Text File option. This opens the Insert Text window which allows you to choose the file you want to insert. In a similar way you can insert pictures by copying them from other Microsoft® Office applications, inserting image files or choosing images from clip art collections. To insert a picture you need to select the Insert menu then highlight the Pictures option to reveal a short menu of options. Figure 4.12 shows the Picture menu options. You can insert a clip art image, a picture saved in a folder or import an image from a digital camera or scanner using these functions. When they appear in the publication they are often too large and need to be resized using the handles.

On the Objects toolbar is the Picture Frame tool which allows you to create a picture frame within your publication. Once you have positioned your picture frame, the Insert Picture window opens so that you can select a picture file to place in the frame.

When you first select these options you may be presented with a message indicating that the functions need to be installed from

Figure 4.12 Picture options

the Microsoft® Office master disks. If this happens, seek help unless you are confident that you can install the functions. They convert files to a format that Microsoft® Publisher can accept. Clip art collections provided by Microsoft® Office are often not installed on the computer and need
to have the CD-ROMs which hold them inserted in the correct drive so that they can be accessed.

Manipulate images

Microsoft® Publisher provides a variety of functions to help you manipulate images. These include:

- flipping the image
- resizing the image
- cropping the image

To flip or rotate an image you need to select it (i.e. click on the image to enclose it in a frame) and then choose the Arrange menu and highlight the Rotate or Flip option to reveal a sub-menu. This offers a range of functions including:

- Free rotate
- Rotate left 90°
- Rotate right 90°
- Flip horizontal
- Flip vertical

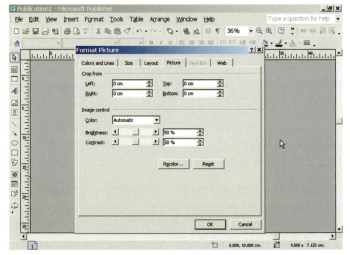

Figure 4.13 Format Picture window

To resize an image you need to select it and then choose the Format menu and the Picture option. This opens the Format Picture window (figure 4.13) that allows you change the size of the image, crop and also rotate it. The options are provided under several tabs displayed across the top of the window.

Amend text

The functions to manipulate and amend text that are available in many Microsoft® Office applications are also offered in Microsoft® Publisher. You can therefore cut, copy, paste, insert, delete and find and replace text. The process is very similar to other applications in that you need to highlight it and then select the required function. Text is inserted by clicking the pointer in the location where you want to add to or amend it. The find and replace functions operates in an identical way to other Microsoft® Office applications.

Lines and borders

All Microsoft® Publisher objects are enclosed in frames which are invisible when printed unless they are turned into borders. Microsoft® Publisher provides you with the functions to enclose frames with lines of different thicknesses or more artistic surrounds. These are available by selecting the Format menu and Text Box to reveal Format Text Box. If you select the Colors and Lines tab you will see the basic line and borders tools. Click on the Border Art button to open the Border Art window of options (Figure 4.14). These functions are only available if the frame you are enclosing is highlighted (i.e. handles showing).

Figure 4.14 Format Text Box – Color and Lines tab

In the Format Text Box and Border Art window you can experiment with different choices of line styles. These appear in the preview area.

On the Objects toolbar (i.e. down the left side of the working area) are several tools that allow you to add lines and simple shapes. These are:

- Line tool
- Oval tool
- Rectangle tool
- Autoshapes tool

Figure 4.15 shows the four tools.

Figure 4.15 Objects toolbar tools

Exercise 40

Importing text and pictures

1. Load Microsoft® Publisher by selecting the Start button, highlighting the All Programs option and clicking on the Microsoft® Publisher item or by double clicking on the Microsoft® Publisher icon on the desktop.

2. Microsoft® Publisher will appear (Figure 4.3).

3. If you have only recently completed the previous exercise (i.e. in this session), select the File menu and you will see the Landscape Columns file at the bottom of the menu. This can be loaded by clicking on it. Alternatively at the bottom of the New Publication task pane in the Open a Publication section you will see the file Landscape Column that you can load by clicking on it.

   If you completed the exercise some time ago then you will need to load it from your floppy disk. Insert the disk into the drive and select the File menu then the Open option to reveal the Open Publication window. Select 3½ Floppy (A:) in the Look in box by clicking on the down arrow button to reveal a list of options. This will reveal the files on your floppy disk. Double click on the Landscape Column publication to load the file or single click on it and then on the Open button.

4. The publication will appear in the work area. If you click within the text frame you will see the location of the flashing cursor. Move the cursor to one line below the heading (Guinea Pigs) by pressing the Enter key with the cursor at the end of the heading.

5. In Unit 1, you undertook an exercise and created some text about guinea pigs. We are now going to import this text file into the publication. Highlight the text frame, select the Insert menu and the Text File option to reveal the Insert Text window. Insert your floppy disk containing the Guinea Pigs file or, if you do not have the file, any other text file containing a short passage since this is a practice publication.

6. Select 3½ Floppy (A:) in the Look in box by clicking on the down arrow button to reveal a list of options. This will reveal the files on your floppy disk. Double click on the Guinea Pigs file to load it or single click on it and then on the Open button.

7. The text file will load into your publication starting at the cursor and flowing across the three columns. If it overflows the columns you will see a message appear asking if you want the automatic flow of text to be undertaken. Click on Yes to accept the automatic flow. Another message will appear asking if you want Microsoft® Publisher to create a new page. Again click on Yes and a final message telling you a new page has been created will appear. Click on OK to remove it and look at your publication.

   You should see a new page with three columns and below the work area you will see the numbers 1 and 2, with 2 highlighted indicating that it is the page you are considering. If you click on 1 then the first or original page will appear. Figures 4.16 and 4.17 show the two pages.

8. The next step is to insert a picture into your publication. Select the Insert menu, highlight the Picture option and click on Clip Art. This will reveal the Insert Clip Art task pane on the left of the display. In the search text box enter animals and click on

continued

Search. A selection of animal related images will appear. Explore the pictures and choose one by clicking on it to open a menu. Choose the Insert option and the image will appear in your publication.

9   You can move the picture or resize it using the mouse pointer in the same way as with the text frame. Experiment with moving the image, including placing the picture inside the text frame. You will see the text move to make room for the image. This shows that you can stack frames on top of each other.

10 With the image inside it, resize the text frame to occupy the whole page and observe what happens.

11 The publication should now look similar to Figure 4.18. Close the Insert Clip Art task pane.

12 You can change the alignment of the text using the Formatting toolbar. Centre the heading text (Guinea Pigs) by highlighting the words and using the Center icon on the toolbar. Change the imported text to Comic Sans (or a font of your choice), character size 12 and justify by again highlighting the text and using functions on the toolbar.

13 Select the Format menu and Text Box option to reveal the Format Text Box.

Figure 4.16 Page one

Figure 4.17 Page two

Figure 4.18 Amended publication

Producting an e-publication

141

continued

Explore the options to provide a border for your publication with a line dividing the columns. Your publication should look similar to Figure 4.19 if you have used the guinea pig text.

14 Save your publication by selecting the `File` menu and the `Save` option. The Save As window will not appear since the system assumes you are updating your previously saved file Landscape Column. If you wanted to create a new saved file then you would need to select the `Save As` option. This would reveal the Save As window for you to enter a new file name.

15 Close the application by clicking on the `Close` button on the top right-hand corner of the window or by selecting `File` and then the `Exit` option.

Figure 4.19 Final publication

Spacing

It is important that the appearance of the text serves the purpose you intend. Often you have only a limited amount of space in which to fit a range of information (i.e. text and pictures). This requires you to balance the content of your publication and is especially true when you have a publication divided into columns. Microsoft® Publisher provides functions with which you can adjust the spacing of your text. These are available in the `Format` menu within the `Character Spacing`, the `Line Spacing` and the `Indents and Lists` options when the text frame is highlighted.

The Character Spacing window allows you to shrink or stretch the characters. You need to highlight the text you want to work on and then increase or decrease the scaling using the up and down arrows. You can see the effects in the sample area at the bottom of the window.

Figure 4.20 Line spacing

The Line Spacing window (Figure 4.20) provides the means of setting the space between lines of text, and before and after paragraphs, letting you finely adjust the presentation between columns or over a page. The changes can be seen in the sample area to help you judge its effects.

By using Indents and Lists (Figure 4.21), you can indent the left and right edges of the text or the first line of your paragraph. The sample area allows you to see the effects of your changes. By setting an indent you will provide a standard look to your publication. It is normal to standardise publications (e.g. the first line of each paragraph is indented in the same way). To create a first line indent click on the down arrow box next to the Preset area. This will display a list of options including 1st Line Indent. Click on the option and you will see the effect in the sample area.

You can also access the Line Spacing window using the button at the bottom of the Indents and Lists window.

Having the ability to change the character size and font of the text with line spacing means you can carefully adjust the balance of each page. It requires some experimentation to gain the best results.

Figure 4.21 Indents and Lists

Printing

A key factor in desktop publishing is the printing of your publication. You can do this with your own local printer or you can save the publication as a file on a disk to take it to an external printer.

Before printing your publication it is important to check your work. A spell checker is available by selecting the Tools menu, highlighting Spelling and clicking on Spelling. This will identify spelling mistakes. However, there are other possible errrors within a publication, such as the insertion of a blank frame. These can be identified using the Design Checker which is opened by selecting the Tools menu and the Design Checker option. This will open a window which allows you to specify what parts (e.g. pages) of the publication you want to check. A final and probably the best check is simply to read and review the publication yourself.

To print your publication you select the File menu, then the Print option and click on the OK button. The printer will print your publication using the standard default settings.

More practice

Activity 1

1 Load Microsoft® Publisher by selecting the Start button, highlighting the All Programs option and clicking on the Microsoft® Publisher item or by double clicking on the Microsoft® Publisher icon on the desktop.

2. Select the **By Blank Publications** option in the Start from a design section of the task pane. Click on the **Poster** option on the right of the display.

3. Microsoft® Publisher will appear. The blank poster will occupy the centre of the work area with the Publication Designs task pane on the left. Close the task pane.

4. Your task is to create a poster for an open garden event in a village.

5. Using **Page Setup** in the **File** menu, set the orientation to Portrait and select the paper size to be 45 × 60 cm.

6. Using the **Layout Guides** in the **Arrange** menu, set the margins to 2.5 cm.

7. Create a text frame to cover the top quarter of the poster and enter Open Gardens as a heading using a character size of 72 and a font called Tahoma (or a font of your choice). Centre and embolden the heading.

8. Using the **Insert** menu and **Picture** option, select and insert a relevant item of clip art.

9. Finally, insert a second text frame at the bottom of the poster.

10. Enter the address where tickets can be obtained for the show using Tahoma (or a font of your choice) and a character size of 72 (e.g Tickets are available at the Post Office). Present the text effectively.

11. Now enclose your three frames in suitable borders using the **Format** menu and the **Text Box** or **Picture** option. Remember that the border tool operates on a frame.

12. Save your poster by selecting the **File** menu and the **Save** option.

13. Print your poster by selecting the **File** menu, the **Print** option and the **OK** button.

14. Close the application by clicking on the **Close** button on the top right-hand corner of the window or by selecting **File** and then the **Exit** option.

Activity 2

1. Load Microsoft® Publisher by selecting the **Start** button, highlighting the **All Programs** option and clicking on the **Microsoft® Publisher** item or by clicking on the **Microsoft® Publisher** icon on the desktop.

2. Select the **By Blank Publications** option in the Start from a design section of the task pane. Click on the **Full Page** option on the right of the display.

3. Microsoft® Publisher will appear. The blank full page will occupy the centre of the work area with the Publication Design task pane on the left of the display. Close the task pane.

4. Your task is to create a newsletter for a community group.

5. Using **Page Setup** in the **File** menu, set the layout to custom, size 20 × 30 cm and the orientation to Portrait.

6. Using the **Layout Guides** in the **Arrange** menu, set the margins to 1.5 cm.

7. Create a text frame to cover the whole page. Using the **Text Box** option within the **Format** menu (remember the text frame must be highlighted), divide the page into three columns with a spacing of 0.4 cm and margins of 0.15 cm.

8 Create a second text frame across the top of the page (over the first text frame) in which to place your heading. Enter the heading Community Newsletter in Arial Black with a character size of 36.

9 Select the **Insert** menu and **Picture** option and insert an appropriate clip art picture into the publication. Position the image in the centre of the newsletter, below the heading and covering the three columns.

10 Create another text frame in the bottom right-hand corner of the page in the third (right-hand) column. This is going to give the Community group's address for correspondence. So enter the address below:

> Community Group
> Green Community Centre
> New Walk
> New Town

11 Use the **Line Spacing** option on the **Format** menu to set the line spacing to 2.

12 Save your newsletter by selecting the **File** menu and the **Save** option. You have effectively created a master document for future editions. You can add the remaining text depending on the news when the newsletter is issued. Save the file as Newsletter.

13 Import a text file into the newsletter. You can choose any file but ideally it should be only a short piece of text. Use the **Insert** menu and the **Text File** option.

14 Observe how the text flows around your image frame and down the columns.

15 Using the Indents and Lists window, indent the paragraphs by 1 cm (remember to highlight all the text you want included) and then set the line spacing between lines to 1.5, and 1 before and after each paragraph.

16 Change the text font to Arial (or a font of your choice) and character size to 12 (or a size of your choice). Set the alignment to justify (remember to highlight all the text you want included). Try to produce a balanced newsletter.

17 Surround the whole newsletter with an appropriate border and with faint lines separating the columns. Enclose the address and heading frames in separate borders.

18 Save the newsletter under a new file name by selecting the **File** menu and the **Save As** option. Use the name New Newsletter.

19 Print your revised newsletter by selecting the **File** menu, **Print** option and the **OK** button.

20 Close the application by clicking on the **Close** button in the top right-hand corner of the window or by selecting **File** and then the **Exit** option.

Wizard

Microsoft® Publisher, like many Microsoft® Office applications, provides you with the means to create a publication quickly, using a variety of standard templates and designs. This exercise is included because it is a practical way of rapidly producing acceptable publications which you may find useful.

Activity 3

1. Load Microsoft® Publisher by selecting Start button, highlighting All Programs and clicking on the Microsoft® Publisher option or double clicking on the Microsoft® Publisher icon on the desktop.

2. Select the By Publication Type option in the Start from a design section of the task pane. Click on the Art Boxes Newsletter option (or select another one if this doesn't appear) on the right of the display.

3. Microsoft® Publisher opens with the chosen newsletter at the centre of the work area with the Newsletter Options task pane on the left of the display. A message may appear telling you that Publisher will enter your personal details automatically into the newsletter. Click on the OK button if this happens and a window will open for you to select your personal information. Press the Update button.

4. On the left of the newsletter display is the task pane. When you are ready, click on the Colour Schemes option to open up a range of choices. Select one you like and then click on the Newsletter Options. You will be asked if you want one- or two-sided printing and whether to include the customer address. Make your choices and then click on Publication Designs and again you will be presented with choices. Make your decisions and click on Page Content which asks you how many columns would you like in your newsletter. Make your choice and click on Font Schemes which will present you with a variety of options. Choose one.

5. You have created a template for your publication. If you click on the newsletter you can see the different frames and these allow you to enter text, import pictures, etc.

6. Explore the different options until you are sure that you understand how the process works.

7. Close the application by clicking on the Close button in the top right-hand corner of the window or by selecting File and then the Exit option.

SUMMARY

1. **Load Microsoft® Publisher:** Use either the Start button and the All Programs menu or double click on the Microsoft® Publisher icon on the Microsoft® Windows® desktop.

2. **Close:** Click on the File menu item and the Exit option or click on the Close button in the top right-hand corner of the application window.

3. **Save a file onto a floppy disk:** Insert a floppy disk into drive A: and click on the File Menu and Save. Select the 3½ floppy (A:) and enter the file name.

   Having saved a file once, you can update it by clicking on the File Menu and Save without the Save As window appearing again. It simply overwrites the original file.

4. **Set page size and orientation:** Select the File menu then the Page Setup option. This will reveal the Page Setup window.

5. **Set guides:** Select the Arrange menu then the Layout Guides to reveal the Layout Guides window.

6 **Insert a text frame**: Select the Text Box tool on the Objects toolbar. The mouse pointer will change to a crosshair to allow you to position your text accurately.

Position the top left-hand corner where you would like to locate the frame and then, holding the mouse button down, move the pointer down to form a rectangle.

7 **Move and resize a frame**: Position the mouse pointer over a handle and the pointer will change shape (a double-ended arrow). By holding down the mouse button, you can change the shape of the frame. Position your mouse pointer over the frame lines away from the handles and the pointer will change shape (crossed, double-ended arrows). By holding down the mouse button, you can move the frame.

8 **Change font and character size**: Highlight the text. Select the small down arrow button to the right of the character size box to reveal a list of sizes. Click on the size of your choice. Select the small down arrow button to the right of the font box to reveal a list of fonts. Click on the font of your choice.

9 **Serif and sans serif fonts**: The list of fonts includes those that are of type serif and sans serif. A serif font has small flags on the ends of the characters (i.e. they are more fancy) while a sans serif does not (i.e. they are more plain).

10 **Alignment**: Highlight the text and select the respective icons from the Format toolbar.

11 **Inserting text and pictures**: Select the Insert menu and the Text File option. This opens the Insert Text window which allows you to choose the file you want to insert.

Select the Insert menu, highlight Picture to reveal the three options of Clip Art, From File and From Scanner or Camera. Alternatively, text and pictures can be copied and pasted from other Microsoft® Office applications.

12 **Lines and borders**: Select the Format menu and Text Box to reveal the Format Text Box window.

13 **Drawing and Shape tools**: Select the tools (i.e. line, oval, rectangle and AutoShapes) from the Objects toolbar.

14 **Character and line spacing**: Select the Format menu and either the Character Spacing or the Line Spacing options with the text frame highlighted. This will reveal either the Character Spacing or Line Spacing windows.

15 **Indent paragraphs**: Select the Format menu and the Indents and Lists option with the text frame highlighted. This will reveal the Indents and Lists window.

16 **Checking**: Select the Tools menu, highlight the Spelling option to reveal a short menu and click on Spelling.

Select the Tools menu and the Design Checker option. This will open a window which allows you to specify what parts (e.g. pages) of the publication you want to check.

17 **Printing**: Select the File menu, then the Print option and click on the OK button.

18 **Flip or rotate an image**: Select the image (i.e. click on the image to enclose it in a

frame) and then choose the **Arrange** menu and highlight the **Rotate or Flip** option to reveal a submenu. This offers a range of functions.

19. **Resize an image**: Select the image, choose the **Format** menu and the **Picture** option to open the Format Picture window. Select the **Size** tab to resize image using scale function.

20. **First Line Indent**: Select the **Format** menu and the **Indents and Lists** option. Click on the down arrow box next to the Preset area. This will display a list of options including 1st Line Indent. Click on the option and you will see the effect in the sample area.

Chapter 5

Unit 5

Creating an e-presentation

This chapter will help you to:
- identify and use presentation graphics software correctly
- set up a slide layout
- select fonts and enter text
- import and insert images correctly
- use the drawing tools
- format slides and presentation
- re-order slides and produce printed handouts
- manage and print presentation files

Assessment

This unit does not assume any previous experience of using a computer. However, you may find it useful to have completed Unit 1: File management and e-document production. You will be assessed through a practical realistic assignment which is designed to allow you to demonstrate your knowledge and skills against each objective. Your tutor can provide you with more guidance.

Presentation applications

Microsoft® PowerPoint® is a presentation application. It provides the resources to create presentations in the form of overhead projector slides, computer presentations and handouts. It is used extensively in both business and education. A sales manager may develop a presentation to persuade customers to buy a new product, a teacher may use it as a visual aid to make a subject more understandable and a manager may employ the application to explain changes in the organisation.

This chapter is based on Microsoft® PowerPoint® XP and Figure 5.1 shows the Microsoft® PowerPoint® interface. It is an application with many functions to assist in producing exciting and interesting presentations by providing a wide range of templates, graphic images and text tools.

When you load Microsoft® PowerPoint® it starts with a display divided into four areas. These are:

- toolbars and menu bar
- a blank slide occupying the work area
- New Presentation task pane on the right of the display – this provides access to recently created presentations (Open a presentation section) and assistance with developing new presentations (New section)
- Tabs pane on the left of the display which provides two different ways of gaining an overview of the presentation you are creating

Figure 5.1 Microsoft® PowerPoint®

New blank presentation

We are going to create a new blank presentation so we need to click on the Blank Presentation option in the New Presentation task pane, New section. The display will change replacing the New Presentation task pane with the Slide Layout task pane (Figure 5.2). This provides a variety of layouts that you can use to design your slides. When the pointer is placed on a layout then a small label will appear giving you the name of the layout. You can select a layout either by clicking on the layout so that it appears in the work area or by clicking the down arrow box which, if clicked, opens a menu of options including Insert New Slide.

Figure 5.2 shows the title layout which is used to begin a presentation. At the moment the slide is transparent. Microsoft® PowerPoint® provides you with a variety of tools to add background colours and an overall design to your slides. These are available within the Format menu and Slide Design option. When you select this option the Slide Layout task pane will be replaced with the Slide Design task pane (Figure 5.3).

The Slide Design task pane offers three different sets of designs:

- Design Templates – different layouts for the slides
- Color Schemes – different combinations of colours for the slides
- Animation Schemes – different animations for the slides

When you select one of the options the section below changes to show

Figure 5.2 Blank presentation

the different choices. In Figure 5.3 the Design Template option has been chosen so the area is a scroll box with a variety of designs. To select a design you click on it and you will see it appear in the working area.

Once you have established the design of the slides you can then add the text that forms the message of your presentation. The title template offers you two text boxes in which you can add text. These are the title and subtitle. After clicking in the boxes, you simply enter text from the keyboard.

A presentation consists of several slides. Once you have completed the title slide, you then need to add a new blank slide. This is done by selecting the Insert menu and then the New Slide option (Figure 5.4). This will insert a new slide into the work area, in this case, a Title and Text slide (Figure 5.5). However, you can change this slide by choosing a new layout from the Slide Layout task pane that also appears when a new slide is inserted. The design of the new slide (e.g. background colours) remains the same as the first slide. It is important in any presentation that the slides are consistent, as this helps the audience to understand the presentation. If each slide is different, with multiple designs and colours employed, there is the danger that the people watching the presentation will be distracted from the message.

The new slide text layout is chosen in the same way as previously discussed (i.e. click on the selected layout), allowing you to present information in several different ways and to include illustrations in the slide. Some options are:

Figure 5.3 Slide design

Figure 5.4 Insert menu – New Slide option

Figure 5.5 New slide

- title and text in a single rectangle
- title and text presented in two parallel rectangles
- title and text in one rectangle with a chart or other image in another

Each layout shows the text or image areas enclosed in a rectangle. These are called placeholders and can either be transparent (i.e. no border) or enclosed in a border.

The rest of the presentation can be developed in this way by adding slides one by one. Microsoft® PowerPoint® lets you edit your slides so it is possible to develop a presentation rapidly by outlining each slide and then completing the presentation later.

Although New CLAiT does not require you to use Microsoft® PowerPoint®'s more advanced features, the application does provide the means of animating slides so that your text can appear to fly onto the slide from almost any direction. The transition from one slide to the next can be made interesting by a variety of means. Some of these features are available in the Slide Show menu.

Organisations tend to develop standard house styles for all presentations carried out by their staff. Organisations have often produced their own design templates including features such as company logos and colour schemes. It is useful to find out if your employer has a house style since you will be expected to follow it and also it may save you a lot of preparation time.

Exercise 41

Creating a presentation

1 Load Microsoft® PowerPoint® using either the All Programs menu or the Microsoft® PowerPoint® icon on the desktop.

2 Select the Blank Presentation option from the New section of the New Presentation task pane. This will open the Title Slide layout. Select the Format menu and Slide Design option to open the Slide Design task pane. Explore the different design templates and select the Blends design template. Enter CLAiT 2006 as the title.

3 Create a second new slide using the Insert menu and New Slide option. A Title and Text layout will appear. Enter the following bullet points:

- Level 1 Qualification

- Certificate – 3 Units

and the Title – CLAiT 2006. You can insert new bullet points by pressing the Enter key at the end of the previous line (e.g. after entering Qualification).

If you make a mistake and identify it immediately you can delete the text by using the Backspace key. If you do not notice it until the slide is finished then click in the text where the error is. This will move the cursor to the location and you can now delete or insert text at this position.

An alternative way of dealing with mistakes is to use the Undo button on the Standard toolbar (Figure 5.6). If you place the cursor over the Undo or Redo icons then a message will appear to help you identify them. Undo removes the last action you have

continued

carried out. You can use Undo repeatedly so that you can remove several actions. You can effectively undo the undo action by using the Redo button on the Standard toolbar. Practise using Undo and Redo.

To move to another slide you can use the scroll bar on the right of the display or click on the slide list to the left-hand side of the display. Practise by returning to the first slide and then to the second one.

Figure 5.6 Undo and Redo

4 Create a third slide using the Insert menu, entering the following bullet points under the same title of CLAiT 2006:

- Mandatory unit
- Optional units

5 Create a fourth and final slide, entering the following bullet points under the same title of CLAIT 2006:

- Thank you
- Insert your name

Figure 5.7 shows the final slide within the Microsoft® PowerPoint® work area. Notice that on the left-hand side of the display there is an overview of the four slide presentation you have created.

6 It is important to check your presentation for spelling mistakes to avoid embarrassing yourself when you show your slides. To check your slides select the Tools menu and the Spelling option. If you have entered the text correctly then a message 'The spelling check is completed' will

Figure 5.7 Final slide

continued

appear. If the check reveals mistakes they will be shown within the Spelling window and alternative spellings will be offered for you to choose from.

7 Save the presentation you have created on to a floppy disk. This procedure is the same in all Microsoft® Windows® applications – you save a presentation, spreadsheet, database or graphic image in exactly the same way.

   – insert a floppy disk into drive A:

   – click on the File menu item and a menu will open showing a list of options.

   – Select Save and a window will open.

8 Click in the box File name and Enter A:\CLAIT 2006. Click on the Save button on the right of the window. You have now saved your presentation as a file called CLAIT 2006. You may hear the drive A: working during this process.

9 To run the slide show you have created select the View menu and then click on the Slide Show option. The presentation will fill the screen and you can move between slides by clicking the left mouse button. When the presentation is over you will return to Microsoft® PowerPoint®. Alternatively select the Slide Show menu and the View show option.

10 You can close Microsoft® PowerPoint® now by clicking on the File menu item and a menu will appear with a list of options. At the bottom of the list is the option Exit. An alternative way is to click on the Close button in the top right-hand corner of the application window.

Editing your presentation

As with other Microsoft® Office® applications, you are able to add, delete and replace parts of your presentation using functions such as:

- Cut, copy and paste (Figure 5.8)
- Search and replace (Figures 5.9)

Cut, copy and paste work by using the mouse pointer to highlight the text or object you want to edit. Highlighting is undertaken by clicking the mouse pointer at the chosen location and holding down the left mouse button while dragging it over the text or object. The text is shown to be highlighted by the background darkening. When the selected text is highlighted you can release the mouse button. To cut or

Figure 5.8 Standard toolbar – Cut and Copy

copy the highlighted area you click on the Standard toolbar icon (Figure 5.8). These functions are also available on the Edit menu (Figure 5.9).

The Cut function removes the highlighted area completely and you can then move it to a new location by using the mouse pointer. A new location is selected by positioning the pointer and clicking. The new position is identified by the cursor being moved (i.e. in the same way as the cursor is moved in Microsoft® Word). Now click on the Paste option or icon and the cut section is placed back into the presentation. The Copy function operates in the same way except that the original highlighted area is not removed.

Figure 5.9 Edit Menu

Cut and Copy are very useful functions since a key element in any presentation is consistency. These functions allow you to ensure quickly and effectively that identical elements are present on all slides (e.g. titles, company logos, etc.).

Presentations often consist of many slides and if you need to change some text on every slide it can be a long and tedious process. Microsoft® PowerPoint® provides a way of finding a particular section of text of any length and replacing it with an amended phrase. This is not only fast but also free from errors such as spelling mistakes caused by having to enter replacement text from the keyboard.

Search and replace is available as an option on the Edit menu called Replace. A window will appear (Figure 5.10) with two text boxes. Click in the top box and enter the words you wish to find then click in the lower box and enter the words you want to replace them with. There are also two options shown by the tick boxes in the bottom left-hand corner of the window:

- Match case
- Find whole words only

Match case means that the search will locate only these phrases that are identical in case (e.g. capitals) to the text entered in the window. Find whole words only restricts the search to matches that are entire words, otherwise the search finds words that are parts of longer words (e.g. a search for car will match with carton, care and handcart). This option is important if you are searching for a single word.

Once you have completed the two text boxes you can start the search by clicking on the Find Next button. The search starts from the location of the cursor and proceeds through the presentation. Whenever a match is located you have the choice of replacing it by clicking on the Replace button which changes that single entry. You then need to click on Find Next again to continue the search. An alternative is to click on Replace All which will change all the matches to the new text. Use this option only if you are completely certain that you want to change them all.

Slide order

An important function available in Microsoft® PowerPoint® is the ability to the change the order of the slides. This is provided in the View menu within the Slide Sorter option. When this is selected the display changes to show all the slides (Figure 5.11). Slides can then be dragged and dropped into a new order using the mouse pointer. Clicking on the slide you wish to move and holding down the left mouse button allows you to move to a new position.

If you highlight a slide with a single click you can also Cut, Copy and Paste slides using the functions on the Standard toolbar and within the Edit menu.

Figure 5.10 Replace

Figure 5.11 Changing the slide order

Exercise 42

Editing a presentation

1 Load Microsoft® PowerPoint® using either the All Programs menu or the Microsoft® PowerPoint® icon on the desktop.

2 In the New Presentation task pane in the Open a presentation section there should be a list of files. Double click on the CLAIT 2006 file shown in the list. The CLAIT 2006 presentation will be loaded, but remember to have your floppy disk inserted in the A: drive.

3 Using the Replace function in the Edit menu, change the title text from CLAIT 2006 to CLAIT 2006 Qualification on all four slides.

4 Using the Cut function, move the text Level 1 Qualification from the second slide to the subtitle box on slide one and amend the text by deleting the word Qualification.

continued

5 Change the order of the slides by moving slide three to make it slide two.

6 Spell check the presentation. Figure 5.12 shows the revised presentation.

7 Save the presentation you have created on to a floppy disk. This procedure is the same in all Windows applications – you save a presentation, spreadsheet, database or graphic image in exactly the same way.

   – insert a floppy disk into drive A:

   – click on the File menu item and a menu will open showing a list of options.

   – Select Save As and a window will open

Figure 5.12 Revised presentation

8 Click in the box File name and Enter A:\CLAIT 2006 revised. Click on the Save button on the right of the window. You have now saved your presentation as a file called CLAIT 2006 revised. You may hear drive A: work during this process.

9 To run the slide show you have created, select the View menu and then click on the Slide Show option. The presentation will fill the screen and you can move between slides by clicking the left mouse button. When the presentation is over you will return to Microsoft® PowerPoint®. Alternatively select the Slide Show menu and the View show option.

10 You can close Microsoft® PowerPoint® now by clicking on the File menu item and a menu will appear with a list of options. At the bottom of the list is the option Exit. If you click on Exit then Microsoft® PowerPoint® will close. An alternative way is to click on the Close button on the top right-hand corner of the application window.

Enhancing your presentation

Microsoft® PowerPoint® has a variety of functions that allow you enhance your presentation. Many of these functions are similar to those available in other Microsoft® Office applications (e.g. Microsoft® Word) and include:

- slide orientation
- background colour
- bold, italics and underline

- alignment
- bullet points
- change fonts and character size
- indent text (i.e. promote and demote text)
- insert graphics (i.e. pictures and charts)

Orientation

The orientation of the slides can be either landscape or portrait and is selected by using the Page Setup function in the File menu. This also allows you to choose the orientation for printing the handouts, overview and any notes.

Background

In a similar way you can apply a background colour to your slides through the Format menu and the Background option to open the Background window. This window lets you choose the colour of the background and apply it to all slides or to an individual one. Good practice is to have one consistent background through out the presentation.

Formatting

The Formatting toolbar (Figure 5.13) provides access to the functions that enable you to embolden text, write in italics, underline, align, change fonts and alter the size of characters. Microsoft® Office provides a wide range of fonts and character sizes. If you click on the small down arrow alongside the Font and Font Size boxes on the toolbar, a menu of options will drop down. Click on the selected option. You can do this before you enter text so that the words you enter will appear in the font and size of your choice or you can change the text you have already entered.

To change already entered text you must first highlight it and then make your choice from the drop-down menus. The font and size of your text is critical for an effective presentation since you are seeking to capture your audience's attention. The font must be attractive and interesting to the audience but must not distract from the message you are presenting. The size of characters must be selected carefully to ensure that the slides are visible from the back row, and it is useful to test your slides in the room. It is also important to check the legibility of your slides since colour combinations that appear very effective on the screen can be poor when projected or printed on to an overhead projector slide.

Promote and demote text

Microsoft® Powerpoint® provides tools to promote and demote text. This essentially means that you can

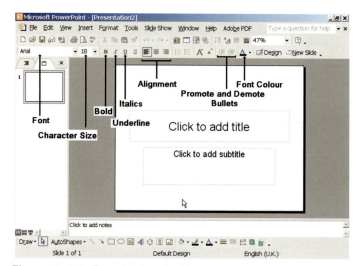

Figure 5.13 Formatting toolbar

structure your bullet points to enhance the main points and show the difference between main and subsidiary issues. By highlighting the text and selecting either the Promote or Demote icons on the Formatting toolbar you can add or remove an indent. This is the same as using the Tab key to indent your text.

These options offer you a variety of ways to emphasise your message and draw the attention of your audience to the critical points. Fonts, character size, bold, italics and underlining all make text stand out.

Alignment

Another useful function is alignment. You can align your text so that it is left, centre or right aligned. Left aligned means that the text starts parallel to the left margin and is uneven on the right edge (i.e. the normal way text is presented). Right aligned means that text is aligned parallel to the right margin and is uneven on the left. This is an unusual way to present text and is rarely used in a presentation. Centre aligned means that the text is centred down the middle of the slide. In presentations, centred is frequently used to draw the audience's attention to the words. Left is also used since it is the most readable way of presenting text.

In a similar way to the use of bold, italics and underline, you can select the alignment before entering the text by clicking on the icon on the Formatting toolbar or you can choose to change the alignment later. Highlight the words you wish to align and click on the appropriate alignment icon. You can align a single word, a sentence, a paragraph, a slide or indeed the entire presentation or you can combine all three ways.

Bullet points

An important device in a presentation is the bullet point list. This is a simple list of items beginning with a symbol (e.g. numbers or geometric symbols) to differentiate it from the rest of the text. It is useful since during a presentation you will be using the slides to indicate the key points of the topic which can be shown as individual bullet points.

Microsoft® PowerPoint® provides a selection of bullet points to choose from, accessed from the Format menu. By clicking on the Format menu item, the drop-down menu is revealed and you can click on the Bullets and Numbering option to show the Bullets and Numbering window. Figure 5.14 shows some bullet symbol options and the Picture button provides access to a wider variety. The Numbered tab reveals styles of numbering that can be used as bullets. You need to explore the wide range of options.

Figure 5.14 Bullets and Numbering

A Microsoft® PowerPoint® template assumes you are using bullet points so it will automatically provide lists. However, you can change the default setting by clicking on the Format menu, selecting Bullets and Numbering and choosing a bullet style. Your chosen style will then appear as you enter the text. However, you can alter the bullet at any time by highlighting the item and choosing a new style. You can change a single item or a whole list.

Illustrations

Pictures can make a presentation more interesting. Use the Picture options on the Insert menu to insert images at any point in your presentations. However, when you are selecting the layout of each slide there are several that include pictures.

To insert a picture into a slide you need to click on the Insert menu item, highlight the Picture option and a second menu will appear to the right of Insert. This provides you with various choices. Clip Art images are provided with Microsoft® PowerPoint® to help you design presentations. From File allows you to select images you have created yourself or have bought. We will consider only the Clip Art option.

By clicking on Clip Art you open a library of pictures to select from. Figure 5.15 shows you the Insert Clip Art pane that is initially displayed. This allows you to search for the clip relevant to a particular topic.

The pane display will change to show the results of your search (i.e. a series of images). To select a picture. You need to click on it, and a short menu of options will appear. The top option will place the image on your slide. However, at this point you may get an error message telling you the pictures are on another disk. This is the Microsoft® Office installation disk and if you have it, you need to place this disk in the CD-ROM drive.

Figure 5.15 Clip Art

The image will either be placed at the cursor or, if your slide has no cursor showing, in the middle of the slide (Figure 5.16). A frame surrounds the image and, if you move the mouse pointer over the image, it changes to a star shape. By holding down the left mouse button when it is over the image you can drag it around the slide and position it. You fix the image by releasing the mouse button and clicking away from the graphic. However, if you click on the graphic image again, the frame will reappear and you can move it to a new position.

Figure 5.16 Position image

An alternative approach is to select a slide layout that includes pictures and to click on the clip art icon. The Select Picture window will appear which allows you to search for a clip art image and insert it in the way described above.

Lines and drawings

Microsoft® PowerPoint® offers functions that enable you to add lines and drawn shapes such as rectangles, ovals and autoshapes (i.e. many different outlines). These are available on the Draw toolbar. In addition you can shade objects or fill the shapes with colour using the Fill Color and Line Color functions. You can colour text, insert three-dimensional shapes and add special effects to text (i.e. WordArt). Figure 5.17 illustrates the Draw toolbar functions.

Figure 5.17 Draw toolbar

Exercise 43

Enhancing your presentation

1 Load Microsoft® PowerPoint® using either the All Programs menu or the Microsoft® PowerPoint® icon on the desktop.

2 In the New Presentation task pane in the Open a presentation section there should be a list of files. Double click on the CLAIT 2006 revised file shown in the list. The CLAIT 2006 revised presentation will be loaded, but you must have inserted your floppy disk which contains the presentation file.

3 During this exercise you are going to use the various Microsoft® PowerPoint® functions to enhance your presentation. The first step is to emphasise the titles on each slide and in particular on the opening one. On the initial slide, change the title font to Algierian (or another you feel has impact), the character size to 48 and embolden it. You need to highlight the title and then select the font, character size and the bold option. Once you have made your selections, simply click away from the highlighting to see the changes made. You may need to widen the text box to allow the title to appear on a single line.

4 Next change each title on the other slides to Algierian but with character size 44.

5 The slide bullet points were produced using the default options so you need to change them to a bullet symbol of your choice. Systematically highlight each list of bullet points and select another bullet symbol (i.e. Format menu, Bullets and Numbering option). It is worth exploring the different options to identify one you like and feel is appropriate.

continued

6. Now change all the other text to a font and character size different from the title (e.g. Arial). Explore the different options until you find a font that looks good. Remember to highlight the text and use the font and character options on the Formatting toolbar.

7. Centre your bullet points (e.g. using the alignment icons on the Formatting toolbar) and check to see if you feel this is appropriate way of presenting the text. If you do not like the way it appears, change to left aligned.

8. Insert a graphic image on the opening slide to provide interest. Remember to move to this slide by using the scroll bar and then select the **Insert** menu, highlight the **Picture** option and click on **Clip Art**. Try to pick an image appropriate to the study of an information and communication technology qualification. Move the image around the slide until you place it in an appropriate spot.

9. While the image is enclosed within its frame, placing the mouse pointer over an edge will change its shape to a double-headed arrow (Figure 5.18). If you hold down the left mouse button you can change the shape of the picture. Try to alter the size of the image. You will need to pull the corner to avoid distorting the image.

Figure 5.18 Inserting a picture

10. Change the background colour of all the slides (**Format** menu, **Background** option and Background window). Use the **Preview** option in the Background window to explore the different colours.

11. Spell check your presentation (**Tools** menu and **Spelling** option).

12. Save the presentation you have created on to a floppy disk. This procedure is the same in all Microsoft® Windows® applications. You save a presentation, spreadsheet, database or graphic image in exactly the same way:
    - insert a floppy disk into drive A:
    - click on **File** menu item and a menu will open showing a list of options
    - select **Save As** and a window will open.

13. Click in the box **File name** and Enter A:\CLAIT 2006 revised2. Click on the **Save** button on the right of the window. You have now saved your presentation as a file called CLAIT 2006 revised2. You may hear drive A: work during this process.

14. To run the slide show you have created, select the **View** menu and then click on the **Slide Show** option. The presentation will fill the screen and you can move between

> ### continued
>
> slides by clicking the left mouse button. When the presentation is over you will return to Microsoft® PowerPoint®. Alternatively select the Slide Show menu and the View show option.
>
> 15 You can close Microsoft® PowerPoint® now by clicking on the File menu item and a menu will appear with a list of options. At the bottom of the list is the option Exit. If you click on Exit then Microsoft® PowerPoint® will close. An alternative way is to click on the close button on the top right-hand corner of the application window.

Headers and footers

You can add headers and footers to your slides in a similar way to other Microsoft® Office applications. This is very useful in a presentation since you can automatically date and number your slides as well as add any standard comments. As part of the assessment you will be asked to identify your slides by inserting your name and study centre number in the footer. To add a header and footer, select the View menu and the Header and Footer option. This reveals a window (Figure 5.19) in which the Slide tab provides you

Figure 5.19 Header and Footer

with options to select the date and time which are automatically updated, number your slides and add text as a footer. The other tab, Notes and Handouts, lets you add headers and other footers to your handouts and notes.

Printing your presentation

So far, we have considered how to create a presentation which appears on the computer screen or which could be projected using a data or video projector. However, in many cases you will want to print your slides to provide a set of handouts or to be able to project them on an overhead projector (OHP), which involves printing them on transparencies. There are different types of transparencies depending on your printer (i.e. laser and inkjet). It is important to check that you are using the correct type since using the wrong one may result in poor slides or even damage your printer.

To print your slides you need to click on the File menu and the option Print. This will reveal the Print window (Figure 5.20). The Print window is divided into areas. These are:

- Printer – this shows you the name of the printer that will be used
- Print range – there are a variety of options which you select by clicking on the radio

buttons. The All option prints the whole presentation. Current slide prints only the slide being viewed at that moment. Selection prints the area of the slide which has been highlighted and Slides allows you to select some of the slides by entering their numbers in the text box alongside

- Copies – this allows you to print more than one copy and to collate them
- Print what – by clicking on the small down arrow at the end of the box, a list of options is revealed allowing you to print slides (transparencies), handouts, notes pages and outline view.

The different Print what options are:

- slides – prints the images on to transparencies and paper
- handouts – prints the slides on to paper so that each person in your audience has a copy of your presentation to take away
- notes pages – you can add notes to your slides so that the audience gets a copy of the slides and your speaking notes
- outline view – this is a list of just the text of the whole presentation. It is useful to help you check that you have not left out any important points

Figure 5.20 The Print dialog box

Exercise 44

Printing

1 Load Microsoft® PowerPoint® using either the All Programs menu or the Microsoft® PowerPoint® icon on the desktop.

2 In the New Presentation task pane in the Open a presentation section there should be a list of files. Double click on the CLAIT 2006 revised2 file shown in the list (Figure 5.21). The CLAIT 2006 revised2 presentation will be loaded,

Figure 5.21 Open Presentation

but you must have inserted your floppy disk which contains the presentation file.

> **continued**
>
> 3. You are going to print your slides and produce audience notes (i.e. a handout).
> 4. Print your slides on to paper initially to check how they look.
>
>   Transparency film is quite expensive so it is worth checking before you waste it. Transparencies are loaded into the printer in the same way as paper but make sure you are using the correct type of transparency for the printer (e.g. inkjet or laser transparencies). It can damage your printer if you use the wrong type. Read the instructions on the transparency box as you may need to insert them in a particular way.
>
> 5. You will be using the default settings to print. Microsoft® PowerPoint® defaults to printing slides as landscape images but handouts, notes pages and outlines as portrait images. Defaults can be changed.
>
> 6. Print your slides (**File** menu, **Print**, change **Print what** to Slides (it may already be set to this option) and **OK** button). The default is to print all your slides so you do not need to change the Print range settings.
>
> 7. Print handouts (**File** menu, **Print**, change **Print what** to Handouts and **OK** button). The default is to print six thumbnail images on each page and therefore since your presentation comprises four slides, four thumbnail images of the slides will be printed. If you look to the right of the Print dialog box you will see how the thumbnails will appear.
>
> 8. Print the notes pages (**File** menu, **Print**, change **Print what** to Notes Pages and **OK** button). In this case your presentation is printed on four sheets with a copy of the slide at the top and a space below for any notes you may have added.
>
> 9. Print outline view (**File** menu, **Print**, change **Print what** to Outline View and **OK** button). The outline is printed on a single sheet.
>
> 10. Take a moment to consider the different printer outputs. You can close Microsoft® PowerPoint® by clicking on the **File** menu item and a menu will appear with a list of options. At the bottom of the list is the option **Exit**. If you click on **Exit** then Microsoft® PowerPoint® will close. An alternative way is to click on the **Close** button on the top right hand corner of the application window.

Master slides

There is a special type of slide called a Master Slide which allows you to define the fonts, character sizes, colour and layout that will be used throughout your presentation. This is very helpful in ensuring that you provide a consistent appearance to your slides. Anything you place on the master slide will appear on all the slides.

When you start a new presentation you create a master slide by selecting the **View** menu, highlighting the **Master** option and clicking on **Slide Master**. The master slide appears (Figure 5.22). In some cases a toolbar called Slide Master View will also appear – drag it towards the toolbars and you will see it join the other toolbars. To define fonts, click on an area and then change the font, character sizes and other features (e.g. insert picture). These features will be reproduced throughout the presentation.

Once you have defined your master, go ahead with designing each slide and you will see the standard features appear on each of them. If you want to make a change, then by altering the master slide you can change all the slides.

Exercise 45

Master slide

1. Load Microsoft® PowerPoint® using either the All Programs menu or the Microsoft® PowerPoint® icon on the desktop.

2. Select Blank Presentation from the New Presentation task pane.

3. Select the File menu and the Page Setup option to set the slide orientation to Landscape.

4. Select the View menu and highlight the Master option to reveal an additional menu. Select the Slide Master option to reveal the outline of the master slide (Figure 5.22). A toolbar called Slide Master View may appear. Drag it towards the toolbars and it will join them.

5. In order to change or add borders to the top text box you need to right click in the placeholder and select the Format Placeholder option. This opens the Format Autoshape window (Figure 5.23). Change the line colour to black by clicking on the down arrow at end of the color box and you will see that the title placeholder will be enclosed in a black rectangle.

6. You can amend the master layout by left clicking within the text placeholders. Change the text of the title area to Arial, character size 36 and bold. The title should be centred.

7. The first level bullet should be Arial, character size 24 and left aligned.

8. The second level bullet should be Arial, character size 20, left aligned and indented from the first level bullet. The bullets should be separated by one character space. Delete the other bullet levels.

9. Click in the footer and enter your name, automatic date and time. The slide number should be displayed on the bottom right of the slide (i.e. View menu and Header and Footer option).

Figure 5.22 Master slide

continued

10. Change the background colour to cyan by selecting the Format menu and the Background option to reveal the Background window. Click on the down arrow to reveal colours, select cyan then click on the Apply to All button. You will see the background colour change.

11. Save the presentation you have created on to a floppy disk. This procedure is the same in all Microsoft® Windows® applications: you save a presentation, spreadsheet, database or graphic image in exactly the same way:

    – insert a floppy disk into drive A:

    – click on File menu item and a menu will open showing a list of options.

    – select Save and a window will open.

12. Click in the box File name and enter A:\Master. Click on the Save button on the right of the window. You have now saved your presentation as a file called Master. You may hear drive A: work during this process.

Figure 5.23 Format Autoshape window

More practice

Activity 1
Sell a product

1. Load Microsoft® PowerPoint® using either the All Programs menu or the Microsoft® PowerPoint® icon on the desktop.

2. You are going to develop a presentation to sell the Wireless Laser Printer (WLP). Microsoft® PowerPoint® is often used for sales presentations.

3. Create a master slide by selecting the View menu, highlight the Master option and choose the Slide Master option.

4. Select the Landscape orientation using the File menu and Page Setup option.

5. Select the font Tahoma, character size 40 and bold for the title placeholder at the top of the slide. Centre the title.

6. Select the font Times New Roman, character size 36 and italics for the first level bullet point. The bullets are left aligned. Delete the other bullet levels – this presentation only employs level 1 bullets. Choose a bullet character.

7 Enter your name, automatic date and time in the footer (`View` menu and `Header and Footer` option). The slide number should be shown on the bottom right-hand side of the slide.

8 The background colour should be white (select the `Format` menu and `Background` option).

9 Save the presentation using the file name Sales.

10 Create slide 1 by selecting the `View` menu and choosing the `Normal` option. This will open the title template in the working area. Insert the title Wireless Laser Printer and select a clip art image below the title placeholder (i.e. `Insert` menu and `Pictures` option).

11 Insert a new slide (`Insert`, `New slide` and select a layout with title and text areas).

12 Insert Wireless Laser Printer on the title bar and then add the following bullets:

- No Cables
- Radio Communication
- Under £200

13 Insert a new slide (`Insert`, `New slide` and select a layout with title and text areas).

14 Insert Wireless Laser Printer as the title and the following bullets in italics:

- 10 pages per minute
- 600 dots per inch
- Quiet operation
- Design life 100,000 pages
- 3 Year warranty

15 Insert a new slide (`Insert`, `New slide` and select a layout with title and text areas).

16 Insert Wireless Laser Printer as the title and the following bullets in italics:

- Acme Printer Company
- 234 New Way, Birmingham
- Info@acmestar.co.uk
- Your name, Sales Representative

17 Spell check your presentation.

18 Save the presentation you have created on to a floppy disk with the file name Sales (`File` menu and `Save` option).

19 Print your slides and a handout with all the slides on one page (`File`, `Print` option and `OK` button).

20 To run the slide show you have created, select the `View` menu and then click on the `Slide Show` option. The presentation will fill

Figure 5.24 Sales presentation

the screen and you can move between slides by clicking the left mouse button. When the presentation is over you will return to Microsoft® PowerPoint®. Alternatively select the Slide Show menu and the View show option. Figure 5.24 shows slide 3.

21 You can close Microsoft® PowerPoint® now by clicking on the File menu item and a menu will appear with a list of options. At the bottom of the list is the option Exit. If you click on Exit then Microsoft® PowerPoint® will close. An alternative way is to click on the Close button in the top right-hand corner of the application window.

Activity 2
Amend a presentation

1 Load Microsoft® PowerPoint® using either the All Programs menu or the Microsoft® PowerPoint® icon on the desktop.

2 In the New Presentation task pane in the Open a presentation section there should be a list of files. Double click on the Sales file shown in the list. The Sales presentation will be loaded, but you must have inserted your floppy disk which contains the presentation file.

3 Change the orientation of the presentation from landscape to portrait (File menu and Page Setup option).

4 Change the text on slide 3 from 10 pages per minute to 25 pages per minute.

5 Add a line below the bullet point text on slides 2, 3 and 4 (Line icon on Drawing toolbar).

6 Save the presentation with the new file name Sales Revised (File menu and Save As).

7 Print the four slides as handouts with 4 slides on a page (File menu, Print option, Print what section and OK button).

8 Change the order of the slides so that slide 3 becomes slide 2 (View menu and Slide Sorter option). Figure 5.25 illustrates the process. Compare the appearance of the slides in portrait orientation with your earlier presentations in landscape.

9 Print the outline view of the presentation with your name as a footer for this printout (i.e. View menu, Header and Footer option and Notes and Handouts tab).

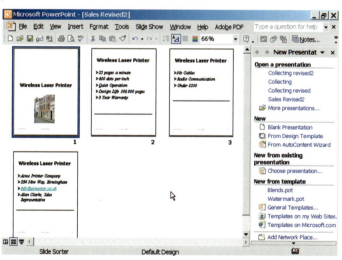

Figure 5.25 Order slides

10 Save the amended presentation as the file Sales Revised2 (File menu and Save As).

11 To run the slide show you have created, select the View menu and then click on the Slide Show option. The presentation will fill the screen and you can move between slides by clicking the left mouse button. When the presentation is over you will return to Microsoft® PowerPoint®. Alternatively select the Slide Show menu and the View show option.

12 You can close Microsoft® PowerPoint® now by clicking on the File menu item and a menu will appear with a list of options. At the bottom of the list is the option Exit. If you click on Exit then Microsoft® PowerPoint® will close. An alternative way is to click on the Close button in the top right-hand corner of the application window.

Activity 3
Explain a hobby

1. Load Microsoft® PowerPoint® using either the All Programs menu or the Microsoft® PowerPoint® icon on the desktop.
2. You are going to develop a presentation to explain why collecting postcards is interesting and fun. Microsoft® PowerPoint® is often used to explain a subject to an audience.
3. Create a master slide by selecting the View menu, highlight the Master option and choose the Slide Master option.
4. Select Landscape orientation using the File menu and Page Setup option.
5. Select the font Times New Roman, character size 44 and bold for the title placeholder at the top of the slide. Centre the title.
6. Select the font Arial, character size 36 and italics for the first level bullet point. The bullets are left aligned. Choose a bullet character. Delete the other bullet levels.
7. Enter your name, an automatic date and time in the footer (View menu and Header and Footer option). The slide number should be shown on the bottom right-hand side of the slide.
8. The background colour should be yellow (select the Format menu and Background option).
9. Save the presentation using the file name Collecting.
10. Create slide 1 by selecting the View menu and choosing the Normal option. This will open the title layout in the working area. Change the title layout by selecting the layout showing a title placeholder at the top of the slide and text placeholder below from the Slide Layout task pane on the right of the display. Insert the title Postcard Collecting and then add the following bullets to the text placeholder:

    - Postcards are over 100 years old
    - 1896 in Great Britain
    - Thousands of collectors
    - All ages and backgrounds
    - Many different themes e.g. local history

11. Insert a new slide (Insert, New slide) and select a layout with title and text areas. Insert Postcard Collecting in bold as the title and the following bullets:

    - Wide price range
    - From 10p to many pounds
    - Photographic to artist-drawn cards
    - Local history
    - Many books to explain the hobby

12. Insert a new slide (<u>Insert</u>, <u>New slide</u>) and select a layout with title and text areas. Insert *Postcard Collecting* in bold as the title and the following bullets:

    - Many collectors fairs
    - Postcard clubs
    - Monthly magazine
    - Dealers
    - Websites

13. Insert a new slide (<u>Insert</u>, <u>New slide</u>) and select a layout with title and text areas. Insert *Postcard Collecting* in bold as the title and the following bullets:

    - Visit the postcard display
    - Ask any questions

14. Spell check your presentation. Figure 5.26 shows the first slide of the collecting presentation.

15. Save the presentation you have created on to a floppy disk:

    - insert a floppy disk into drive A:
    - click on <u>File</u> menu item and a menu will open showing a list of options.
    - Select <u>Save</u> and a window will open.

Figure 5.26 Collecting presentation slide 1

16. Click in the <u>File name</u> box and enter A:\Collecting. Click on the <u>Save</u> button on the right of the window. You have now saved your presentation as a file called Collecting. You may hear the drive A: work during this process.

17. Print your slides and a handout (<u>File</u>, <u>Print</u> option and <u>OK</u> button).

18. To run the slide show you have created select the <u>View</u> menu and then click on the <u>Slide Show</u> option. The presentation will fill the screen and you can move between slides by clicking the left mouse button. When the presentation is over you will return to Microsoft® PowerPoint®. Alternatively select the <u>Slide Show</u> menu and the <u>View show</u> option.

19. You can close Microsoft® PowerPoint® now by clicking on the <u>File</u> menu item and a menu will appear with a list of options. At the bottom of the list is the option <u>Exit</u>. If you click on <u>Exit</u> then Microsoft® PowerPoint® will close. An alternative way is to click on the <u>Close</u> button in the top right-hand corner of the application window.

Activity 4
Edit Collecting presentation

1. Load Microsoft® PowerPoint® using either the <u>All Programs</u> menu or the <u>Microsoft® PowerPoint®</u> icon on the desktop.

2. In the New Presentation task pane in the Open a presentation section there should be a list of files. Double click on the Collecting file shown in the list. The Collecting presentation will be loaded, but you must have inserted your floppy disk which contains the presentation file.

3. Demote bullet point two in slide 1 – *1896 in Great Britain* – Arial, 28

4. Demote bullet point four in slide 1 – *All ages and backgrounds* – Arial, 28

5. Demote bullet point five in slide 1 – *Many different themes e.g. local history* – Arial, 28

6. Demote bullet point two in slide 2 – *from 10p to many pounds* – Arial, 28

7. Save the presentation with the new file name Collecting Revised (`File` menu and `Save As`).

8. Print the four slides as handouts with 2 slides on a page (`File` menu, `Print` option, `Print what` section and `OK` button).

9. Change the order of the slides so that slide 3 becomes slide 2 (`View` menu and `Slide Sorter` option).

10. Print the outline view of the presentation with your name as a footer for this printout (i.e. `View` menu, `Header and Footer` option and `Notes and Handouts` tab).

11. Save the amended presentation as the file Collecting Revised2 (`File` menu and `Save As`).

12. To run the slide show you have created select the `View` menu and then click on the `Slide Show` option. The presentation will fill the screen and you can move between slides by clicking the left mouse button. When the presentation is over you will return to Microsoft® PowerPoint®. Alternatively select the `Slide Show` menu and the `View show` option.

13. You can close Microsoft® PowerPoint® now by clicking on the `File` menu item and a menu will appear with a list of options. At the bottom of the list is the option `Exit`. If you click on `Exit` then Microsoft® PowerPoint® will close. An alternative way is to click on the `Close` button in the top right-hand corner of the application window.

Other ideas

If you would like to practise then the following list of ideas for presentations might be useful. Design presentations to:

- introduce new employees to your workplace
- explain why you deserve a pay rise
- explain a hobby or interest (e.g. collecting postcards, keeping guinea pigs or walking)
- help new computer users understand the uses of information and communication technology
- help people new to the Internet to search for information

SUMMARY

1. **Load Microsoft® PowerPoint®**: Use either the Start button and the All Programs menu or double click on the Microsoft® PowerPoint® icon on Microsoft® Windows® desktop.

2. **Close**: Click on the File menu item and the Exit option or click on the Close button on the top right-hand corner of the application window.

3. **Save a file on a floppy disk**: Insert a floppy disk into drive A: and click on the File menu and Save. Select the drive (3½ Floppy (A:)) and enter the file name.

   Having saved a file once, you can update it by clicking on the File menu and Save, without the Save As window appearing again. It simply overwrites the original file.

4. **Start a new presentation**: Select the option Blank Presentation from the New Presentation task pane on the right of the display.

5. **Select new layout**: Select a layout by clicking on the desired layout in the Slide Layout task pane to reveal a menu. Select Insert New Slide from the menu.

6. **Delete text**: You have two keys (i.e. Backspace and Delete) which both work from the position of your cursor.

   Backspace key – this removes text, character by character, to the left of the cursor position.

   Delete key – this removes text, character by character, to the right of the cursor position.

   There is also undo and redo. Undo removes the last action you have undertaken, while redo carries out the actions removed by undo. Undo can be used to remove text that has just been typed.

7. **Select design template**: Select the Format menu and the Slide Design option to open the Slide Design task pane on the right of the display. Choose a design.

8. **Spell check**: Select the Tools menu and the Spelling option.

9. **Change Slide Order**: Select the View menu and the Slide Sorter option.

10. **Insert graphics**: If you have used a graphics template then you need to double click on the image area to access the clip art search window. Search for a suitable image.

    Select the Insert menu, highlight the Picture option to reveal another menu of options. Select the Clip Art item to open the Insert Clip Art pane.

    You may see an error message telling you the pictures are on another disk. This is the Microsoft® Office installation disk and you need to place this disk, if you have it, in the CD-ROM drive.

11. **Move the image**: Place the mouse pointer over the image and the pointer will change to indicate that the picture can be dragged by holding down the left mouse button.

12. **Change the font, character size and text characteristics** (bold, italics and underline): Highlight the text you want to change. Change the font and/or character size by selecting

the item in the drop-down list on the Formatting toolbar. Change the text characteristics (i.e. bold, italics and underline) by selecting the icon on the Formatting toolbar.

13. **Change the text alignment**: Highlight the text you want to change. Select the alignment option by clicking on the icon on the Formatting toolbar.

14. **Replace text**: Select the <u>E</u>dit menu and the <u>R</u>eplace option. The Replace window appears. Enter the text you want to replace in the Fi<u>n</u>d what: box and the replacement text in Re<u>p</u>lace with: box.

15. **Bullets**: Select the F<u>o</u>rmat menu and the <u>B</u>ullets and Numbering option. The dialog box gives you a range of styles to choose from.

16. **Orientation**: Select the <u>F</u>ile menu and the Page Set<u>u</u>p option.

17. **Background**: Select the F<u>o</u>rmat menu and the <u>B</u>ackground option to open the Background window.

18. **Header and Footer**: Select the <u>V</u>iew menu and the <u>H</u>eader and Footer option.

19. **Printing**: Select the <u>F</u>ile menu and the <u>P</u>rint option.

20. **Masters**: Select the <u>V</u>iew menu, highlight the <u>M</u>aster option and click on <u>S</u>lide Master, Ha<u>n</u>dout Master or <u>N</u>otes Master.

Chapter 6

Unit 6

E-image creation

This chapter will help you to use a drawing package to:

- identify and use drawing software correctly in accordance with laws and guidelines
- use basic file handling techniques for the software
- download digital pictures from a digital camera
- import, crop and resize images
- enter, amend and resize text
- manipulate and format page items
- manage and print artwork

Assessment

This unit does not assume any previous experience of using a computer. However, you may find it useful to have completed Unit 1: File management and e-document production. You will be assessed through a practical realistic assignment which is designed to allow you to demonstrate your knowledge and skills against each objective. Your tutor can provide you with more guidance.

Drawing applications

There are many computer applications concerned with the production and manipulation of images. You can capture them using digital cameras and scanners, purchase collections known as clip art or simply create your own from scratch. Almost anyone can create pictures using a computer drawing package. Computer pictures are called graphics. Microsoft® Windows® has a drawing application built into it called Microsoft® Paint (Figure 6.1) which provides you with tools to draw lines, curves, circles and rectangles as well as to add colour to your images and change the orientation of the image. Microsoft® Word has built-in drawing tools (select View menu, highlight the Toolbars option and click on Drawing).

There are two types of graphic images:

- bitmaps
- vectors

A bitmap image is composed of dots called pixels. The more pixels in a given amount of space (e.g. a square inch) the clearer the image, that is the higher the resolution of the picture. Each pixel is associated with the number of colours that can be displayed. An 8-bit image can use 256 colours while a 24-bit image can use 16.7 million colours.

Vector images are defined by mathematical formulae rather than pixels. This defines the start and finish of the line and allows it to be easily changed. Vector images can be

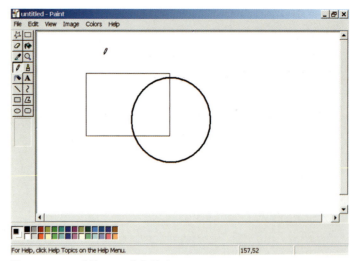

Figure 6.1 Microsoft® Paint

resized and still stay in perfect proportion. Although you can change a bitmap image, it will often distort if the change is too radical. However bitmaps can probably show more detail than vector images since every pixel of the image is employed.

This chapter is based on CorelDRAW® 10, a professional vector drawing package with numerous useful tools for working with bitmaps and vectors.

File formats

Graphics created by a painting or drawing package are stored on the computer as files. There are a variety of file formats that are used to represent graphics. The main ones are:

- JPEG – Joint Photographic Expert Group is a bitmap format which is used extensively on the World Wide Web. Files which are in JPEG format are shown with an extension .jpeg or .jpg
- GIF – Graphics Interchange Format is a bitmap format which is also used extensively on the World Wide Web. Files in GIF format are shown by the extension .gif
- TIFF – Tagged Image File Format is a bitmap format widely used in the graphics industry. Files in this format are shown by the extension .tif
- Microsoft® Windows® bitmap – this is the standard format for graphics in the Microsoft® Windows® operating system. Files in this format are shown by the extension .bmp
- Microsoft® Windows® Metafile – this is the Microsoft® Windows® vector graphics standard format. Files in this format are shown by the extension .wmf
- Encapsulated Postscript – this is a vector file format which is shown by the extension .eps

There are many other graphic file formats which have been designed for specific tasks. It is possible to convert from one to another but in some cases this will affect the quality of the image.

CorelDRAW®

Figure 6.2 shows the CorelDRAW® Application. When it is loaded, a window overlays the application offering you a variety of choices in the form of six icons. These are:

- New Graphic – to start a new image
- Open Last Edited – to allow you to continue working on the last image
- Open Graphic – to open an existing image
- Template – to open a standard template
- CorelTUTOR – to access a tutorial on how to use CorelDRAW®
- What's New? – provides you with an overview of CorelDRAW®

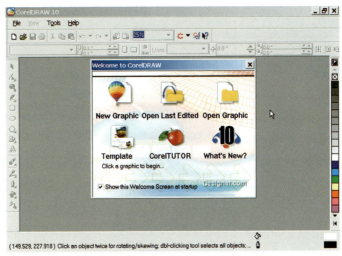

Figure 6.2 CorelDraw®

You should select the New Graphic icon (Figure 6.2) and the overlay window will close revealing the main application display (Figure 6.3). The centre of the display shows the document area in which you can create a new graphic image. On the left is the Toolbox containing a variety of the drawing tools, on the right is the colour palette which allows you to select drawing and painting colours and on the top are the menu and toolbars. The nearest toolbar to the work area shows the size of the document that you are creating. In Figure 6.3 it shows an A4 page. The toolbars in CorelDRAW® change according to the action you are undertaking which can be confusing initially.

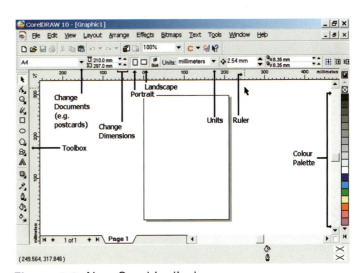

Figure 6.3 New Graphic display

Exercise 46

Explore CorelDRAW®

1 CorelDRAW® is opened by either selecting the Start button, highlighting All Programs and clicking on the CorelDRAW® item or by double clicking on the CorelDRAW® icon on the Microsoft® Windows desktop.

2 Select the New Graphics icon.

3 Explore the different menus and toolbars.

> **continued**
>
> 4 Explore the use of the drawing tools. Change the size of the drawing document using the down arrow on the toolbar near to the A4 box (left-hand side of the toolbar).
>
> 5 Select the `File` menu and locate the `Import`, `Print` and `Save` options.
>
> 6 Move your mouse pointer across the document and observe the rulers. You should see that the pointer's position is shown on each ruler. This is intended to help you position items on the page.
>
> 7 Locate the colour palette on the right-hand side of window.
>
> 8 Continue to explore until you are comfortable with finding your way around the application.
>
> 9 Close the application either by selecting the `File` menu and the `Exit` option or by clicking on the `Close` button in the top right-hand corner of the window.

New image

When you select the `New Graphic` icon, the default document is an A4 page. This can be changed by using the arrow keys on the toolbar (Figure 6.3). You can select from a wide range of different documents (e.g. different page sizes, envelopes and postcards), change the actual size of the page, choose either landscape or portrait orientation and even alter the units of measurement of the page size (e.g. millimetres or inches).

Importing images

Pictures can be provided by:

- scanning images
- taking pictures using a digital camera
- selecting from collections of clip art
- drawing and painting your own graphics

CorelDRAW® can work with images from any source. Clip art collections of many thousands of images can be bought and used. If you have access to a scanner or digital camera, you can use them to produce pictures. CorelDRAW® can enhance and extend these images. It is possible for the application to add captions to a digital picture explaining the different parts of the image.

CorelDRAW® provides a straighforward way of importing images that allows you to:

- crop the images (i.e. cut away parts of the picture you do not need)
- resize images
- precisely position imported images on your art work

To import an image you need to select the `File` menu and the `Import` option. This reveals the Import window (Figure 6.4). The first step to importing an image is to locate the folder in which it is stored on your computer. Do this by clicking on the down arrow at the end of the Look in box which will reveal a list of drives on which the folder could be stored.

If you select C: (the computer's internal hard disk) the work area will be filled with all the folders stored on that disk. To see what is in each folder, you need to click on it and it will open to show you its contents. This could be more folders and again, you need to click on them to reveal their contents.

Figure 6.4 Import window

If you click on A:, the work area will show you the contents of the floppy disk. By clicking on D: you access the CD-ROM drive and if a CD-ROM is inserted you will be able to see its contents. Clip art is often distributed on CD-ROMs since they can hold hundreds and in some cases thousands of images.

Figure 6.4 shows a folder called Pictures which is stored on the hard disk (i.e. C:). These images are the result of taking digital photographs, using screen capture software and drawing applications. It is good practice to set the Files of type to All File Formats using the down arrow button near the box. This will show you all the files available whereas other options will only reveal files of the type selected. This can sometimes confuse in that it can seem that the image you want has disappeared.

To identify the image, the window has a preview feature. If you click in the Preview tick box (a tick will appear) you can see each file that you highlight. Figure 6.4 shows an image of a garden water feature. You can review the images until you find the one you want. When you have identified the correct picture, click on the Import button.

In the middle of the Import window is a small box which in Figure 6.4 has the words Full Image in it. The down arrow next to the box, if clicked on, will reveal other options. These are:

- Full Image – this is the most straightforward option in that the chosen image is imported unchanged
- Crop – this opens a further dialog box to allow you to identify what parts of the image you want to keep (Figure 6.5). It provides you with a preview of the image
- Resample – this lets you change the resolution of an image and reduce its size (Figure 6.6)

The Crop and Resample Image windows enable you to manipulate the

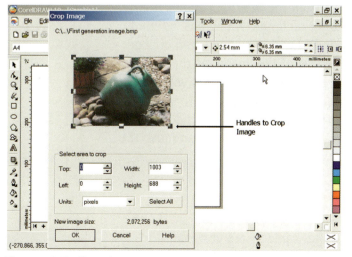

Figure 6.5 Crop image

image after you have chosen to import it and when this has been done, the image is inserted into the document by clicking on the OK button.

When importing the image into the main application area, you need to choose where to place it. This is done using a changed mouse pointer which allows you to position the top left-hand corner of the image precisely. Figure 6.7 shows the positioning of an image. The positioning pointer is placed at the desired point and the mouse button clicked. The image will now appear enclosed in a frame with a number of black squares (called handles). If the mouse pointer is placed on the handles it changes to a double headed arrow. If the mouse button is held down after the pointer has changed shape, you can drag the shape of the image around. The enclosure is removed by clicking away from the image and can be replaced by clicking on the image.

Figure 6.8 shows external and internal handles. Internal handles are located at each corner of the image and let you skew the image using the mouse pointer which changes shape to that of a large arrowhead. Further out from the internal handles is a larger rectangle which has external handles with which you can change the size of the image. At the centre of the image is a cross. If you place your mouse pointer over this cross it turns into a star. By holding down the mouse pointer, you can move the image to new positions.

Digital camera

Digital cameras are very useful to capture images. Pictures taken with a

Figure 6.6 Resample image

Figure 6.7 Positioning an imported image

Figure 6.8 Handles

digital camera can be imported directly into CorelDRAW® by using the File menu and highlighting the Acquire Image option to reveal a short menu (Figure 6.9). Select Select Source to open the Select Source window (Figure 6.10) in order to pick the digital camera and then Select to choose the image from the camera. The camera must be linked to the computer and this is normally achieved using a cable supplied with the camera which plugs into the USB port on the computer.

Digital cameras are usually provided with software so that pictures can be transferred into a folder on a computer. Images can then be imported from this folder into CorelDRAW® as an alternative to directly selecting the pictures from the camera.

Figure 6.11 shows the Get Pictures window which opens when the Acquire option is selected. It allows you to highlight images to import into CorelDRAW®. They are imported when you click on the Get Pictures button in the CorelDRAW® working area.

Figure 6.9 Importing images from a digital camera

Figure 6.10 Select Source

Figure 6.11 Imported digital image

Exercise 47

Importing an image

1 CorelDRAW® is opened either by selecting the Start button, highlighting All Programs and clicking on the CorelDRAW® item or by double clicking on the CorelDRAW® icon on the Microsoft® Windows® desktop.

2 Select the New Graphics icon.

3 Select the File menu and Import option to reveal the Import window. Identify the folder in which the images are stored and use the preview facility to review the images. Select the Crop option and double click on the picture's file name. The image will appear in the Crop window (Figure 6.5).

4 Use the enclosure handles to crop the chosen image. Figure 6.12 shows before and after cropping. You can use the handles for large crops and then Select area to crop for precise detail.

5 When you are ready, click on the OK button and the positioning pointer will appear on the document for you

Before **After**

Figure 6.12 **Cropping**

to position the image precisely. Locate the picture in the centre but in the top half of the page and click. The image of the water feature or your own picture will be placed on the document. In some cases the image will be larger than the page and you will need to use the handles to resize the picture to fit the page.

6 Figure 6.13 shows the image on the document.

7 By clicking on the centre cross you will see the handles change shape. If you place your mouse pointer on these handles it too will change shape (i.e. a partial circle with arrows on each end or parallel arrows facing opposite directions). The partial circle will allow you to rotate the image while the parallel arrows enable

Figure 6.13 **Image**

continued

you to skew the image. Experiment with the two pointers by holding down the mouse button to move the image.

8 Skew the image. Turn it upside down and at 45 degrees (Figure 6.14).

9 When the image is enclosed in its handles it is possible to copy or cut it using the functions on the Edit menu and the options Cut , Copy and Paste . These are also available on the Standard toolbar.

10 Select the Edit menu and the Copy option and then Paste . If you observe carefully you will see the image flicker. You now have two images of the garden water feature, one placed precisely on top of the other, so drag the top image down the page by clicking on the image and holding down the mouse button. You can paste as many copies of the image as you want.

Figure 6.14 Skewed image

11 Delete the first image – you do this by clicking on it to enclose it and then either select the Edit menu and the Delete option or you can press the keyboard's Delete key.

12 An alternative approach to manipulation is to use the Arrange menu and the Transformations option. This provides access to the Transformation window which is positioned alongside the graphic image. Explore the options (e.g. mirror to produce a Edit Bitmap Image mirror image). To remove the window click on the cross in the top right-hand corner of the window.

13 Bitmapped images can also be edited. Click on the right mouse button to reveal a menu and select the Edit Bitmap option (Figure 6.15). This enables you to undertake detailed changes to the image.

14 Experiment with changing the image.

15 Save the image by selecting the File menu and the Save option. This will reveal the Save Drawing window.

Figure 6.15 Bitmapped image

continued

You need to decide where you will save your image. This is done by clicking on the down arrow near the Save in box to reveal a list of options (Figure 6.16). Insert a disk into the floppy drive and select 3½ Floppy (A:). Click in the File name box and enter Imported Image. Click on the Save button. Your image is now saved as the file Imported Image.

16 Close the application either by selecting the File menu and the Exit option or by clicking on the Close button on the top right-hand corner of the window.

Figure 6.16 Save

Exercise 48

Change resolution

1 CorelDRAW® is opened either by selecting the Start button, highlighting All Programs and clicking on the CorelDRAW® item or by double clicking on the CorelDRAW® icon on the Microsoft® Windows desktop.

2 Select the New Graphics icon (Figure 6.17).

3 Select the File menu and Import option to reveal the Import window. Identify the folder in which the images are stored and use the preview facility to review the images. Select the Resample option and double click on the picture's file name. Click on the Import button. The image will appear in the Resample window (Figure 6.6). Change the resolution to 30 pixels/inch and click on the OK button.

Figure 6.17 New Graphics icon

continued

4 The positioning pointer will appear on the document for you to position the image precisely. Locate the picture in the centre but in the top half of the page and click. In this example the image of a ship with tugboats will be placed on the document. In some cases the image will be larger than the page and you will need to use the handles to resize the picture to fit the page (Figure 6.18).

5 Experiment with changing the image.

6 Save the image by selecting the File menu and the Save option. This will reveal the Save Drawing window. You need to decide where you will save your image. This is done by clicking on the down arrow near the Save in box. This will reveal a list of options. Insert a disk into the floppy drive and select 3½ Floppy (A:). Click in the File name box and enter Resampled Image. Click on the Save button. Your image is now saved as the file Resampled Image.

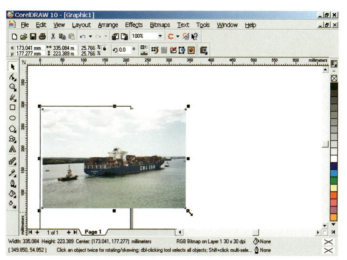

Figure 6.18 **Resize image**

7 Close the application either by selecting the File menu and the Exit option or by clicking on the Close button in the top right-hand corner of the window.

Exercise 49

Digital camera

1 CorelDRAW® is opened either by selecting the Start button, highlighting All Programs and clicking on the CorelDRAW® item or by double clicking on the CorelDRAW® icon on the Microsoft® Windows® desktop.

2 Select the New Graphics icon.

3 Connect your camera to the computer using the cables supplied with it.

4 Select the File menu, highlighting Acquire Image option to reveal a shortcut menu. Select Select Source to open the Select Source window in order to pick the digital camera and then Acquire to choose the image from the camera.

5 A window will open showing you the images stored on your camera. They may be shown as a series of small images (thumbnails), as a list of files or other variations depending

continued

on your camera. It is probably best to select the thumbnails option (Figure 6.19) if it is offered so you can browse the images and pick the ones you need.

6 To select an image, highlight it by clicking on the picture and then on Get Pictures.

7 The image will appear on your page in CorelDRAW®.

8 Experiment with manipulating the image.

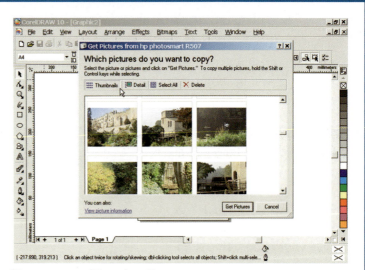

Figure 6.19 Thumbnails

9 Save the image by selecting the File menu and the Save option. This will reveal the Save Drawing window. You need to decide where you will save your image. This is done by clicking on the down arrow near the Save in box. This will reveal a list of options. Insert a disk into the floppy drive and select 3½ Floppy (A:). Click in the File name box and enter Digital Image. Click on the Save button. Your image is now saved as the file Digital Image.

10 Close the application either by selecting the File menu and the Exit option or by clicking on the Close button on the top right-hand corner of the window.

Create a graphic image

To create a graphic image you need to employ the tools available in the CorelDRAW® toolbox which are available on the left edge of the application window (Figure 6.3 shows the different tools). You can draw squares, circles, rectangles, ellipses, triangles, straight and curved lines as well as freehand drawings. Tools used to manipulate an imported image are also available. To help you identify the tools, a label appears when you position the pointer over them.

Interactive fill

You can fill a shape you have created by selecting the Interactive Fill tool by clicking on it to reveal a series of options and then a colour from the palette (right-hand side of the application). This can be done after or before creating the shape but if you have created the shape you must select it to indicate the one that you want the colour to act on. If you select the Interactive Fill Tool and Colour before selecting a shape then a window (Uniform Fill) will warn you.

Freehand tool

The Freehand tool is used to draw lines. If you click on the small arrow in the botton corner of the icon then a series of versions of the tool appear. They include:

- Freehand tool – to draw freehand rather like a pencil
- Interactive Connector tool – allows you to connect points and so draw straight lines)

Exercise 50

Creating an image

1 CorelDRAW® is opened either by selecting the Start button, highlighting All Programs and clicking on the CorelDRAW® item or by double clicking on the CorelDRAW® icon on the Microsoft® Windows® desktop.

2 Select the New Graphics icon.

3 Click on the Freehand tool and try to draw a diagonal line across the page (top left to bottom right). The pointer takes the form of cross hairs to help position the start and finish of the line. You start by clicking where you want to begin and dragging the line to the opposite corner then clicking the button again when you want to finish. If you place the mouse pointer over the tool icons then a label will appear to identify them.

4 The line will be surrounded by an enclosure of handles and a central cross. If you place the pointer over the centre you will see it change into a star (Figure 6.20). If you hold down the mouse button you can drag the line around. Try to move the line.

5 If you place the pointer over a handle it changes shape to a double-headed arrow and if you hold down the mouse button, you can reshape the line. Experiment with the different handles. You can use the Undo and Redo icons on the Standard toolbar to retrace your steps.

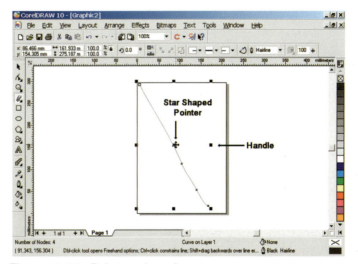

Figure 6.20 Pointer changing

6 If you click again on the centre you will see the handles turn into curved arrows (Figure 6.21). These curved handles are used to rotate or skew the line using the mouse pointer. The mouse pointer turns into a partial circle and, if you hold down the button, you can rotate the line; or the pointer turns into two parallel lines which you can use to skew the image. Experiment with rotating and skewing the line.

continued

7. Draw a curved freehand line by clicking where you want to start and releasing the button where you want to stop. Notice that along the curve are small squares or handles. If you place your pointer on one of these it will change shape into a large arrow. If you hold down your mouse pointer you can manipulate the shape of the line. Experiment with reshaping the line.

Figure 6.21 Handles change into curved arrows

8. Click on the Pick tool and then on the shapes you have created. They will be enclosed and if you press the Delete key, the shape will disappear. Clear all the shapes you have created.

9. Click on the Interactive Fill tool and the colour palette (select red). A window will appear called Uniform Fill you should choose the Graphic option and the OK button.

10. Click on the Rectangle tool. The pointer will once more change into a crosshair and you again start by clicking and holding down the tool. If you move diagonally you will see a rectangle appear. Draw a square using the rulers as a guide (Figure 6.22). The square will be enclosed and filled with red. You can change the shape by moving the handles or move the square by using the central cross. You can even drag the image off the page into the surrounding area. This is a useful place to store objects until you are ready to use them. Again if you click on the centre cross or double click with the Pick tool you access the rotational handles. Experiment with rotating the square.

Figure 6.22 Rectangle

11. Click on the Interactive Fill tool and the colour palette (yellow).

12. Click on the Ellipse tool and attempt to draw an ellipse within the square which will fill with the colour yellow. You will need to drag the ellipse handles to achieve the outcome (Figure 6.23).

continued

13 Click on the Interactive Fill tool and the colour palette (blue).

14 Click on the Freehand tool and draw a triangle within the square. Your picture should resemble something similar to Figure 6.24.

15 Continue to experiment with the different tools until you are confident that you can use them. If you find that the enclosure disappears and you cannot get it to reappear then you are probably clicking with the ordinary mouse pointer when you need to use the Pick tool.

16 Save the image by selecting the File menu and the Save option. This will reveal the Save Drawing window. You need to select the location where you will save your image. This is done by clicking on the down arrow near the Save in box to reveal a list of options. Insert a disk into the floppy drive and click 3½ Floppy (A:). Click in the File name box and enter Graphical Shapes. Click on the Save button. Your image is now saved as a file entitled Graphical Shapes.

Figure 6.23 Draw an ellipse

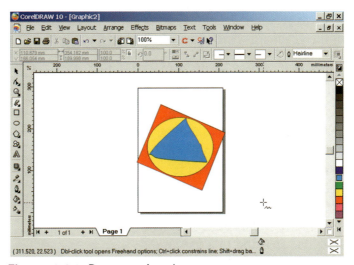

Figure 6.24 Draw a triangle

17 Close the application either by selecting the File menu and the Exit option or by clicking on the Close button in the top right hand corner of the window.

Line thickness

In the exercise we used quite thin lines but CorelDRAW® allows you to vary line thickness using a toolbar option shown in Figure 6.25. You change the thickness of the lines by selecting the Freehand tool, clicking on the down arrow next to the line thickness box to choose from the list of options and then drawing your line. The thickness will be transferred to the other tools (e.g. rectangles will have the new line thickness). When you select the thickness, this may reveal a message which may not make a lot of sense to you at this point in time. Simply click on the OK button.

You can adjust the thickness of a line that was drawn earlier by selecting it (i.e. enclosing it in handles) using the Pick tool and then choosing the line thickness. This is the general way to edit a shape using the various tools provided by CorelDRAW®.

Figure 6.25 Line thickness

Using text

Located in the toolbox is a Text tool which you use to draw a rectangular area in which you can enter text from the keyboard. When you select the Text tool, a new toolbar is opened in the application (Figure 6.26) which allows you to select fonts, character sizes, embolden, write in italics and underline text. This is done by clicking on either the icons or on the down arrows to reveal lists of options. Notice the pointer changes shape to a cross hair with the letter A outside of the text rectangular area and to a bar inside the box.

Figure 6.26 Text

Exercise 51

Using text

1 CorelDRAW® is opened either by selecting the Start button, highlighting All Programs and clicking on the CorelDRAW® item or by double clicking on the CorelDRAW® icon on the Microsoft® Windows® desktop.

2 Select the New Graphics icon.

3 Select the Text tool and create a text rectangle on the document. Then select Arial Black font and character size 48. The cursor flashes in the text rectangle to show you where the text is going to be inserted (Figure 6.27). Type the text:

This is text

continued

4 You can edit your work by using the Backspace key to delete text or insert the cursor by clicking in the required place using the mouse pointer. Insert 'a' between 'is' and 'text' (i.e. This is a text) and then the word rectangle after the word 'text'. It should now read:

   ### This is a text rectangle

   If you have not made your text box large enough you may not see the word 'rectangle'. You need to resize the box and it will then appear.

Figure 6.27 Text rectangle

5 The text rectangle is enclosed in a similar way to the graphic images and if you place the mouse pointer over the handles you can resize it. The text remains unchanged. To change its size requires it to be highlighted using the mouse and a new character size chosen from the toolbar.

6 Change the text size to 36.

7 The text rectangle can be moved using the centre handle and the mouse pointer which changes into a star when placed over the centre handle. By holding down the mouse button you can drag the rectangle to a new position.

8 If you select the Pick tool and double click with it on the text rectangle you will see the rotational and skew handles appear. These allow you to rotate or skew the text. Explore the options.

9 You can enter coloured text by selecting the Text tool and then clicking on your choice of colour in the palette on the right-hand side of the application window. Type the text:

   ### This is coloured text

   using an Arial font, size 72 in red. Figure 6.28 shows the results of entering the two pieces of text.

Figure 6.28 Text

continued

10 An alternative approach is to select the menu and the Transformations option (Figure 6.29). Explore the options.

11 When the text rectangle is enclosed you can cut, copy and paste its contents or delete the whole rectangle. Experiment with making copies and deleting them. The options are available on the Edit menu.

12 When you are confident you can enter, amend and manipulate text then close the application by either selecting the File menu and the Exit option or clicking on the Close button in the top right-hand corner of the window.

Figure 6.29 Transformation options

Print

The quality of an image depends on its resolution but there are considerable differences between viewing an image on the screen and printing the graphic on paper. The quality of monitors and printers varies considerably. A typical monitor may have a resolution of 72 dots per inch while a printer will often print using 300, 600 or 1200 dots per inch. To print a screen image using a high resolution may produce a larger or smaller print image compared with the display. It is not a matter of what you see is what you get (WYSIWYG) since the translation between screen and paper often means a change in size. However, CorelDRAW® helps by presenting your image on a distinct size of page so that you can see how it will look when printed.

CorelDRAW® shows you the size of the document on which you are creating your images and enables you to change its size using the toolbar. If you change the document size after creating an image you will see the page changes size but the image stays the same. This indicates that you need to resize the picture. When the image is enclosed by handles (highlighted) you can see the exact size of the graphic on the toolbar. If you move the handles to resize the image, the figures on the toolbar will change accordingly.

CorelDRAW® provides you with tools to specify how your images are going to be presented. To print an image, select the File menu and the Print option to reveal the Print window. At the bottom of the Print window is a Print Preview button so you can see how the image will appear when printed. When you are satisfied, return to the Print window by clicking on the Close button and then on the OK button to print.

More practice

Activity 1
Design the artwork for a postcard

1 CorelDRAW® is opened either by selecting the **Start** button, highlighting **All Programs** and clicking on the **CorelDRAW®** item or by double clicking on the **CorelDRAW®** icon on the Microsoft® Windows® desktop.

2 Select the **New Graphics** icon.

3 Select Japanese PostCard from the toolbar list (Figure 6.30) and give the postcard a landscape orientation.

4 Click on the **Freehand** tool and draw a straight line down the centre of the card using the rulers as a guide (**Interactive Connector** tool may be helpful). Click on the **Rectangle** tool and draw a rectangle to show where the stamp should be placed. Click again on the **Freehand** tool to draw the four lines for the name and address to be written. If you draw one you can use copy and paste to produce the others.

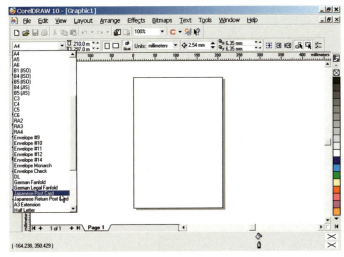

Figure 6.30 Japanese postcard

5 Click on the **Text** tool and insert the word 'To' aligned with the bottom of the stamp. Use Arial font and size 18 characters.

6 Click on the **Freehand** tool and change the line thickness to 0.706. If a message appears simply click on the **OK** button. Click on the **Rectangle** tool and draw a border around the other side of the postcard.

7 With the rectangle you have just created enclosed within its handles, select the **File** menu and the **Import** option. Crop the image so that it will fit the space available. Import an image into the rectangle and using its handles, resize and position the image to fill the rectangle. In this example I have used a picture of a street scene taken with a digital camera (Figure 6.31). You can use anything that is available.

8 If you want to make the image unusual you can flip it using the

Figure 6.31 Street scene

Mirror buttons. You will see them on the toolbar when the image is enclosed (if you place your mouse pointer over options on the toolbar, labels will appear to help you identify them – the Mirror buttons are near the centre of the toolbar). Try it and see what happens (Figure 6.32). You can retrace your steps using the Undo icons or options on the Edit menu. This toolbar also shows you the exact dimensions of your image.

9. Save the image by selecting the File menu and the Save option. This will reveal the Save Drawing window. You need to select the location where you will save your image. This is done by clicking on the down arrow near the Save in box to reveal a list of options. Insert a disk into the floppy drive and select 3½ Floppy (A:). Click in the File name box and enter Postcard. Click on the Save button. Your image is now saved as the file Postcard.

Figure 6.32 Mirror Buttons flipping image

10. Select the File menu and the Print option to reveal the Print window. Click on the Print Preview button and check your postcard. If you are happy, click on the Close button to return to the Print window and then on the OK button.

11. Close the application by either selecting the File menu and the Exit option or clicking on the Close button on the top right-hand corner of the window.

Activity 2
Design art work for a compact disc

1. CorelDRAW® is opened either by selecting the Start button, highlighting All Programs and clicking on the CorelDRAW® item or by double clicking on the CorelDRAW® icon on the Microsoft® Windows® desktop.

2. Select the New Graphics icon.

3. Insert a size of 430 mm by 430 mm by clicking in the size boxes on the toolbar and entering the new size (Figure 6.33). You are going to create the art work for a music CD.

4. Select the Freehand tool and change the size of line to 0.706. Select the Rectangle tool and click on the red colour in the palette. Draw a rectangle inside the document leaving a small margin around the outside. You should see a red rectangle form.

Figure 6.33 New size

5. Select the Ellipse tool and draw a small circle outside the document area. It will be filled with red. However, while it is still enclosed, click on the yellow colour in the palette and you will see the circle change colour. Now copy the circle using the Copy and Paste functions on the Edit menu or the toolbar icons. Remember that the pasted circle will appear on top of the original shape so will need to be dragged away. When you have three circles, move them to form a diagonal across the red rectangle.

6. Select the Text tool and draw a text rectangle away from the document area and type:

   Rock Music

   using a font and character size of your choice.

7. Rotate the text until it is at a 45 degree angle. Copy the text twice more and drag it so that it rests diagonally across each circle. Your CD cover should look something like Figure 6.34.

8. Experiment with the design to improve its appearance (e.g. rotate the text so that it is at different angles).

9. Save the image by selecting the File menu and the Save option. This will reveal the Save Drawing window. You need to select the location where you will save your image. This is done by clicking on the down arrow near the Save in box. This will reveal a list of options. Insert a disk into the floppy drive and select 3½ Floppy (A:). Click in the File name box and enter CD Cover. Click on the Save button. Your image is now saved as the file CD Cover.

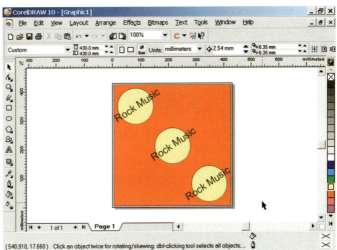

Figure 6.34 CD cover

10. Select the File menu and the Print option to reveal the Print window. Click on the Print Preview button and check your cover (Figure 6.35). If you are happy, click on the Close button to return to the Print window and then on the OK button.

11. Close the application either by selecting the File menu and the Exit option or clicking on the Close button on the top right-hand corner of the window.

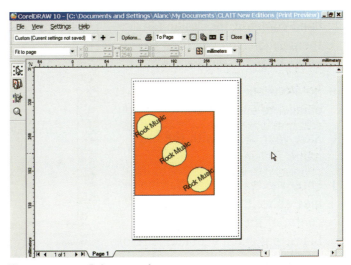

Figure 6.35 Print preview

Activity 3

On the website (www.hodderclait.co.uk) associated with this book you will find the following images:

- Canal in Winter
- Countryside in Winter
- Winter Walk

Using them or your own graphics create the design outlined in Figure 6.36 ensuring that the images maintain their original proportions and are not distorted. However, you can resize them.

1. Create a design that is A1 size and landscape orientated.

2. Change the background colour to green (Interactive Fill tool, Palette and Rectangle tool)

3. Create a polygon (five sided) shape covering the middle of the rectangle (Polygon tool). Fill this area with white.

4. Import the image Winter Walk and insert it inside the polygon (File menu and Import function). You will need to resize the image to ensure it fits.

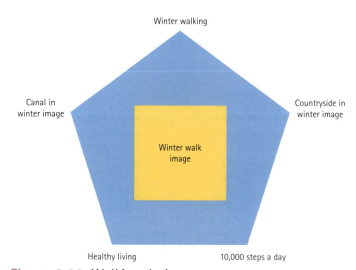

Figure 6.36 Walking design

5. Save your design with the file name Walking.

6. Import the image Canal in Winter and insert it in left-hand corner of the design outside the polygon. You will need to resize the image to ensure it fits.

7. Rotate the image until its base is parallel to one side of the polygon (Figure 6.37)

8. Import the image Countryside in Winter and insert it in the right-hand corner of the design outside the polygon. You will need to resize image to ensure it fits.

9. Rotate image until its base is parallel to one side of the polygon

10. Save your design with the file name Walking.

11. Enter the text Winter Walking in blue above the polygon in the centre of the design using Arial Black font and a character size of 100.

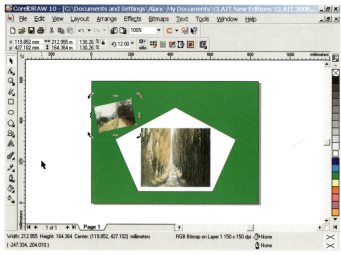

Figure 6.37 Rotating image

12. Enter the text Healthy Living in yellow and rotate it by 90 degrees anticlockwise. Use Times New Roman font and a character size of 100 and embolden the text.

13. Insert Healthy Living on the left-hand side of design.

14. Enter the text 10,000 steps a day in yellow and rotate it by 90 degrees clockwise. Use Times New Roman font and a character size of 100 and embold the text.

15. Insert 10,000 steps a day on the right-hand side of design.

16. Save your design with the file name Walking. Figure 6.38 illustrates the final design.

17. Print your design in colour and then compare your work with the outline (Figure 6.36) for accuracy.

18. Close the application.

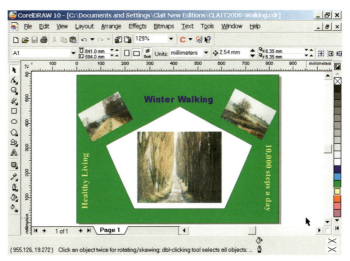

Figure 6.38 Walking

Activity 4

On the website (www.hodderclait.co.uk) associated with this book you will find the following images:

- Boat
- Harbour
- Sea at night
- Sailing Boat

Using them or your own graphics create the design outlined in Figure 6.39 ensuring that the images maintain their original proportions and are not distorted. However, you can resize them.

1. Create a design which is 400 × 600 mm size and portrait orientated.

2. Change the background colour to yellow (Interactive Fill tool, Palette and Rectangle tool).

3. Create a circle covering the middle of the rectangle. Fill this area with white.

4. Import the image Sea at

Figure 6.39 Outline design

night and insert it inside the circle (File menu and Import function). You will need to resize the image to ensure it fits.

5 Save your design with the file name Cruising.

6 Import the image Harbour and insert it in the bottom left-hand corner of the design outside of the circle. You will need to resize image to ensure it fits (Figure 6.40).

7 Rotate image until it is at 45 degrees to the edge of the design.

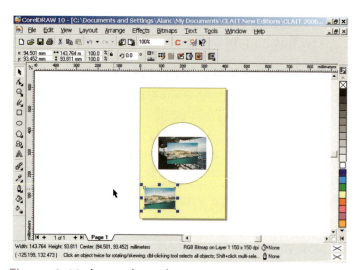

Figure 6.40 Image insertion

8 Import the image Sailing Boat and insert it in the bottom right-hand corner of the design outside of the circle. You will need to resize the image to ensure it fits.

9 Rotate the image until it is at 45 degrees to the edge of the design.

10 Save your design with the file name Cruising.

11 Enter the text Cruising in red across the top of the design using Bahamas Font and a character size of 100.

12 Enter Relax and enjoy in blue using Bahamas font and a character size of 100 on the left-hand side of design. Rotate the text anticlockwise so that it fits without overlapping the circle or title.

13 Enter the text Food and drink in blue using Bahamas font and a character size of 100. Rotate the message clockwise so that it fits without overlapping the circle or title.

14 Save your design with the file name Cruising. Figure 6.41 illustrates the final design.

15 Print your design in colour and then compare your work with the outline (Figure 6.39) for accuracy.

16 Close your application.

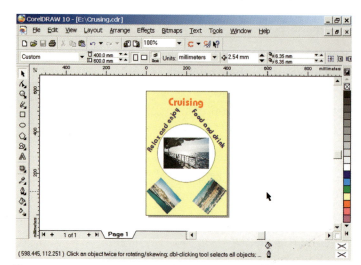

Figure 6.41 Cruising

SUMMARY

1. **Open CorelDRAW®**: Select the Start button, highlight All Programs and click on the CorelDRAW® item or double click on the CorelDRAW® icon on the Microsoft® Windows® desktop. Select the New Graphics icon.

2. **Close CorelDRAW®**: Select the File menu and the Exit option or click on the Close button on the top right-hand corner of the application window.

3. **New image**: Use the arrow buttons on the toolbar to select from options to choose page sizes or different types of documents, change the actual size of page, landscape or portrait orientation and alter the units of measurement of page size (e.g. millimeters or inches).

4. **Import images**: Select the File menu and the Import option to reveal the Import window.

5. **Crop or resample image**: Select from full image, crop and resample by clicking on the down arrow to the right of the box on the Import window. This will reveal the Crop and Resample windows which allow you to manipulate the image. Click on the OK button when ready.

6. **Edit bitmaps**: Right click on the image and select Edit Bitmap.

7. **Manipulate images**: By clicking on the image, you enclose it with handles. Using the mouse pointer you can resize and move images.

   Click again on the centre or double click using the Pick tool and the handles will turn into curved arrows. The curved handles allow you to rotate or skew the line using the mouse pointer. When the mouse pointer turns into a partial circle, hold down the button and then you can rotate the line. When the pointer turns into two parallel lines, you can use them to skew the image. Alternatively select the Arrange menu and the Transformation option.

8. **Digital camera images**: Select the File menu, highlighting the Image option to reveal a short menu. Select the Select Source to open the Select Source window in order to pick the digital camera and then Acquire to choose the image from the camera.

9. **Line thickness**: Select the Freehand tool, click on the down arrow next to the line thickness box on the toolbar to choose from the list of options and draw line.

   Adjust the thickness of a line by selecting it (i.e. enclosing it in handles) using the Pick tool and then choosing the line thickness.

10. **Draw a graphic image**: Click on the various tools in the toolbox on the left edge of the application window. These allow you to draw squares, circles, rectangles, ellipses, triangles, straight or curved lines and freehand drawings.

11. **Print**: Select the File menu and the Print option to reveal the Print window. Click on the Print Preview button to see how the image will appear when printed. Click on the Close button and then on the Print button.

Chapter 7

Unit 7

Web page creation

> This chapter will help you to create a web page by:
> - identifying and using appropriate software correctly
> - importing, formatting and placing text and image files
> - inserting relative, external and email hyperlinks
> - managing and printing web pages

Assessment

This unit does not assume any previous experience of using a computer. You may find it useful to have completed Unit 1: File management and e-document production. You will be assessed through a practical realistic assignment which is designed to allow you to demonstrate your knowledge and skills against each objective. Your tutor can provide you with more guidance.

What is a web page?

When surfing the World Wide Web, you read and interact with many different documents. These are known as web pages which, when linked together, are called websites. A web page is created using a special language called Hypertext Markup Language or HTML. This allows you to design the presentation of the page's information (i.e. text and images) so that anyone viewing the page using an application called a web browser can see the information. HTML supplies the browser with the instructions to create a web page from different elements such as text, pictures, sounds and videos. The HTML code is simply a text document with special commands (i.e. HTML commands) embedded in the text. HTML commands are sometimes known as tags. They tell the browser to, for example, show an image, underline text or enclose an area in a border. The images, text and sounds are not HTML but rather separate files which the code locates and presents in the browser. HTML is a language that organises information into an attractive, interesting and readable form.

A web page can be as long as you want it to be. It can contain a vast amount of information or only a single item. The designer decides on the contents and the length of the page. Many web pages need their users to scroll down them to access their contents. It is good practice to limit the length of a page to no more than four A4 sheets. This minimises the possibility of users getting lost and confused within the page. This possibility is increased when web pages are linked to others using hyperlinks. These are places on the page which, when clicked on with a mouse pointer, cause the browser to jump to a new page. Links can be single words or phrases, pictures, icons and almost anything else. There are a number of common conventions in designing links and possibly the most well known is the underlined word which signals that it is a link to another page.

HTML applications

Originally, to design a web page you had to understand the HTML language in depth. However, several HTML editors using a WYSIWYG (What You See Is What You Get) approach are now available. You can visually create a page so that you can see how it appears as you design it. This is obviously easier than writing lines of code and having to visualise mentally the resulting page which normally leads to the final appearance being different to that which you intended so you are forced to amend the code.

Word processors (e.g. Microsoft® Word) and desktop publishing applications can convert their documents into HTML automatically. This is a useful productivity tool when you want to place a document you have created on to a web page quickly. However, the precise presentation of the information is often different in a browser to that created in the word processor. You are converting between two different formats and there is often a need for a degree of compromise between them. If you rely on using a word processor to develop all the content for a web page it will rapidly come to look like an office noticeboard while a professional HTML editor will add quality and impact to the raw information.

This chapter is based on Microsoft® FrontPage® XP, an editor capable of developing complex web sites with many different web pages. We will only be considering a limited range of its capabilities but it will provide you with the foundation to develop your knowledge and skills later.

Microsoft® FrontPage® XP

Microsoft® FrontPage® is loaded either by clicking on the Start button, highlighting All Programs and then selecting the Microsoft® FrontPage® item or by double clicking on the Microsoft® FrontPage® icon on the Microsoft® Windows® desktop. Figure 7.1 shows the application. This consists of:

- menu and toolbars – these provide the various functions available to you and are similar to those in other Microsoft® Office applications
- Web document window – this is the area in which you create, view and edit your page
- New page or web task pane – this provides access to many of the functions required when creating a new page
- Views bar – this provides you

Figure 7.1 Microsoft® FrontPage® XP

with access to the different views available to you and, in our case, the view of the web page
- Workspace tabs – these three tabs give you access to the different modes of operation:
  - Normal – to edit the page in WYSIWYG mode
  - HTML – to edit the HTML code directly
  - Preview – to see what the page may look like in a browser

Exercise 52

Exploring Microsoft® FrontPage®

1. Load Microsoft® FrontPage® either by clicking on the Start button, highlighting All Programs and then selecting the Microsoft® FrontPage® item or by double clicking on the Microsoft® FrontPage® icon on the Microsoft® Windows® desktop.

2. Maximise the application window to fill the display using the Maximise button in the top right-hand corner of the application window.

3. Turn the view to Page by clicking on the Page icon in the Views Bar if this is not already set. Turn the workspace to Normal by clicking on the Normal workspace tab.

4. The web document area should be clear now. The top of the area should show new_page_1.htm indicating that you are working on the first page – .htm is the extension for the HTML files.

5. The cursor will be flashing on the top line of the area. Type:

   This is a new page.

6. If you click on the HTML workspace tab you will see the code to present this simple text (Figure 7.2).

7. This shows some of the HTML tags such as:

   <html> marks the start of the HTML commands

   </html> marks the end of the HTML commands

   <head> marks the beginning of an HTML document

   <body> shows the start of the main body of a document

   </body> shows the end of the main body of a document

   <p> indicates the start of a paragraph

Figure 7.2 HTML code

> **continued**
>
> Other tags are:
>
> <b> </b> bold and end bold, respectively
>
> <a href> </a> hypertext link, start and end, respectively
>
> If you are interested in creating a simple page using HTML then try the optional exercise at the end of the chapter.
>
> 8 Click on the Normal workspace tab.
>
> 9 Explore the different options comparing menus and toolbar layouts with other Microsoft® Office applications. Try to locate:
>
> - the Insert menu and the File and Picture options
> - the File menu and the Open, Save, Print and Exit options
> - the Formatting menu and the Background option
>
> 10 Continue to explore the application until you are confident that you can find your way around the interface.
>
> 11 Close the application by selecting the File menu and Exit option or by clicking on the Close button on top right-hand corner of the window. You may be asked if you want to save your work; on this occasion, click on the No button.

Designing a web page

Before you begin to design a page it is useful to consider what you intend to achieve and who will be reading its contents. Microsoft® FrontPage® provides a variety of options and the main mistake new designers make is to use too many of them. You could display a page with dozens of different fonts, a wide range of character sizes, lots of colour, several pictures and lots of emphasis. In practice, the overuse of the different design elements will result in a poor page which is difficult to read and understand. It is good practice to keep your designs simple.

For example

- Colour can add interest so a background colour is a useful device to enhance a web page.
- Various character sizes help draw the reader's attention to the content of the page but they should not be overused.
- Pictures add interest to a page but are best used when they relate to the text.
- The use of bold and italics to emphasise particular pieces of text is effective so long as it is not used too often.

Entering and emphasising text

Microsoft® FrontPage® provides you with two ways of picking fonts and character sizes. Firstly, you can select the down arrow button to the right of the Font or Font Size box to reveal a list of options. When you enter text it is in the font and size you have chosen. Alternatively, you can also change them by highlighting the text and then selecting the font and size.

The size of characters is shown in two different ways – the normal points way that is used in all the Microsoft® Office applications (e.g. character size 10) and also in HTML sizes. The two sizes are both shown on the Formatting toolbar (Figure 7.3).

Example

HTML	Points
1	8
2	10
3	12
4	14

You can enter text which is bold, in italics or underlined by either selecting the option initially and then entering the text or by highlighting and changing them later.

You can align text and pictures on your page by using the alignment options on the toolbar. Again this can be done prior to inserting the text or picture or afterwards by highlighting the object and then making the selection. Figure 7.3 shows the different options available on the Formatting toolbar.

You can align a whole page or vary the alignment down the page. This means, for example, you can have a heading and a picture centred, while the main body of words is left aligned. This is often an effective way of indicating the relationship of different elements on the page (e.g. headings).

A web page needs to present an engaging image to visitors so that they will read the content and return for more on another occasion. When you are designing the display you need to control the flow of text

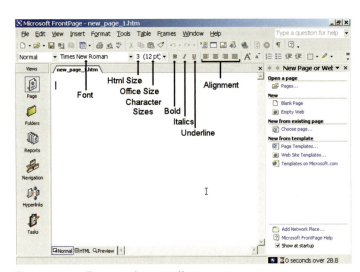

Figure 7.3 Formatting toolbar

around the page. In a sense you are guiding the user around your material. You can do this by combining the different elements of the page together to control the flow of text (e.g. tables of information, text, pictures and using alignment). It is useful to plan your page and a few moments spent sketching out how you think it should look are often repaid by an attractive page.

Some simple design considerations are:

- Keep it simple and concise
- Make it easy to find information

- Be consistent
- Show relationships between the different parts of content

You can use the different elements to define areas of the page which can serve different purposes. For example, news can always be centred and appear beneath the title. By left or right aligning an image you allow yourself to present text alongside it thus giving the visual message that the text relates to the image. A blank space can separate different topics. You need to consider what you are trying to achieve and plan your page to achieve it.

Checking text

A web site potentially may be viewed by thousands of people so it is very important that you check the spelling, grammar, layout and number of words displayed. Microsoft® FrontPage® provides you with a spell checker (**Tools** menu) and if you prepare your text in Microsoft® Word and import it then you can use its **Spelling and Grammar** checker and **Word Count** tool. Users of websites rarely read every word. They browse or scan the material for interesting content. It is therefore useful to minimise the amount of text displayed. The **Word Count** tool in Word is therefore useful to checking how much text you intend to show.

Exercise 53

Creating a web page

1. Load Microsoft® FrontPage® either by clicking on the **Start** button, highlighting **All Programs** and then selecting the **Microsoft® FrontPage®** item or by double clicking on the **Microsoft® FrontPage®** icon on the Microsoft® Windows® desktop.

2. Maximise the application window to fill the display using the **Maximise** button in the top right-hand corner.

3. Turn the view to Page by clicking on the **Page** icon in the Views bar if this is not already set. Turn the workspace to Normal by clicking on the tab. Select the **Blank Page** option from the New Page or Web task pane.

4. We are going to create a simple web page for a company called First Generation.

5. Select Arial font and a character size of 36 (using the Formatting toolbar) and enter the main heading as First Generation Company. Centre this heading by highlighting the text and clicking on the centre alignment icon.

6. Press Enter twice to move the cursor down the page.

7. The next step is to insert a suitable picture to gain the attention of the users. Do this by selecting the **Insert** menu, highlighting the **Picture** option and clicking on the **Clip Art** item. This will reveal the Clip Art task pane which allows you to search for pictures related to a particular theme. The results of the search are shown as thumbnail images from which you can select an image by clicking on it. A menu box appears and provides you with the option to insert the image.

You may get a message telling you that the clip art requires you to insert the Microsoft® Office master CD-ROM into the appropriate drive since the clip art is stored

continued

on this disk. You can also insert your own pictures by selecting <mark>From File</mark> instead of the <mark>Clip Art</mark> option and then direct Microsoft® FrontPage® to the folder containing your images.

8. Since you have already chosen centre alignment, your image will be placed in the centre of the page. The cursor will be flashing alongside the image so that if you select left, centre or right alignment the image will move to relate to that alignment. Explore the different alignments and position the image where you feel is best.

9. If you click on the picture you will see the image enclosed within squared dots (i.e. handles). If you place your pointer on these dots the pointer will change shape and if you hold down the mouse button you can change the shape of the image. Experiment with this to resize your picture. Figure 7.4 shows the picture handles and the changing shape of the cursor.

Figure 7.4 **Image changes**

10. Press Enter to move the cursor down the page. We will next enter the links to the rest of the site.

11. Type, leaving five spaces between each word, the following text:

    Contacts   Products   Prices   News

12. You have created a simple page. Preview the page and look at the HTML code for this page. Check the layout and proofread the text to make sure it is correct.

13. Insert a floppy disk into the computer's drive. To save your web page select the <mark>File</mark> menu then the <mark>Save</mark> option to reveal the <mark>Save As</mark> window. You need to choose the location in which to store your page by clicking on the down arrow at the end of the <mark>Save in</mark> box. This will reveal a list. Click on the floppy disk option. You will then see this appear in the box. Now click in the <mark>File name</mark> box and enter from the keyboard the name 'First_Generation_Company.htm' (it may appear automatically) and click on the <mark>Save</mark> button. You will hear the drive and the publication will be saved on the floppy disk as a file called First_Generation_Company.htm.

14. You may be presented with a second window asking if you want to save the embedded files. In this case it means the Clip Art image. Click on the <mark>OK</mark> button and the window will clear. The embedded file will be saved to the floppy disk.

15. Now print the page by selecting the <mark>File</mark> menu and the <mark>Print</mark> option to reveal the Print window. Click on the <mark>OK</mark> button to print the page using the printer default settings.

continued

16 Change the workspace tab to HTML and print the code using the same procedure. You will now have printouts of the code and the visual presentation of the page.

17 Close the application by selecting the `File` menu and `Exit` option or by clicking on the `Close` button on the top right-hand corner of the window.

Standard toolbar

The Standard toolbar provides a range of tools (Figure 7.5) which include alternative ways of inserting pictures, printing and saving using the toolbar buttons. In addition, the `Undo` and `Redo` icons allow you to recover from making a mistake. You can reverse what you have done by clicking on `Undo`. If you make an error in using `Undo`, then you can reverse this with `Redo`.

As with other Microsoft® Office applications you can cut, copy and paste text and pictures around a web page or between Microsoft® Office applications and Microsoft® FrontPage®. These functions operate by highlighting the text or picture and then selecting the `Cut` or `Copy` icon. The cut function removes the highlighted area and you can paste it (relocate) into a new position by placing the cursor at the desired location and clicking on the `Paste` icon. The `Copy` function works in the same way but does not remove the original text or picture.

Figure 7.5 Standard toolbar

Inserting text files

Although you can enter text from the keyboard, it is also possible to import text as files or paste it from other Microsoft® Office applications into your web page. To import a text file, position the cursor at the location on the page where you want the text to be inserted. Using the `Insert` menu (Figure 7.6) and the `File` option you can import text into the page. Once the file option is selected, the Select File window is opened which allows you to choose the file to be inserted.

Figure 7.6 Insert menu

In order to select a file you need to know where it is located within your computer or on your floppy disk. To find the location, click on the down arrow button to the right of the Look in box. A list of drives will appear (Figure 7.7) such as floppy disk and C:. C: is normally the designation for the computer's internal hard disk in which most files are stored within folders. In Figure 7.7 you will see that below C: is a folder called Documents and Settings. This is one of the various folders stored on the hard disk.

Figure 7.7 Select file

If you click on C: you will see the folders stored on the disk appear in the work area. To discover what each folder contains, double click on it and its contents will appear in the work area. When you locate the text file you want to include, you can either double click on it or single click to insert its name in the File name box and then on the Open button. The text file will then be opened on the web page.

Exercise 54

Inserting a text file

1. Load Microsoft® FrontPage® either by clicking on the Start button, highlighting All Programs and then selecting the Microsoft® FrontPage® item or by double clicking on the Microsoft® FrontPage® icon on the Microsoft® Windows® desktop.

2. Maximise the application window to fill the display using the Maximise button in the top right-hand corner.

3. Turn the view to Page by clicking on the Page icon in the Views bar if this is not already set. Turn the workspace to Normal by clicking on the tab. Select the Blank Page option from the New Page or Web task pane.

4. We are going to insert a text file into a simple web page. It is important to check the text file for spelling and grammar errors and to undertake a word count to ensure the correct number of words are displayed. This can be done in Microsoft® Word before the file is imported into Microsoft® FrontPage®.

5. If you have undertaken the word-processing unit you will have created some text files that you will have saved to a floppy disk. This exercise is based on inserting one of them although you can use any text file you like.

6. Insert the floppy disk containing the file into the drive. Position your cursor three lines down the new page by using the Enter key. Select the Insert menu and the File option to reveal the Select File window. Choose the floppy disk option in the Look in box and double click on the text file of your choice. We are going to select the Invasion of Russia

continued

(created earlier in a word-processing exercise). If your disk appears blank this may be because the 'Files of type' box contains a type not present on the disk. You will need to change it by clicking on the down arrow button at the end of the box and selecting All Files (*.*) which will look for files of all types. It is good practice always to set the box to this option.

7. Observe what happens. You may briefly see a message saying that the file is being converted into HTML code and then the file will appear on the page (you may miss it if you blink). You are now free to enhance its appearance but before we attempt that, look at the file in the HTML workspace. See if you can identify the paragraph breaks from the HTML code (<p>).

8. Highlight the title Invasion of Russia and change its font to Arial, size 24 and centre it.

9. Highlight the rest of the passage and change the font to Times New Roman and size 12.

10. Above the title Invasion of Russia insert the page heading 'Military History' using Arial but in size 36. Centre the text and embolden it.

11. Insert an appropriate clip art or other image between the page heading and the passage title. Left align the picture. Experiment with resizing the image to get the best effect.

12. You have created another simple page (Figure 7.8). Notice that you need to scroll the page in order to see the whole content. Preview the page and consider its HTML code. It is also important to check the spelling and grammar of your web page. A webpage will potentially be seen by thousands of people so it is important that it is perfect.

13. Insert a floppy disk into the computer's drive. To save your web page, select the **File** menu then the **Save** option to reveal the Save As window. You need to choose the location in which to store your page by clicking on the down arrow at the end of the **Look in** box. This will reveal a list. Click on the floppy disk option. You will then see this appear in the box. Now click in the **File name** box and enter the name Military_History.htm and click on the **Save** button. You will hear the drive and the publication will be saved on the floppy disk as a file called Military_History.htm.

Figure 7.8 Military history page

14. You may be presented with a second window asking if you want to save the embedded files. In this case this means the clip art or other image. Click on the **OK** button and the window will clear.

> **continued**
>
> 15 Now print the page by selecting the File menu and the Print option to reveal the Print window. Click on the OK button to print the page using the printer default settings.
>
> 16 Change the workspace tab to HTML and print the code using the same procedure. You will now have printouts of the code and the visual presentation of the page.
>
> 17 Close the application by selecting the File menu and Exit option or by clicking on the Close button in the top right-hand corner of the window.

Background colours and images

Colour can create attractive and interesting designs. Microsoft® FrontPage® provides the tools to change the background colour of your page or to use a picture as the background. Your text is thus presented on top of the picture or colour. When selecting a colour ensure that it provides a contrast to the text colour (or foreground colour) and thus makes the text legible.

The background colour or picture is set using the Format menu and the Background option. This will reveal the Page Properties window (Figure 7.9). The background settings can be seen on the Background tab display.

At the top of the display is the Background picture checkbox. This is activated by clicking in the small blank square in front of the item. A small tick will appear in the square and the box alongside the Browse button becomes white. You can insert the source of the picture in the box (e.g. A:\Picture.gif) which

Figure 7.9 Background colour

will become the background image. If you cannot remember the exact location of the image you can browse the hard disk or floppy disk to locate it by clicking on the Browse button. This opens the Select Background Picture window from which the image can be selected. This window also provides access to the Clip Art gallery.

Below this area of the window is the section dealing with colour. There are five options to choose from:

- Background – the default is white
- Text – the default is black
- Hyperlink – this shows the colour of hyperlink text, with the default blue
- Visited hyperlink – this shows the colour of hyperlink text when a link has been used in the past, with the default of purple

- Active hyperlink – this shows the colour of hyperlink text when a link is currently active, with the default of red

The link colours are fairly standard and should not be changed. The normal text colour is black and should also not often need to be changed, unlike background colours. If the down arrow to the right of the Background box is clicked then a palette of colours is revealed. To select a new background colour click on it and it will then appear in the box.

Exercise 55

Changing background colours

1. Load Microsoft® FrontPage® either by clicking on the Start button, highlighting All Programs and then selecting the Microsoft® FrontPage® item or by double clicking on the Microsoft® FrontPage® icon on the Microsoft® Windows® desktop.

2. Maximise the application window to fill the display using the Maximise button in the top right-hand corner.

3. Open the file First_Generation_Company by inserting the floppy disk into the drive then selecting the File menu and Open option to reveal the Open File window. Change the Look in box to floppy disk and you should see the file in the work area. If it is not visible then check that the Files of type box reads All Files (*.*). The file should now be visible and you can load it by double clicking on its name. The First Generation Company page should now appear.

   Alternatively in the New Page or Web task pane to the right of the display in the section Open a page you may see First_Generation_Company listed. If you click on the name the web page will open.

4. Explore the different background colours, checking the effects the colour has on the image and text. In particular make sure the text is legible. Figure 7.10 shows an example.

Figure 7.10 Change background colour

5. When you are confident, save the revised page and close Microsoft® FrontPage®.

Graphics file formats

If you add pictures or other graphic elements (e.g. borders, lines and shapes) to your web page then its storage size will increase. This can be important if your space for storing the website is limited or you anticipate many users who will not have access to a high speed (broadband) link.

In general it is good practice to minimize the size of your images by physically resizing them and also by saving them in file formats suitable for the web. The main formats used for web page images are:

- JPEG
- GIF
- PNG

You can convert images to these formats by right clicking on the picture and selecting the Picture Properties option. This opens the Picture Properties window that lets you convert the image to one of the above formats.

Hyperlinks

An important feature of web pages is their ability to be connected (or hyperlinked) both to other pages within the same site and to other sites. There are four main types of hyperlink available to you when you are designing a web page. These are:

- A simple hyperlink between two pages you have created. This will allow you to design a route through the site you are building.
- A hyperlink to a file stored on your computer so that you have access to extra material on your page. You could load a Microsoft® PowerPoint® presentation to explain an idea or subject to your users.
- A hyperlink to a web page which is part of another site on the World Wide Web. This is a widely used link and most sites have many of this type.
- A hyperlink to an email editor to allow you to send an email to a chosen location. You could use this link to let your users comment on the design of the page or to order products advertised on the page or any other communication need.

Hyperlinks are activated by clicking on them and usually take one of two main forms: an underlined word or phrase, or a picture. The picture can be an icon, a large image or even the whole screen.

Microsoft® FrontPage® gives you access to the hyperlinks through the Insert menu and the option Hyperlink to reveal the Insert Hyperlink window (Figure 7.11). You will see the location and name of the web page you are working on. In this example it is the First Generation Company, stored on a floppy disk. If you wanted to change the page you would use the Look in box, employing the same method you have used to save or open a file.

The window provides you with the means of creating four types of link. These are shown as four icons displayed below Link to. From top to bottom the icons enable you to:

Figure 7.11 Insert Hyperlinks

- link to an existing file or webpage
- link within the current document
- link to a new document
- link to email location

Exercise 56

Creating and testing hyperlinks

1. Load Microsoft® FrontPage® either by clicking on the Start button, highlighting All Programs and then selecting the Microsoft® FrontPage® item or by double clicking on the Microsoft® FrontPage® icon on the Microsoft® Windows® desktop.

2. Maximise the application window to fill the display using the Maximise button in the top right-hand corner.

3. Open the file First_Generation_Company by inserting the floppy disk into the drive and selecting the File menu and Open option to reveal the Open File window. Change the Look in box to floppy disk and you should see the file in the work area. If it is not visible then check that the Files of type box reads All Files (*.*) and change it to this option. The file should now be visible and you can load it by double clicking on its name. The First Generation Company page should now appear.

   Alternatively in the New Page or Web task pane to the right of the display in the section Open a Page you may see First_Generation_Company listed. If you click on the name the webpage will open.

4. When we designed this page we provided four potential links at the bottom of the page. These are:
   - Contacts
   - Products
   - Prices
   - News

5. We will create links from each of these.

6. The contacts link is intended to allow users of the page to email the company to ask for information, ask questions or comment on the page.

7. Highlight the word Contacts to identify it as the link you are going to create. Select the Insert menu and the Hyperlinks option to open the Insert Hyperlinks window.

8. In the Text to display box at the top of the window you should see Contacts displayed. In the work area in the centre of the window you should see A:\First_Generation_Company.htm (open) displayed. Click on the icon to create an email link – this is the fourth down from Link to. It will open a new window (Figure 7.12).

9. Enter webmaster@firstgeneration.co.uk in the E-mail address box (Figure 7.12) and click on the OK button. The window will close returning you to the web page.

continued

10 Observe the Contacts link and you will see that it has changed colour to blue and is underlined which indicates that it is a link. Change the workspace tab to Preview and we will test the link.

11 Click on the Contacts link in Preview mode. You should see the email page for the system that is set up on the computer you are using appear. The email address will be included in the blank email page. It is important to test each link to ensure it does what you intend.

Figure 7.12 Email hyperlink

12 Return to Normal mode by clicking on the Normal workspace tab. Highlight Products and again open the Insert Hyperlinks window. You are going to link the page to an existing web page on the World Wide Web. Select the Existing File or Web Page icon. Click on the World Wide Web icon which is the second icon to the right of the Look in box. This opens your browser so you can locate your chosen page. Find the page you want to link to and then press the Alt and Tab keys to return to Insert Hyperlink window. You should see the page's address in the address box at the bottom of the window. Click on the OK button.

If you make a mistake you can remove the link by clicking on the Remove Link button on the Insert Hyperlinks window once you have highlighted the link on your web page.

13 You have created a link from the First Generation Company page to the web page of your choice. When you selected the OK button you will return to the First Generation Company page.

14 You should see the word 'Products' has changed colour to blue, indicating a link has been established.

15 Test the link by changing to the Preview workspace and clicking on Products and you will see your page appear if the link has been correctly established. Click on the Normal workspace tab to return to the First Generation Company page.

Figure 7.13 Link to a file

continued

16. Highlight Prices and again open the Insert Hyperlinks window. You are going to create a link to a New Document. Click on Create New Document and the display will change (Figure 7.14) asking you to enter the path to the new document. The figure shows a link to a document called New Document stored on a floppy disk. Click on the OK button to return to the First Generation Company Page.

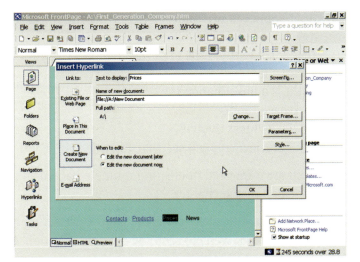

Figure 7.14 New Document link

17. You should see the word 'Prices' has changed colour to blue, indicating a link has been established.

18. The last link is between News and another part of the page. The first step is to create a bookmark on the page to link to. Highlight the word Generation in the title and select the Insert menu and the Bookmark option to reveal the Bookmark window. This will display Generation and you need to confirm the bookmark by clicking on the OK button. Highlight News and access the Insert Hyperlinks window. Click on the button called Place in This document. The display will change to show a heading Bookmark and a link to Generation. Highlight Generation and click on the OK button and you will return to the First Generation Company Page.

19. You should see the word 'News' has changed colour to blue, indicating a link has been established.

20. Test the link by changing to the Preview workspace and click on News and you will see your view of the page change to focus on the word generation. The link has moved you within the page. Click on the Normal workspace tab to return to the First Generation Company page.

21. Insert a floppy disk into the computer's drive. To save your First Generation Company web page, select the File menu then the Save As option to reveal the Save As window. You need to choose the location in which to store your page by clicking on the down arrow at the end of the Save in box. This will reveal a list. Click on the floppy disk option. You will see this appear in the box. Now click in the File name box and type the name Links.htm, then click on the Save button. You will hear the drive and the publication will be saved on the floppy disk as a file called Links.htm.

22. You may be presented with a second window asking if you want to save the embedded files. In this case this means the clip art image. Click on the OK button and window will clear.

continued

23. We are going to explore the effects of editing the HTML code. Click on the `HTML` workspace tab which will reveal the code. Experiment with changing the code and use Preview to see the effects of the change.

    Try removing `<p align="center">` from the line `<p align="center"><font face="Arial" size="7">First Generation Company</font></p>` by highlighting it and pressing the Delete key.

    In the Preview you will see that the title is now left aligned.

    If you are interested in creating a simple page using HTML then try the optional exercise at the end of the chapter.

24. When you are finished, close the page by selecting the `File` menu and `Close`. You will be asked if you want to save the changes. Click on `No` since you do not want to save the changes to the code.

25. When you edit code it sometimes will not take effect since Microsoft® FrontPage® is still working from the original code. It is therefore necessary to reload pages after saving the changes.

26. Now Print the page by selecting the `File` menu and the `Print` option to reveal the Print window. Click on the `OK` button to print the page using the printer default settings.

27. Change the workspace tab to `HTML` and print the code using the same procedure. You will now have printouts of the code and the visual presentation of the page.

28. Close the application by selecting the `File` menu and `Exit` option or by clicking on the `Close` button in the top right-hand corner of the window.

Link resources

When creating links, you have to remember that the resources you are linking to must be available when the web page is part of the website. There is no point linking to a file which, when the page is on the World Wide Web, is not available.

All the linked resources must therefore be retained and it is good practice to save everything to the same folder or floppy disk. In these exercises you have been asked to save everything to a floppy disk. When you were saving your pages you were prompted to save the embedded files. This is a function of Microsoft® FrontPage® that tries to help you retain all the data required for the web page. If you need to practise or develop your file management skills then consider Unit 1.

More practice

Text files and images are available at http://www.hodderclait.co.uk/.

Activity 1

1. Load Microsoft® FrontPage® either by clicking on the Start button, highlighting All Programs and then selecting the Microsoft® FrontPage® item or by double clicking on the Microsoft® FrontPage® icon on the Microsoft® Windows® desktop.

2. Maximise the application window to fill the display using the Maximise button in the top right-hand corner.

3. Turn the view to Page by clicking on the Page icon in the Views bar if this is not already set. Turn the workspace to Normal by clicking on the tab.

4. We are going to create a simple web page about the hobby of collecting stamps.

5. Select the Blank Page option from the New Page or Web Task Pane and enter the heading Stamp Collecting in a font of your own choice in size 36.

6. Centre the heading and insert a clip art image suitable for the subject, centred on the page. Resize the image as appropriate. Alternatively insert the image Stamps (available at http://www.hodderclait.co.uk/.

7. Below the picture enter, in a font of your choice and in size 12, the following text. Or insert the text file Stamp Collecting. In both cases the text should be left justified. Remember to check the text file for spelling and grammar mistakes and to count the number of words.

    Stamp Collecting is the largest collecting hobby in the world. It attracts people of all ages and backgrounds. This site aims to help people discover more about stamp collecting. The links below provide access to more information about the hobby. You can email me by clicking on E-mail link. To link to the introduction page click on Introduction. If you click on the picture you will be linked to other sites about stamp collecting.

8. Leave two blank lines and enter:

    Last updated by (your own name) on (the date)

9. Establish links from the word email to an email address, from the word Introduction to a new page and from the picture to web site http://www.stampcollecting.co.uk. In all cases, highlight the text or picture and select Insert menu and the Hyperlink option to reveal the Insert Hyperlink window. The link text should be size 14. The new page should be called introductionstamps2.htm.

10. Test your links using the Preview workspace tab.

11. Select a suitable background colour.

12. Check your web page to ensure you have followed all the instructions. Proofread the page to check spelling, grammar and layout.

13. Figure 7.15 shows the page design in Preview mode. Notice that the cursor changes shape when over a link (i.e. the image).

14. Insert a floppy disk into the computer's drive. To save your web page, select the File menu then the Save option to reveal the Save As window. Choose the location in which to store your page by clicking on the down arrow at the end of the Look in box. This will reveal a list. Click on the floppy disk option. You will then see this appear in the box. Now click in the File name box and type the name Stamp_Collecting.htm and click on the Save button.

You will hear the drive and the file will be saved on the floppy disk as Stamp_Collecting.htm.

15 You may be presented with a second window asking if you want to save the embedded files. In this case this means the clip art or Stamps image. Click on the OK button and the window will clear.

16 Now Print the page by selecting the File menu and the Print option to reveal the Print window. Click on the OK button to print the page using the printer default settings.

Figure 7.15 Stamp collecting

17 Change the workspace tab to HTML and print the code using the same procedure. You will now have printouts of the code and the visual presentation of the page.

18 Close the application by selecting the File menu and Exit option or by clicking on the Close button on the top right-hand corner of the window.

Activity 2

This activity involves developing the Stamp Collecting web page produced in Activity 1 so you can simply continue the exercise or load the saved files.

1 Load Microsoft® FrontPage® either by clicking on the Start button, highlighting All Programs and then selecting the Microsoft® FrontPage® item or by double clicking on the Microsoft® FrontPage® icon on the Microsoft® Windows® desktop.

2 Maximise the application window to fill the display using the Maximise button in the top right-hand corner.

3 Open the file Stamp_Collecting by inserting the floppy disk into the drive and selecting the File menu and the Open option to reveal the Open File window. Change the Look in box to floppy disk and you should see the file in the work area. If it is not visible then check that the Files of type box reads All Files (*.*) and change it to this option. The file should now be visible and you can load it by double clicking on its name. The Stamp Collecting page should now appear.

Alternatively in the New Page or Web task pane to the right of the display in the section Open a Page you may see Stamp_Collecting listed. If you click on the name the web page will open.

4 Start a new paragraph leaving a blank line between the paragraphs. Type the text in the same font and character size as used for the original text:

There are other hobbies with strong links to stamp collecting such as postcard, first day covers and postmark collecting. Many stamp collectors are also involved with these pastimes.

5 Add a sub-heading Background above the original paragraph leaving a blank line between the heading and the paragraph. Use Tahoma with a character size of 14 and embold the heading.

6 Now centre align the last line of text 'Last updated by Your Name on Monday, 19th December 2005'

7 Check your web page to ensure you have followed all the instructions. Proofread the page to check spelling, grammar and layout.

8 Figure 7.16 shows the design of this page.

9 Save your revised web page.

10 You may be presented with a second window asking if you want to save the embedded files. In this case this means the clip art image. Click on the OK button and the window will clear.

11 Now Print the page by selecting the File menu and the Print option to reveal the Print window. Click on the OK button to print the page using the printer default settings.

Figure 7.16 Revised stamp collecting

12 Change the workspace tab to HTML and print the code using the same procedure. You will now have printouts of the code and the visual presentation of the page.

13 Close the application by selecting the File menu and the Exit option or by clicking on the Close button on the top right-hand corner of the window.

Activity 3

1 Load Microsoft® FrontPage® either by clicking on the Start button, highlighting All Programs and then selecting the Microsoft® FrontPage® item or by double clicking on the Microsoft® FrontPage® icon on the Microsoft® Windows® desktop.

2 Maximise the application window to fill the display using the Maximise button in the top right hand corner.

3 Turn the view to Page by clicking on the Page icon in the Views bar if this is not already set. Turn the workspace to Normal by clicking on the tab. Select the Blank Page option from the New Page or Web Task Pane.

4 We are going to create a simple web page about a community group.

5 Enter the heading East Wolds Community Group in a font of your own choosing in size 36. Centre the heading. Leave one blank line and then enter the text below in a font of your choice but in size 14. Or insert the text file East Wolds. Remember to check for spelling and grammatical errors and to count the number of words displayed.

The East Wolds Community Group was founded in 1996 with the aim of supporting the development of the environment within East Wolds village and the people who live in the parish. The group have several main programmes of work underway including:

- Preserving the local wild life
- Ensuring access to the countryside
- Maintaining footpaths

6 Fully align this text.

7 Leave two blank lines and type:

   Last updated by (your own name) on (the date)

   Centre this text.

8 Change the background colour to green.

9 Insert a suitable clip art or saved image (i.e. East Wolds) appropriate to the subject centred on the page between the bottom line of text (e.g. 3. Maintaining footpaths and Last updated...). Resize the image as appropriate.

10 Leave two blank lines below the image and insert the text below to act as links using a font of your choice and a character size of 18. Centre them.

   East Wolds   Contact

11 Establish links from the words East Wolds to a new page and from the word Contact to an email address. In both cases, highlight the text and select the Insert menu and the Hyperlink option to reveal the Insert Hyperlink window.

12 Test the links using the Preview workspace tab. Spell check your page.

13 Figure 7.17 shows the design of this web page.

14 Insert a floppy disk into the computer's drive. To save your web page select the File menu then the Save option to reveal the Save As window. Choose the location in which to store your page by clicking on the down arrow at the end of the Save in box. This will reveal a list. Click on the floppy disk option. You will then see this appear in the box. Now click in the File name box and type the name

Figure 7.17 East Wolds

East_Wolds_Community_Group.htm (this may be inserted automatically) and click on the Save button. You will hear the drive and the file will be saved on the floppy disk.

15 You may be presented with a second window asking if you want to save the embedded files. In this case this means the clip art image. Click on the OK button and the window will clear.

16. Now change the alignment of the three bullet points to left aligned and indent them.

17. Add a fourth bullet point

    ■ Developing an archive of village life

18. Change Last updated by to Edited by. Reduce character size to 10.

19. Check your web page to ensure you have followed all the instructions. Proofread the page to check spelling, grammar and layout.

20. Save your amended page. Figure 7.18 shows the new page.

21. Now Print the page by selecting the File menu and the Print option to reveal the Print window. Click on the OK button to print the page using the printer default settings.

22. Change the workspace tab to HTML and print the code using the same procedure. You will now have printouts of the code and the visual presentation of the page.

Figure 7.18 Amended East Wolds page

23. Close the application by selecting the File menu and Exit option or by clicking on the Close button in the top right-hand corner of the window.

Activity 4 Optional exercise
Writing HTML

1. HTML files are simply plain text files and they can be created by many text editors including Microsoft® Notepad which is supplied as part of Microsoft® Windows®.

2. To load Microsoft® Notepad, select the Start button, highlight All Programs, Accessories and click on Notepad.

3. Enter the text below:

   <html>
   <head>
   <TITLE>A Basic Page</TITLE>
   </head>
   <body>
   <H1>This is the first heading of the Page</H1>
   <P>This starts the first paragraph</P>
   <P>A new paragraph</P>
   <P>Yet another paragraph</P>
   </body>
   </html>

4 This uses only a few tags. These were:

<html> marks the start of the HTML commands
</html> marks the end of the HTML commands
<head> marks the beginning of the HTML document
</head> marks the end of the heading
<body> shows the start of the main body of a document
</body> shows the end of the main body of a document
<H1> marks the start of first heading
</H1> marks the end of first heading
<P> marks the start of a paragraph
</P> marks the end of a paragraph

5 Insert a floppy disk in the computer's drive. To save your web page select the **File** menu then the **Save As** option to reveal the Save As window. Choose the location in which to store your page by clicking on the down arrow at the end of the **Save in** box. This will reveal a list. Click on the floppy disk option. You will then see this appear in the box. Now click on the **File name** box and type the name HTMLexample.htm and click on the **Save** button. The extension .htm is vital or your browser will not recognise the code. You will hear the drive and the file will be saved on the floppy disk.

6 Close the application by selecting the **File** menu and **Exit** option or by clicking on the **Close** button on the top right-hand corner of the window.

7 Without connecting to the Internet open Microsoft® Internet Explorer or another browser either by clicking on the **Start** button, highlight **All Programs** and then selecting **Microsoft® Internet Explorer** or by double clicking on the **Microsoft® Internet Explorer** icon on the Microsoft® Windows® desktop.

8 Click on the address box and enter A:\HTMLexample.htm and press Enter. Your page will be displayed.

9 Close the application by selecting the **File** menu and **Close** option or by clicking on the **Close** button on the top right hand corner of the window.

SUMMARY

1 **Load Microsoft® FrontPage®**: Click on the **Start** button, highlight **All Programs** and then select the **Microsoft® FrontPage®** item or double click on the **Microsoft® FrontPage®** icon on the Microsoft® Windows® desktop.

2 **Close Microsoft® FrontPage®**: Select the **File** menu and the **Exit** option or click the **Close** button on the top right-hand corner of the window.

3 **Save file on a floppy disk**: Insert a floppy disk into the computer's drive. Select the **File** menu and the **Save** option to reveal the Save As window. Click on the down arrow at the end of the **Look in** box. This will reveal a list. Click on the floppy disk option. Now click in the **File name** box and enter from the keyboard the name of the file then click on the **Save** button.

4. **Alignment**: Highlight the text and select the respective icons (i.e. Left, Right, Centre or Justify) from the formatting toolbar.

5. **Select fonts and character size**: Highlight the text. Select the small down arrow button to the right of the Font Size box to reveal a list of sizes. Click on the size of your choice.

   Select the small down arrow button to the right of the Font box to reveal a list of fonts. Click on the font of your choice.

6. **Bold, italics and underline**: Highlight the text and select the respective icons (i.e. Bold, Italic or Underline) from the formatting toolbar.

7. **Insert clip art images**: Select the Insert menu, highlight the Picture option and click on the Clip Art item. This will reveal the Clip Art task pane which allows you to search for pictures related to a particular theme. The results of the search are shown as thumbnail images from which you can select an image by clicking on it. A menu box appears and provides you with the option to insert the image.

8. **Insert files**: Select the Insert menu and the File option to reveal the Select File window.

9. **Background colours and images**: Select the Format menu and the Background option. This will reveal the Page Properties window.

10. **Creating hyperlinks**: Highlight the word or image which will form the link. Select the Insert menu and the option Hyperlink to reveal the Insert Hyperlink window.

11. **Print page**: Change the workspace tab to Normal. Select the File menu and the Print option to reveal the Print window. Click on the OK button to print the page using the printer's default settings.

12. **Print code**: Change the workspace tab to HTML. Select the File menu and the Print option to reveal the Print window. Click on the OK button to print the code using the printer's default settings.

13. **Convert image formats**: Right click on the picture and select the Picture Properties option (only available from the Normal tab).

14. **Size of characters**: Character size is shown in two different ways. These are the normal points way used in all the Microsoft® Office applications and also in HTML sizes (e.g. HTML 3 is equal to 12 points).

Chapter 8

Unit 8

Online communication

This chapter will help you use electronic communication to:

- identify and use email and browsing software
- navigate the World Wide Web and use search techniques to locate data on the Web
- transmit and receive email messages and attachments

Assessment

This unit does not assume any previous experience of using a computer. However, you may find it useful to have completed Unit 1: File management and e-document production. You will be assessed through a practical realistic assignment which is designed to allow you to demonstrate your knowledge and skills against each objective. Your tutor can provide you with more guidance.

What is the Internet?

The Internet is essentially a worldwide network linking millions of computers. It was initially developed to allow communication between research organisations and provides users with a range of services including:

- Email (electronic mail)
- the World Wide Web (WWW)

It is possible to send email messages anywhere in the world to anyone having an email account. It is like being able to send a postcard almost instantaneously. It is fast and efficient and many people regard email as one of the major benefits of the Internet.

The World Wide Web comprises an extremely large number of locations called websites which provide

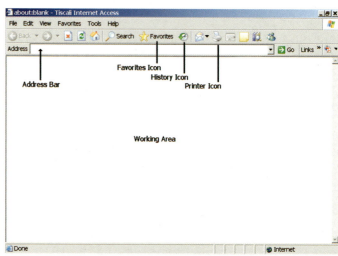

Figure 8.1 Microsoft® Internet Explorer

information about a subject or organisation using text, sound, video and graphics. These sites are located on computers scattered all over the world, linked by telecommunication networks (e.g. telephone lines and optical cables). The World Wide Web uses the Internet to offer information on almost every topic. Visiting websites is is known as surfing the Web and browsing websites.

To explore the World Wide Web you need to use a browser, which is an application designed to allow you to view websites. There are many browsers including:

- Microsoft® Internet Explorer (Figure 8.1)
- Netscape®
- Mozilla Firefox

There are other browsers, including ones developed to help visually impaired users to browse websites by reading the site contents aloud. Microsoft® Internet Explorer is probably the most widely used browser.

To send and receive emails requires access to an email application. Microsoft® Internet Explorer is linked to email software called Microsoft® Outlook® (Figure 8.2) which provides the functions that allow you to send and receive email. There are also a number of other email systems including those that operate from websites.

Figure 8.2 Microsoft® Outlook®

Accessing the World Wide Web

The process of accessing the World Wide Web depends on where you are trying to communicate from. If you are at a college or at work then it is probably very straightforward, involving simply loading the email application or browser. College or work networks are often linked to the Internet automatically. However, at home you will probably need to carry out the additional action of connecting to the Internet through an Internet Service Provider to which you have subscribed. Once you have made your connection, you can then load the browser or email application. If you have broadband (e.g. ADSL) at home then the process will be similar to college or work since many broadband systems offer a continuous link to the Internet although since there are a range of ways of configuring systems there may be differences depending on how the computer and broadband is set up.

Some hotels and other organisations offer wireless connections meaning that if you have a laptop that is wireless-enabled you can access the Internet and send emails through your account simply by being within their buildings. This is becoming increasingly common but arrangements vary and in some cases there are charges or you need to register to use the service.

Surfing the World Wide Web

To locate a particular website you need to know its address (or URL – Uniform Resource Locator). When this is entered into the Address bar and the Enter key is pressed, the browser searches for the website which is then displayed in the browser window.

Website addresses are unique and are structured in a similar way to a postal or street address. The address or URL for the BBC is http://www.bbc.co.uk. This comprises:

- http – Hypertext Transfer Protocol – this tells the browser how to transfer the web page across the Internet so you can view it
- www – World Wide Web
- bbc – host of the website
- co – company
- uk – United Kingdom

The general form is thus http://www.host.typeoforganisation.country. However, websites in the USA do not use a country suffix. Other codes for some organisations and countries are:

- .ac – university/academic
- .com – company
- .co – company
- .edu – educational institution
- .org – charity or not for profit organisation
- .gov – government
- .mil – military
- .net – network
- .be – Belgium
- .ca – Canada
- .dk – Denmark
- .nl – Netherlands
- .ch – Switzerland

Structure of a website

A website consists of a variety of pages each displaying content in the form of text and graphics. Some will also provide sound and video. The pages can vary in length and you often need to scroll them. Each page is linked to the others by hyperlinks which, when clicked on, allow you to jump around the site. A website can be designed so that almost anything can be linked to something else. Links exist to connect items of information within pages as well as between different pages. This can sometimes be confusing since you may feel you have jumped to a new page whereas you have only moved to a new part of the same page. Websites vary in size and can be very large and complex. Figure 8.3 illustrates links between web pages. There can be links such as:

- from an image to a text passage
- from a word to the top of a page

- from an image to another picture
- from the bottom of one page to the top of another
- between pages and within pages

Links may take the form of underlined words, of areas of the screen that change the shape of the mouse pointer when it passes over them or of buttons.

The standard address of a website (e.g. http://www.host.type.country) usually links to what is called the Home page of the site which is rather like the contents page of a book. It normally has links to the main parts of the site but it is also possible to link to individual pages within a website by extending the address (e.g. http://www.host.type.country/ nextpage/otherpages). This is useful when you want to direct people to a particular page but it can be confusing since by following a link you may suddenly find yourself in the middle of a new website. Links can be:

- between pages in a single site
- between pages in different sites
- within a single page

Figure 8.4 illustrates a structure of a simple website. This is presented as a series of layers but websites are often more complex than this with direct links from the home page to major parts of the site ensuring that you do not need to move through each layer. Although this is efficient, it is easy to get lost in a more complex website.

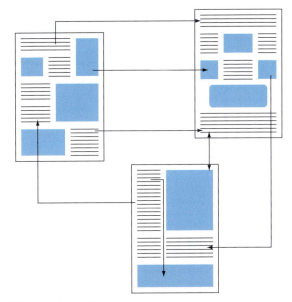

Figure 8.3 Links between web pages

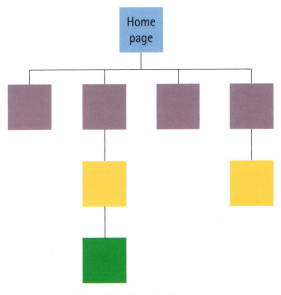

Figure 8.4 Simplified website structure

Exercise 57

Using the browser

Establish a connection to the Internet – this will depend on your location (i.e. home, work or college).

1. Using either the All Programs menu or by clicking on the Microsoft® Internet Explorer icon on the desktop, load the browser. The browser may appear either filling the entire screen or in a window. If you want to expand the window to fill the whole screen, use the Maximise button in the top right-hand corner of the window.

continued

2. Enter http://www.bl.uk/ (this is the website of the British Library) in the Address bar and press Enter. It is vital to be 100% accurate when entering URLs since any mistake will result in your browser giving you an error message suggesting there is no website at that address. When the page appears in your browser, scroll down and view the content. This is the home page so you should be able to locate a menu of the contents of the site.

3. Try to locate the links to other pages. These will take the form of either underlined words, words in a different colour, areas that are highlighted when you move the pointer over them or the mouse pointer changing shape to become a hand.

4. Click on a link that looks interesting and watch what happens. You should see the page disappear and a new one take its place. Often the outline of the page will appear quickly but illustrations will take longer although a frame showing their location may be revealed almost at once. It takes time for the contents of a page to load. The length of time changes depending on the size of the page (i.e. pages containing many illustrations are slow to load), how many people are visiting the site at the same time (i.e. the site gives equal priority to all visitors so if thousands of people are using the site at the same time it will be slow) and the number of people using the World Wide Web (i.e. the more people, the slower the access).

5. Explore the new page and again jump from this to another and so on. Investigate the site and see what you can find.

6. After a few jumps to new pages, it may be difficult to remember the route you have taken. However, you can retrace your steps using the **Back** button on the toolbar which will move you back to the page you jumped from. You can return using the **Forward** button.

7. Use **Back** and **Forward** and observe what happens. You may notice that pages are faster to load in some cases since your computer has stored the contents of the page and can therefore quickly access it.

8. Explore the site until you are confident that you can recognise links, move between pages and use the **Back** and **Forward** buttons.

9. You can jump from one website to another from anywhere, so delete the British Library URL and enter http://www.thebritishmuseum.ac.uk/ in the address bar and press Enter.

10. Observe the new website appear. This is the home page of the British Museum website. Explore this site practising linking to new pages, locating links and retracing your path.

11. When you are confident about navigating sites, close the browser by selecting the **File** menu and the **Close** option or click on the window **Close** button on the top right-hand corner of the browser. You can exit the browser from any page within a site.

Searching a website

Unless the site is small or has limited links, locating precise content is quite difficult if you simply follow the links. A large, complex site can be difficult to use, so many have a facility to search for chosen topics. Figure 8.5 shows a site search facility or search engine that will allow you to locate any content within the site that matches your search words.

Figure 8.5 Site search engine (Reproduced with the permission of Atomz.com)

This search engine works in a similar way to many others in that you enter a word or words and it seeks to match them to content. In this case you are allowed to refine the nature of the match:

- Any words – any of the words you have entered match any word in the content
- All words – all the search words appear in the content in any order
- Exact phrase – the search phrase is matched exactly in the content
- Sound-alike matching – you can match with any words that sound like your search words

The search engine gives a score indicating the closeness of the match. In many cases, search engines give you a number of matches which you can review to see if they are correct. It is normal to start with a very wide search and then to refine it so that you do not get too many to review.

Exercise 58

Search a single site

1 Establish a connection to the Internet – this will depend on your location (i.e. home, work or college).

2 Load the browser using either the All Programs menu or by clicking on the Microsoft® Internet Explorer icon on the desktop. The browser may appear filling the

continued

entire screen or in a window. If you want to expand the window to fill the whole screen, use the **Maximise** button on the top right-hand corner of the window.

3 Enter http://www.niace.org.uk/newsearch.htm in the address bar and press enter – this is the website of the National Institute of Adult Continuing Education (NIACE). This URL will jump you into the page on which the search engine is located.

4 Investigate the site search engine by trying a number of different searches.

5 Enter 'information and communication technology' with option **Any word** (click into the radio button alongside the option) and click on the **Search** button. A list of matches appears with a brief summary describing them to help you identify if it is the correct one. You can display matches without a summary by changing the 'with summary' option (click on the down arrow to select other options).

6 This search reported over 2000 matches and showed the top ten matches. You can change the number displayed by altering the **Show** option (click on the down arrow to select a new number). The number of matches you will find will be different since websites are always changing and developing.

7 If you scroll down to the bottom of the results page you will again find the search engine. Alternatively click on the **Back** button.

8 Search again for 'information and communication technology' with option **All words** and click on the **Search** button. The search engine reports the matches and again displays the top ten.

9 Search again for 'information and communication technology' with option **Exact phrase** and click on the **Search** button. The search engine reports the matches and again displays the top ten.

10 Search again for 'information and communication technology' with option **Exact phrase**, **Dated within last 2 weeks** and click on the **Search** button. The search engine reports the matches and again displays the top ten.

You will have noticed that the more restrictive your search options, the smaller number of matches.

11 Explore the search engine using different combinations of options until you are confident you understand how it works.

12 You can jump to the content matched by clicking on the link shown with each match (e.g. underlined and coloured words). You will have to do this frequently to check if it is what you are searching for. To return, use the **Back** button.

13 When you are confident about searching, close the browser by selecting the **File** menu then the **Close** option or click on the window **Close** button in the top right-hand corner of the browser.

Other opportunities to practise

There are a variety of ways that search facilities work on a website. If you would like to practise your search skills, try using the site search engines on:

- www.thebritishmuseum.ac.uk – The British Museum
- www.bl.uk – The British Library
- www.tate.org.uk – The Tate Gallery
- www.movinghere.org.uk – The Moving Here site

All four sites have powerful search facilities to help you locate information.

Searching the World Wide Web

There are millions of websites covering almost every subject. Many organisations provide search engines to help you locate content on the World Wide Web. They have indexed web pages so that you can search them by using key words. This is similar to searching a single website. However, while it is relatively easy to find the content on a single site using a site search engine, it is far more difficult on the World Wide Web because of the number of sites. World Wide Web search engines search for individual web pages rather than entire sites.

Search engines are essentially large databases of web pages that have been amassed automatically by the engine. This is carried out by using tools called spiders or robots which follow links between pages and index the pages they find. The index is directly related to the words presented on the web pages. When you enter your keywords for the information, you are searching the database and not the World Wide Web itself.

There are many search engines and although they all work in broadly similar ways, there are differences between them. They differ:

- in the range of search options they provide
- in how they present or rank the results of a search

There are two different types of search engine:

- individual
- meta

Individual search engines are essentially what we have been describing. A meta engine does not develop its own database but rather searches the databases of several other individual search engines. They are therefore very useful in finding more elusive content.

Another way of finding content on the World Wide Web is by using devices called directories. Directories are very different from search engines. While you search an engine using key words that you select as being related to what you are seeking, a directory provides you with categories to choose from. The contents of directories are chosen for you. The staff pick sites that they believe you will be interested in so they are in a sense making recommendations whereas a search engine leaves the whole choice to you. Directories are very quick to use while a search engine can take time to identify suitable pages. However, the categories available to you in a directory are limited to what have been identified as popular items (e.g. computers, shopping and holidays), but a search engine places no limits on categories you can search for.

There are many different search engines and directories. The list below shows some examples:

Alltheweb	http://www.alltheweb.com
AltaVista	http://www.uk.altavista.com/
Bigbook	http://www.bigbook.com
Chubba	http://www.chubba.com/
Excite	http://www.excite.com/
Google	http://www.google.com
	http://www.google.co.uk
HotBot	http://www.hotbot.com/
Looksmart	http://www.looksmart.com/
Lycos	http://www-uk.lycos.com/
Northern Lights	http://www.nlsearch.com/
Webcrawler	http://www.webcrawler.com/
Yahoo	http://www.yahoo.com
	http://www.uk.yahoo.com

Search engines can also be used to find individual email addresses. There are several that specialise in locating email addresses.

Bigfoot	http://www.bigfoot.com/
InfoSpace	http://www.infospace.com/
Whowhere	http://www.whowhere.com/
Yahoo People	http://people.yahoo.com/

Meta search engines include:

Dogpile	http://www.dogpile.com/
Metacrawler	http://www.metacrawler.com
Monster Crawler	http://www.monstercrawler.com
Lxquick	http://www.lxquick.com
Ask	http://www.ask.com

Searching is easy to do, but can be difficult to do well. Most search engines offer help in a variety of ways and it is useful to investigate these options. Different search engines operate in different ways so that undertaking an identical search using several will produce different results. The next two exercises are based on comparing the same search using two different search engines (i.e. Altavista and Google).

Exercise 59

Searching the World Wide Web – Altavista

1 Establish a connection to the Internet – this will depend on your location (i.e. home, work or college).

2 Load the browser by using either the All Programs menu or by double clicking on the Microsoft® Internet Explorer icon on the desktop.

3 Enter http://www.uk.altavista.com in the address bar and press Enter – this is the website of Altavista. If you would like to compare this search engine with a directory then visit

continued

http://www.bigbook.com. Study the Altavista search engine and notice that there are options to search for images, audio, video and news.

4   Return to the Altavista home page, Web tab. We will try to locate a hotel in Edinburgh. So enter the word – hotels – into the box of the search engine and select the option which restricts the search to the United Kingdom (click on the radio button – a small circle which when you click on it inserts a dot in its centre to show it is active). Click on the Find button.

The results give several million pages matching the word hotels and also offering a number of sponsored matches about hotels.

5   This is not very useful as there are too many matches. Let's refine the search by adding the word Edinburgh. You should enter – hotels Edinburgh – select the UK option and click on the Search button.

6   The results of this search were still several thousand pages that match the words and also some sponsored matches relating to hotels in Edinburgh. However, the number of matches is significantly reduced.

7   Refine the search by joining the words with a plus sign – hotels+Edinburgh. The engine will now search for pages containing both words.

8   A final search involves enclosing the words in double inverted commas. This normally makes the engine search for pages in which the phrase "hotels Edinburgh" appears. Finally try to reverse the order of the words so enter "Edinburgh hotels".

9   You can jump to any matching web page by clicking on the link (underlined and coloured words) to check if it is what you are looking for. To return to the search engine, use the Back button. Explore the search engine by carrying out a search to find web pages that interest you (e.g. look for pages about a hobby, football team, government or places of interest).

10   When you are confident about searching, close the browser by selecting the File menu and the Close option or click on the window Close button in the top right-hand corner of the browser.

Exercise 60

Searching the World Wide Web – Google

1   Establish a connection to the Internet – this will depend on your location (i.e. home, work or college).

2   Load the browser by using either the All Programs menu or by clicking on the Microsoft® Internet Explorer icon on the desktop.

continued

3. Enter http://www.google.com in the address bar and press Enter. This is the website of the Google search engine (Figure 8.6).

4. Notice that this search engine offers options to search for images, groups, news, Froogle and more. Explore the other options and see if you can find out what Froogle offers.

5. We will try again to locate a hotel in Edinburgh, so enter the word – hotels – into the search box. Click the Google Search button.

   The result of the search are far from useful since there are far too many matches. Let's refine the search by adding the word Edinburgh. You should enter – hotels Edinburgh – and click on the Google Search button.

Figure 8.6 Google search engine

6. A third possible step is to modify the search by joining the words with a plus sign. The engine will search for pages containing both words: hotels+Edinburgh.

7. A fourth search is to enclose the words in inverted commas. This normally makes the engine search for pages that include the phrase "hotels Edinburgh".

8. A final way is to reverse the search words and enter "Edinburgh hotels".

9. Compare the results of the two searches and consider the effectiveness of different search approaches and search engines. It is useful to compare which pages each search engine identified in their top ten.

10. Explore the Google search engine by carrying out a search to find web pages that interest you (e.g. look for pages about a hobby, football team, government or places of interest).

11. When you are confident about searching, close the browser by selecting the File menu and the Close option or click on the window Close button in the top right-hand corner of the browser.

Exercise 61

1. Try searching for hotels in Edinburgh using Yahoo UK (http://uk.yahoo.com).

2. Search engines often provide other services. Try finding out what news and other services the different search engines offer.

Saving information

Browsers provide functions allowing you to save the contents of web pages, images and save the URL so you can return to the page and to print the page. All these functions require the browser to be accessing the chosen web page.

To print the page, select the File menu then the Print option, which will open the Print dialog box. Press the OK button in the Print dialog box and the web page will now be printed using the printer default settings. Web pages are quite often long, so printing a web page can produce several A4 sheets. Figure 8.7 shows the File menu.

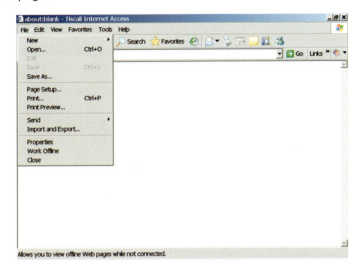

Figure 8.7 File menu

In a similar way, the contents of the web page can be saved by selecting the File menu and the Save or Save As options. This opens the Save dialog box. To save a web page as a file, you need to identify a folder in which to save it. This is done by clicking on the down arrow at the end of the Save in box to open a list of the drives and folders. To select one, single click on it. Once you have selected a folder you can name your file by clicking in the File name box and entering the name using the keyboard. The file can now be saved by clicking the Save button. The latest browsers allow you to save both the text and images unlike the earlier ones which only allowed you to save the text and left gaps where the pictures should be.

You can also save images by positioning the mouse pointer over the picture and right clicking. This will open a menu of options including Save Picture As… . If you select this option then a window called Save Picture will open that offers you the opportunity to select the file name (i.e. in the box at the bottom of the window called File name) and the file type (i.e. in the box at the bottom of the window called Save as type). Usually this will be completed by the system identifying the file. It is often JPEG or GIF since these are widely used on websites. The window also allows you to choose where to save the file by using the Save in box at the top of the window.

Once you have found a useful website it is important to be able to find it again. Microsoft® Internet Explorer lets you save the URLs in a special area called Favorites. To store a URL, you need to be

Figure 8.8 Favorites

accessing the chosen website. You then select the Favorites menu and the Add to Favorites option. Figure 8.8 shows a list of Favorites. To return to a Favorite website you simply click on it. You can organise your Favorites into folders, grouping related sites together.

Another way of returning to a useful website is to use the browser's history records. Microsoft® Internet Explorer keeps records of sites visited. However, this record system is often set to keep the list of sites visited for just a short time so its main task is to allow you to return to a particular site after a session visiting many different websites. Figure 8.9 shows the History record open. It is accessed by clicking on the History button on the toolbar.

Figure 8.9 History

Microsoft® Outlook®

When you first start to use email it has a magical quality. You connect to the Internet, open your email application (e.g. Microsoft® Outlook®) and your emails arrive. What happens is that an email is addressed in the same way as a letter or postcard. This address directs the email to a location on the Internet, normally that of the Internet Service Provider who supplies your access to the Internet, where it is stored on a computer until you collect it. In some cases that may be your employer or college. Often as soon as you connect to the Internet and open your email application, the mail automatically arrives. However, sometimes you will need to request that the email is sent to you (often called downloading) or even establish a link to the Internet before accessing your messages. It depends on your situation.

An important issue to remember is that computer viruses are often distributed by email. You should always protect your computer system with up-to-date virus protection software. Most virus protection applications will allow you to set them so that all incoming and outgoing emails are checked. This is critical to protect your computer.

Microsoft® Outlook® is an email system that also offers many additional features to manage your activities (e.g. diary). You can access it from the All Programs menu or by clicking on the Microsoft® Outlook® icon on the Microsoft® Windows® desktop. This means you can use it independently from Microsoft® Internet Explorer. You do not need to be connected to the Internet in order to use Microsoft® Outlook® to read old emails, to write new emails or reply to one that you have received.

However, to send or receive new emails does require a connection to the Internet. Once you are connected then the emails you have created can be sent. This is like writing letters at home and having to walk to the postbox to post them. This process of writing or reading emails while not being connected is called 'working off-line'. This is important since it will save you the telephone charges associated with being connected.

Figure 8.2 shows you the major features of Microsoft® Outlook®. These are:

- Inbox – this is the folder in which your email is stored when it is received; it is sometimes called the mailbox.
- Outbox – this is the folder in which your emails are stored until they are sent (i.e. before you connect to the Internet).
- Sent Items – this is the folder in which all your emails that have been sent are stored.
- Deleted Items – this is the folder in which emails that have been deleted are stored. This is very useful to help rectify mistakes.
- Drafts – this is the folder in which emails that are only partially written are stored.
- Address book (Open book icon on toolbar) – this provides access to an electronic address book where email addresses can be stored.

Many of these functions are all shown on the left-hand side of the application in the small window marked Folders, with the exception of Address Book which is a toolbar button. Microsoft® Outlook® provides you with these features to ensure that emails are safeguarded and organised. However, you can also use standard Microsoft® Windows® file-saving methods to save emails as files in other folders. This is useful if the email relates to a particular topic and you have already created a folder for other files so that you can keep everything together.

Incoming mail is displayed in the Inbox which you access by clicking on the Inbox function in the Folders list or in the main work area (i.e. right-hand side of opening display). Figure 8.10 shows the Inbox. If you select an email by single clicking to highlight it you will see that the message appears in the window below. Microsoft® Outlook® offers a range of ways of showing messages and these are available in the View menu. To open the message so that it is displayed in a separate window you need to double click on it.

Figure 8.10 Inbox

To save an email in an external folder, highlight the message and select the File menu and the Save As option. This will open Save Message As window. This is identical to other Microsoft® Office applications. You need to:

- Select the drive (e.g. floppy disk) using the Save in box down arrow
- Select a file name using the File name box. Microsoft® Windows® provides you with a name based on the contents of the document but it is always best to name your own files to ensure you can remember them

If you have opened the message the process of saving to an external folder is the same.

You can also save your messages to a folder within the Inbox folder. In order to save your emails to an internal folder you must first create it. The first step is to highlight the Inbox folder within the folders list on the left of the display and then select the down arrow on the

New button on the toolbar. This will open a menu of options from which you should choose Folder to reveal the Create New Folder window (Figure 8.11). You enter the name of the folder you want to create and then click on the OK button. Your new folder is created within the Inbox folder. You could create it within any of the folders.

Once you have started to use email you will rapidly have too many messages to remember them all. It is therefore critical to organise them in folders so you can find them later. Figure 8.12 shows a folder structure which organises the management of messages. Once you have saved a message it is important to remove it from the Inbox or you will quickly have a very long list of messages displayed. To delete an email simply highlight it and press the Delete key on the keyboard or select the Delete option in the Edit menu.

Figure 8.11 Create New Folder

When you want to read a saved email you simply highlight the folder and you will see the saved messages appear in the message area. You are then able to select the message you want to read and it will open so you can view it. When you send emails they are automatically saved in the Sent Items folder.

Figure 8.12 Email folders

Sending messages

To send a new email, click on the New button on the toolbar of Microsoft® Outlook®. This will open the email window (Figure 8.13). The layout of the message window guides you through how to write your message. You need to enter an email address, a subject and the contents of your message. You can also send copies of your message to other people. When you have completed your message, send it by clicking on the Send button. If you are connected to the Internet, the email will be sent immediately. If you are working off-line (i.e. you are not connected to the Internet) then the email is stored in the Outbox and the number stored will be shown in brackets next to the title Outbox.

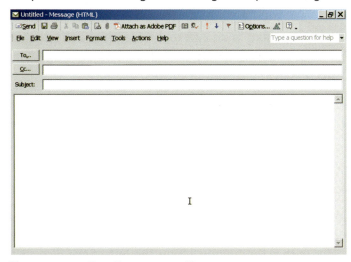

Figure 8.13 Sending an email

You should see the number increase by one when you click on the Send button. The email will be dispatched as soon as you next connect to the Internet.

Emails are normally short messages but other computer files such as spreadsheet, word-processor or presentation files can be attached. This allows far more detailed information to be communicated. Sales staff, for example, can send their expense claims as a spreadsheet file or managers can send their reports as word-processor files. These files are called attachments and they are easily added to the email using the Insert File button (i.e. shown by a paperclip).

Email is very useful in business in that mail carries the sender's details. It automatically gets assigned a date and time of creation so that messages can be more easily traced or kept in order. These features allow detailed records to be straightforwardly maintained. Equally important is that any emails you receive can be kept (e.g. in your folders).

The address of an email follows a standard convention. It is a combination of the user's name with a domain name (often the email's computer host or Internet Service Provider) joined by the @ symbol. Some examples of email addresses are:

- ajones@acme.co.uk
- alison.jones@acme.net
- jones@harry.org.uk
- a.jones@acme.com

Many organisations standardise email addresses so that if you know one email addresses you can work out other ones.

For example

You know one member of staff's email address is d.harrison@acme.co.uk then if you know another person is called James King then his email address may be j.king@acme.co.uk.

Exercise 62

Send an email

1. Load Microsoft® Outlook® using either the All Programs menu or by clicking on the Microsoft® Outlook® icon on the desktop.
2. Open a new message by selecting the New button on the toolbar to reveal the email window (Figure 8.13).
3. If you are studying OCR CLAIT 2006 as part of a class, ask your learning colleagues if you can send them an email or ask a work colleague for their address.

    Enter the following text

        To: e-mail address of your colleague

        Subject: Practice email

        This is my first email and I would be grateful if you would reply to it so that I can see what happens.

        Name

continued

4 Before you send your email check that you have entered the address accurately. It must be 100% correct or it will not be delivered. If you send a message to an unknown address you will receive an error message saying that there is no such address. Often this is the result of a tiny error.

5 Click on the Send button as soon as you have completed the message. If you are not connected to the Internet you will see the message added to the Outbox (number in brackets will increase by one). If you are connected then the message will be sent immediately and a copy placed in the Sent Items folder. Check this folder and see if your message has been added.

6 If you are not connected to the Internet you should then connect and you will see your message sent. It should only take a moment or two.

7 Explore Microsoft® Outlook® by clicking on menus and buttons and investigating the different options. Observe the changes to the display.

8 When you are confident that you understand the layout of the application, close Microsoft® Outlook® by selecting the File menu and the Exit option or click on the window Close button in the top right-hand corner of the application window.

Receiving emails

Emails that have been sent to you will appear in the Inbox which you access by clicking on the Inbox folder in the Folders List or in the main work area (i.e. right-hand side of opening display). Figure 8.10 shows the Inbox. A list of emails is shown in the Inbox which presents you details of who the message is from, its subject and the date and time it was received. This information can be preceded by a symbol (e.g. a paperclip indicates an attachment and an exclamation mark, an important message). If you single click on a message it will be highlighted and its contents revealed in the box below the list. If you double click on the message then it will open fully (Figure 8.14).

When you receive an email you have a variety of options. You can:

- read then delete the message (with the email highlighted or the message window open, select the Edit menu and the Delete option or press the Delete key)
- read and save the message (with the email highlighted or the message window open select the File menu and the Save As option)

Figure 8.14 Open email

- read and reply to the original email sender (with the email highlighted or the message window open, click on the **Reply** button on the toolbar)
- read and reply to everyone who received the original email (i.e. copies) (with the email highlighted or the message window open click on **Reply to All** button on the toolbar)
- read and forward the message to someone else (with the email highlighted or the message window open, click on the **Forward** button on the toolbar and enter the email address of the person you want the message copied to)
- read and copy the message to a folder (with the email highlighted or the message window open, select the **Edit** menu and the **Copy to Folder** option. This allows you to place a copy of the message into one of the existing local folders or in a new local folder. This is useful in that within Microsoft® Outlook® you begin to create a filing system for your communications. Alternatively you could use **Save As** option we discussed earlier)
- read and copy the message to another person (with the email highlighted or the message window open, click on the **Reply** button on the toolbar. Enter the address of the person you want to copy your reply to in addition to the sender in the **Cc** box or delete the senders address and enter the address of the person you are copying the message to)
- print the message (with the email highlighted or the message window open, select the **File** menu and the **Print** option)

Emails are often printed and it is important always to print the email header. This shows the details of the sender, receiver, date sent and subject of the message. This allows you to trace the background to the message and to link it to other related items. It is quite common to print a series of messages to read and answer while travelling and then to send the answers when you return to the office. In order to avoid mistakes it is clearly vital to have the details on the printout. During the assessment for this chapter you will be required to print emails with the headers.

The process of deleting messages from your Inbox once you have acted on them is important since very quickly after starting to use email you are likely to have a vast number of old messages. It is vital that these are organised (e.g. saved into folders) or you will rapidly become confused by the mountain of correspondence.

Some of the emails you receive will be accompanied by attachments. If you look at the top line of the Inbox you will see a variety of headings – one is a paperclip. If you now look down the list of messages, if any have a paperclip it indicates a message with an attachment. These are files of information (e.g. word-processor files). To open an attachment double click on it and it will open, providing you have the appropriate application available on your computer. A Microsoft® Word file requires Microsoft® Word, a Microsoft® Excel® file requires Microsoft® Excel® and so on. If the appropriate application is not present then you will see an error message stating that it cannot identify the application. Once an attachment is open you can save or print it using its application. The appropriate application will be opened automatically by the attachment.

Viruses are frequently transmitted by email attachments. It is therefore important not to open an attachment unless you know who has sent you the message. Equally important is to have up-to-date virus protection software on your computer. Many virus protection systems allow you to check attachments automatically before opening them. It is good practice to check email attachments even if you know the sender. Some viruses automatically send email messages to spread their effects.

Netiquette

Many organisations have established codes of conduct for using email. Email messages are often informal and short making them easy to misunderstand. This has given emails a reputation for causing offense without intending to do so. Many people do not realise that the same laws apply to emails as do to letters (e.g. libel). These codes of conduct are called 'netiquette'. Netiquette rules vary but some widely used ones are:

- never send or reply to a message in anger
- always introduce your message (e.g. Dear... or Hi...)
- always end your messages (e.g. Best Wishes, etc)
- do not include items in an email that you would not send in a letter
- do not send any form of material that could cause offence

There are possibly other rules and it is important to find out what your employer's netiquette code is and to follow it.

Formatting email

Emails are often informal and can easily be misunderstood so it is important to consider how to format messages to make them clear. When creating a new message you can select from a range of formatting options by selecting the Format menu and a series of options including:

- Font
- Paragraph
- Background

The Font options allows you to select the font, style (i.e. underlined, italics or embolden) and character size. The Paragraph offers options to align your message left, right and centre as well as a bullet list, while the Background options offers the possibility of using a picture of your choice as a background for the message or changing the colour of the background.

This range of different options provides powerful ways of presenting your messages to give impact. However, the main purpose of any message is to ensure that the receiver understands it. It is therefore important not to overuse the different features since they can sometimes distract the reader from the message.

Exercise 63

Receiving emails

1 Load Microsoft® Outlook® using either the All Programs menu or by clicking on the Microsoft® Outlook® icon on the desktop.

2 Single click on the Inbox which will be highlighted and a list of emails received will be listed. Email messages that you have not opened are shown in bold. You will possibly find a reply to a previous email but even if no one has sent you a message, Microsoft® Outlook® usually shows a welcome email from the Microsoft® Outlook® team.

continued

3 Single click on a message. You will see the content displayed. This is very useful if you are seeking to check your email rapidly.

4 Double click on a message and you will see the Message window open.

5 Click on the Reply button and a new window will appear (Figure 8.15) showing the original message but it reverses the sender and receiver. In the space above the original message you enter your reply. This enables both the original message and reply to be sent. If this email provokes a response, the email will have the original, the reply and the second reply. Emails can contain the whole communication.

Figure 8.15 Reply

6 Enter a reply that is appropriate to the message you have opened. In my example, I might reply:

> Hi
>
> I hope the donation helps
>
> Keep up the good work
>
> Alan Clarke

7 Click on the Send button as soon as you have finished. If you are connected to the Internet your message will be sent. If you are working off-line then the message will be stored in the Outbox and you will see the number in the box increase.

8 Open the email again and this time, click on Reply to All and you will see the same window (Figure 8.15) open. This is because the original email was sent only to you. If the original message had been copied to other people then your reply would go to everyone. Close the window, select the File menu and the Close option or click on the Close button in the top right-hand corner of the window.

9 **Open the email again** and click on the Forward button. You will see the same window (Figure 8.15) open again but with a blank To line. This lets you send your message to another person. You can also add an extra message. To close the window, select the File menu and the Close option or click on the Close button in the top right-hand corner of the window.

10 Open the email again and click on the Reply button. You will see the same window (Figure 8.15) open again with the sender and receiver reversed. Delete the address in the To box and enter another address (perhaps another student if you are taking a course) and copy the email to the new person.

> ### continued
>
> 11 Repeat step 10 but instead of substituting the address in the To box, insert the address of the person you are copying to in the Cc box.
>
> 12 Compare the Reply, Reply All, Forward and Cc functions.
>
> 13 When you are confident that you understand the three functions, close Microsoft® Outlook® by selecting the File menu and the Exit option or click on the window Close button in the top right-hand corner of the application window.

Attaching files

Attaching files to an email can be very useful. You initially need to start a new email (click on the New button) which opens the Email window (Figure 8.13). To add an attachment, click on the Insert File button (i.e. paperclip) on the toolbar. This will open the Insert File window (Figure 8.16).

This window gives you access to all your saved files. To move around the different drives, use the drop down arrow next to the Look in box and then click on the selected folder or drive. When you have identified the file, double click on it or single click the file and then click on the Insert button. The attached file will appear in your message.

Electronic address book

Figure 8.16 Insert File

An important function that Microsoft® Outlook® provides is the storage of email addresses. You can copy addresses from emails that are sent to you or enter new ones manually. Once you have created an entry in the electronic address book, you can send an email directly from it.

The address book can be opened by selecting the Address Book icon (i.e. an open book) on the toolbar. This opens the Address Book window (Figure 8.17). It will often open in a

Figure 8.17 Address Book

small window which you will need to enlarge to full screen size by selecting the Maximise button in the top right hand corner of the window. You can enter new addresses by selecting the New Entry button which will open a new window with the options:

- New Contact
- New Distribution List

In New Contact you insert an individual address. New Distribution list allows you to create a group of email addresses so that by typing a single name you can send a message to everyone in the group. If you select the New Contact option then you will open the Properties window which resembles a paper address book where you can record names, addresses, email addresses, telephone numbers, etc.

A useful function provided by the Address Book is the ability to send an email from it. If you select the New Message button with an address highlighted, then the email window will open with the email address of the entry inserted (Figure 8.18).

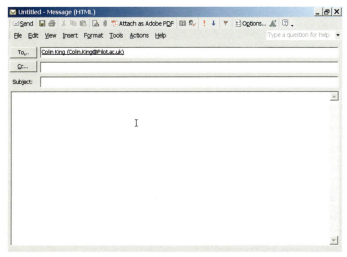

Figure 8.18 Send email

Exercise 64

Using an address book

1 Load Microsoft® Outlook® using either the All Programs menu or by clicking on the Microsoft® Outlook® icon on the desktop.

2 Click the Address Book icon to open the window (Figure 8.17). Click on the New Entry button to reveal the New Entry window and select the New Contact option and click on the OK button to open the Contacts window (Figure 8.19).

3 Add the following information to create a new record

Bill Jones
Acme
11 New Way
Newtown

020 345 7896

b.jones@acme.co.uk

Figure 8.19 Contacts window

continued

When you have completed the entry, click on the `Save and Close` button and you will see the new entry in the Address Book.

4 Try entering the contact details and email addresses of some people you know. If you are using this book as part of a course, ask the other learners for their details. Practise until you are confident of adding new addresses. You can delete entries by highlighting them and selecting the `File` menu and the `Delete` option.

5 If you single click on an address it will be highlighted and by selecting the `New Message` button, you can send an email to this address. If you double click on an address, you can add more information to your record, such as the postal address.

6 Select an address and send a new email. An email window will appear with the address you have selected in the To box. Experiment with the different formatting options (e.g. fonts, character size, alignment and background colours) for presenting your email.

7 Explore the other Address Book functions until you are confident you understand what it can offer you.

8 Close the Address Book window by selecting the `Close` button on the top right-hand corner of the window or the `File` menu and the `Close` option.

9 Close Microsoft® Outlook® by selecting the `File` menu and the `Exit` option or click on the `Close` button on the top right-hand corner of the application window.

Web-based email

Another way of providing yourself with an email account, if you have access to the Internet, is through web-based email suppliers. To send or receive messages you must gain access to the World Wide Web. This has the advantage that you can access your messages from any computer in the world connected to the Internet, although it does have the disadvantage that you must be online to read or send messages.

Almost all the web-based services are free but you will find advertising related to both the sites you have to visit and in some cases the emails you send. In order to establish an account you normally only have to visit the site, complete some online forms, and choose a user name and password. Once this is done you are ready to send and receive email.

Some Internet Service Providers will offer you both a web-based account and one linked to your home computer. This gives you the opportunity of reading and replying to your mail when **you are away from home.**

Company policy and legislation

Although the World Wide Web provides a huge amount of useful information, it also contains offensive material, pornography and information which is incorrect. Many employers have established policies about the use of the World Wide Web. It is critical that you are aware of your organisation's policy.

Companies frequently forbid the use of the World Wide Web to access offensive material and in many cases it is a serious disciplinary offence to breach the policy. The legal position should also be considered. There have been several prominent court cases about using the World Wide Web to access pornography. It is important to be aware of both the law and access policy. In a similar way, learning centres, colleges and libraries which provide public access to the Internet also place restrictions on the use of the system.

Many organisations have also developed policies regarding the use of email which you should be fully aware of. In simple terms, it is always best to include in an email only material you would write in a letter. You are just as liable for what you write in an email as in a letter.

More practice

Activity 1
Locate a website

1 Access the website at www.movinghere.org.uk which is a website allowing people to learn more about migration to Great Britain. It contains a wealth of material. Figure 8.20 shows the home page today but since websites are dynamic, it is likely that it will have changed to some extent when you view it.

We would like to acknowledge The National Archive for their permission to use the screen capture of *Moving Here*.

Figure 8.20 Moving Here

2 Use the site search facility to locate information about stories from Ireland.

3 Save the page as a Favorite so that you can locate it again.

4 Print the web page.

5 On the printout of your web page write your name and the date you located it.

6 Use the links on the website to locate the gallery and return to the home page.

7 Save the Home page as a Favorite so that you can locate it again.

8 Print the Home page and write your name and the date you located it.

9 Close your browser when you have completed the task.

Activity 2
Searching the World Wide Web

1 Using a search engine of your choice, locate a picture of the Fighting Temeraire which is a famous painting by the artist J.M.W. Turner.

2 Use the links to find a page with a copy of the painting.

3 Save the page as a Favorite so that you can locate it again.

4 Print the web page.

5 Write your name on the printout and indicate the painting of the Fighting Temeraire.

6 Close your browser when you have completed the task.

Activity 3
Sending an email message

The website linked to this book (www.hodderclait.co.uk) has an email bin into which you can send emails but you will not get a reply.

1 Using Microsoft® Outlook® or another email editor, send an email message to a friend or colleague. Use the formatting options to present your message in an attractive and effective way.

Title: Practising email

Text: I am learning how to send emails. I would be grateful if you would email me and attach a picture file to the message. I have attached a file with an image.

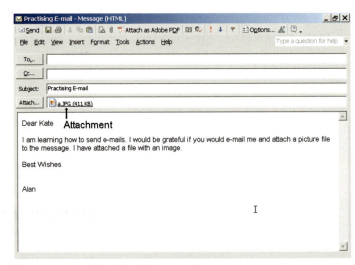

Figure 8.21 Email with attachment

2 Attach an image file to the message (the images used in this book are available from the associated website if you do not have access to one). Figure 8.21 illustrates an example message.

3 Check your message for mistakes.

4 Close Microsoft® Outlook® or your chosen email editor.

Activity 4
Replying to an email

1 Open your email system and access your Inbox to check if you have received any messages.

2 Open the message from your friend and read it.

3 Ensure that the attachment is checked for viruses.

4 Save the email attachment to a folder you have created.

5 Reply to the message.

Many thanks for your help

6 Make sure your email system will save your reply.

7 Send your reply.

8 Close your email system.

Activity 5
Managing email

1 Open Microsoft® Outlook® or another email system and access your Inbox.

2 Create a series of folders to store your emails within the Inbox folder.

3 Create four folders for emails relating to work. They are:
- Proposals
- Confidential Matters
- Staff
- General

Figure 8.22 indicates the structure of the Inbox folders.

4 Close Microsoft® Outlook®.

Figure 8.22 Email folders

Activity 6
Address Book

1 Open Microsoft® Outlook® or another email system and access your Inbox.

2 Open the Address Book and add the following new addresses.

Sheila Davidson
Unicorn Enterprises
234 High Road
Hatson

s.davidson@unicornenterprises.com

Janice Lord
Gold Ltd
Gordon House
Rose Street
Firstville

Janicelord@ltdgold.co.uk

Frank Stevenson
Philips plc
675 Lion Court
Kilston

FS@philplc.co.uk

3 Select an address and send a new email to them.

4 Close Microsoft® Outlook® or your chosen email editor.

Other ideas

- Send an email to a colleague with one of your files (one that you have created in another unit) attached.
- Search the World Wide Web for opportunities to shop for books, compact discs or videos.
- Search the World Wide Web for your favourite football, rugby or cricket team.
- Many websites provide you with the opportunity to email the developers with your feedback so take advantage of this to practise sending emails.
- Many television and radio programmes ask listeners and viewers to send them emails. This will give you an opportunity to practise your emailing.

SUMMARY

1. **Load Microsoft® Internet Explorer**: Use either the **Start** button and the **All Programs** menu or double click on the **Microsoft® Internet Explorer** icon on the Microsoft® Windows® desktop.

2. **Close Microsoft® Internet Explorer**: Click on the **File** menu item and the **Close** option or click on the **Close** button in the top right-hand corner of the application window.

3. **Load Microsoft® Outlook®**: Use either the **Start** button and the **All Programs** menu or double click on the **Microsoft® Outlook®** icon on Microsoft® Windows® desktop.

4. **Close Microsoft® Outlook®**: Click on the **File** menu item and the **Exit** option or click on the **Close** button in the top right-hand corner of the application window.

5. **URL (Uniform Resource Locator)**: Website addresses are unique and consist of http (Hypertext Transfer Protocol), www (World Wide Web), the website host, a code to explain the type of organisation and a country code (e.g. http://www.bbc.co.uk).

   Perfect accuracy is essential.

6. **Links**: Links connect different web pages both within a particular website and to other websites. Links are indicated by underlined words, coloured text, the mouse pointer changing shape (i.e. from an arrow to an hand) or areas being highlighted by the mouse moving across them.

7. **Retracing your route**: Microsoft® Internet Explorer provides you with **Back** and **Forward** buttons. These allow you either to retrace your steps or to return along your route.

8. **Searching**: Complex websites often provide a means of searching for distinct pages. In a similar way there are search engines that will locate websites which relate to a user's interest. The search engines tend to operate by matching words which the users enter describing their interest. They match the words in different ways such as:

   - match with any words entered
   - match with all words entered in any order
   - match with the exact phrase entered

9 **Saving web addresses**: Microsoft® Internet Explorer lets you save URLs so that you can return to the website later. From the chosen website, select the `Favorites` menu and the `Add to Favorites` option to save the URL.

10 **Saving a web page**: Select the `File` menu and the `Save` option.

11 **Save an Image displayed on a web page**: Right click on the image to open a menu of options. Select `Save Image As` to open the Save Image window.

12 **Printing a web page**: Select the `File` menu and the `Print` option.

13 **Create a new email**: Select the `New` button on the toolbar of Microsoft® Outlook® and the Email window will be revealed. Enter your message and address, then click on the `Send` button.

If you are connected to the Internet, the email will be sent immediately.

If you are working off-line (i.e. you are not connected to the Internet) then the email is stored in the Outbox and the number of messages stored will be shown in brackets next to the title Outbox.

14 **Read a message**: Emails are stored in the Inbox. Clicking on the `Inbox` will reveal a list of messages. If you single click on a message, it will be highlighted and its contents revealed in the box below the list. If you double click on the message, then a new window will open, showing the message.

15 **Reply, Forward and Copy messages**: With the message window open, you can reply to the email, forward its contents to another person or copy the message to a folder.

Reply – with the email highlighted or the message window open, click on the `Reply` or `Reply to All` buttons on the toolbar.

Forward the message – with the email highlighted or the message window open, click on the `Forward` button on the toolbar and enter the email address of the person you want the message copied to.

Copy the message to a folder – with the email highlighted, select the `Edit` menu and the `Copy to Folder` option. This allows you to place a copy of the message in one of the existing local folders or a new local folder.

16 **Attached files**: To open an attachment, double click on it and it will open providing you have the appropriate application available on your computer.

To attach a file, start a new email (click on the `New` button) and click on the `Insert File` button (i.e. paperclip) on the toolbar. This will open the Insert File window from where you can select a file.

17 **Save and recall email addresses**: Select the `Address Book` icon (i.e. open book) to open the window. This offers a series of options that allow you to add, delete and send emails.

18 **Send an email using a saved address**: With the Address Book open, highlight the chosen address (single click), select the `New Message` button and a blank email will appear with the To line completed.

19 **Print an email:** With the email highlighted or the message window open, select the File menu and the Print option.

20 **Company policies and legislation:** It is essential to be aware of both your organisation's policy and the law relating to the use of the Internet.

Glossary

Alignment – a way of laying out text, e.g. left aligned means that text is aligned so that its left edge is parallel with the paper's edge when it is printed.

Application – a software program designed to perform a task such as desktop publishing, designing a database or designing a web page.

Bar Chart – a chart which represents numerical information as bars of different lengths.

Bitmap – an image composed of many dots called pixels. The more pixels in a given amount of space (e.g. a square inch) the clearer the image or the higher the resolution of the picture.

Boot – the process that occurs when you switch on the computer. It involves the loading of the operating system (e.g. Microsoft® Windows® XP) and checking of the equipment to ensure that everything is ready for you to use.

Browser – an application which allows you to access a World Wide Web page. Each page has a unique address which is called a URL (Uniform or Universal Resource Locator) which, when entered into the browser, allows it to find the site and view its contents.

Byte – the basic measure of memory. A byte is sufficient memory to store one character (e.g. a letter or a number).

Column Chart – a chart which represents numbers and columns of different lengths.

CPU – Central Processing Unit: a silicon chip which controls the operation of the computer.

Database – a way of storing information so that its contents can be extracted in many different combinations and ways.

Desktop – the main display of the operating system and normally the first display you see after the computer has loaded the operating system (e.g. Microsoft® Windows® XP).

Desktop Publishing – an application which allows text and images to be combined in many different ways so that many different forms of printed document can be designed (e.g. newsletters and posters).

Directory – a list of World Wide Web addresses related to a particular topic or subject.

DTP – see Desktop Publishing

Email – a message which is sent electronically through the Internet or over a local network.

Field – an individual piece of information stored on a database usually as part of a record.

File – a collection of digital (computer) information. There are many types of file such as word-processing, graphic and spreadsheet files.

Floppy Disk – a small magnetic disk on which you can store a small amount of information in the form of files.

Folder – a location on the computer in which you can store files.

Font – characters can be printed and displayed in many different styles. These styles are known as fonts.

Format – a way of structuring the computer information stored in a file on a disk or drive. There are many different types of file format.

Formula – a method of calculating parts of a spreadsheet automatically.

Greyscale – a way of describing an image which is shown in a range of shades of grey rather than in different colours.

GUI – Graphical User Interface: a display in which icons, windows and a mouse pointer interact to produce an easy to use environment.

Hard Disk – a magnetic disk located inside the computer, on which a large amount of information can be stored.

Hardware – the physical components which make up the computer.

HTML – Hypertext Markup Language: a presentation language which is used to design World Wide Web pages so that they can be read using a browser.

HTTP – Hypertext Text Transfer Protocol: specifies how to access documents on the World Wide Web (e.g. http://www.bbc.co.uk)

Hypertext – Pages of a web site are linked together through a number of hypertext connections. These are shown by underlined words, coloured words, icons and graphic pictures. The links allow the user to jump between different parts of the site or even between sites.

Icon – a small picture which represents a computer function or operation.

Internet – a super network of networks which links millions of computers throughout the world.

ISP – Internet Service Provider: a commercial company that provides connections to the Internet for individuals and companies.

KB – Kilobyte: a measure of memory (i.e. 1024 bytes).

Laptop – a portable computer with a screen built into its cover.

Line Graph – a graphical way of comparing two or more sets of numerical information.

MB – Megabyte: a measure of computer memory (approximately a million bytes).

Memory – a measure of the computer's capacity to perform tasks and to store information.

Menu – a method of displaying options.

Operating System – software that provides the instructions to make the hardware work.

Password – a series of alphanumeric characters that limits access to a computer system.

Personal Computer – an individual computer which is normally used by one person at a time.

Pie Chart – a graphical representation of information by showing it as slices of a circle so that the size of each slice is proportional to the data.

Pixel – graphic images are made up of many small rectangular areas which are called pixels.

Port – a way of connecting peripheral devices (e.g. printers) to a computer.

Query – a way of asking a database of information a particular question. Normally, this takes the form of identifying particular combinations of information (e.g. all customers who have ordered more than £100,000 of goods during the last three months).

QWERTY – this is the order of the top line of alphabetical keys on the keyboard.

RAM – Random Access Memory: the computer's working memory in which the computer carries out its functions once it is switched on. It only exists while the machine is on. If the power is switched off, so is the memory.

Record – a group of related fields of information which you find in a database.

Resolution – this is a way of describing the quality of an image, monitor or printer. The quality is described in terms of the dots which make up the image. That is, the more dots the higher the quality of the image, monitor display or printer output.

ROM – Read Only Memory: the computer's permanent memory, built into the structure of the silicon chips. It is not lost if the power is switched off.

Search Engine – an application that allows you to search the World Wide Web for a web page containing information on a specific topic or to search within a website for a particular item of information.

Software – computer programs written to allow you or the computer to carry out certain tasks such as constructing databases.

Sort – a way of presenting information in a spreadsheet or database (e.g. alphabetically).

Surfing – the process of wandering around the World Wide Web in search of interesting information.

Table – the part of a database in which information is stored as a series of records and fields.

URL – Uniform Resource Locator: the unique address of a World Wide Web site that allows a browser to locate the site.

Vector – an image that is defined by mathematical formulae rather than pixels. This defines the start and finish of the line and allows it to be easily changed. A vector image can be resized and it will stay in perfect proportion.

Virus – a computer program designed to cause harm to a computer.

Web page – a document which forms part of a website.

Website – a collection of pages on the Internet.

Word Processor – an application which allows you to create and manipulate documents.

WWW – World Wide Web: a collection of millions of websites and documents spread across the world as part of the Internet.

Window – rectangular area of the screen in which computer applications and information is displayed.

Wizard – Many Microsoft® Windows® applications include Wizards that are used to perform complex tasks more easily by allowing the user to choose between options.

Index

Access 99–127
   adding records 105–6
   amending records 105–6
   applications 99–100
   data entry 104
   database creation 101–4
   deleting records 105–6
   design 120
   editing data 105–6
   entering data 104
   fields 101, 113–14, 117
   inserting records 105–6
   numerical searching 112–13
   printing tables 106–7
   querying 107, 109–11, 118–20, 123
   records 100, 102, 105–6
   reports 113–16, 120–1, 123
   right button menus 105
   saving 110–11, 119
   searching 107, 111–13
   sorting 107–8
   syllabus 99
   tables 101, 104, 116–18, 124
   vs spreadsheets 100
Accessories 14
Accounts 44
Acquire Image 181, 185, 186
Active cells 54
Active sheets 71
Add to Favorites 236
Adding
   data 121
   records 105–6
Adding up figures 59–62
Address Books 237, 244–6, 249
   Delete 246
   Distribution 245
   New Contact/List/Message 245

   Save and Close 246
   using 245–6
Addresses 232
Alignment 41, 65, 137, 159
All Programs 14, 17
All words 230
Alphabetical sorting 107–8
Altavista search engine 232–3
Amending records 105–6
Any word 229, 230
Appearance 14, 38, 41–3
Applications 4
   Access 99–100
   charts/graphs 53–6, 73–4
   CorelDRAW 176–99
   Excel 53–74
   FrontPage 201–23
   HTML 200–23
   icons 5
   opening 5–6
   PowerPoint 149–74
   presentation 149–50
   Publisher 128–48
Apply to All 167
Arrange 130, 138–9, 183, 192
Art 139
   see also Clip Art
As new sheet 82
Ascending sorting 108, 118
Attaching files to email 244
Axes, charts 87

Back 228, 230
Background
   FrontPage 203, 210–11
   Outlook 242
   PowerPoint 158, 162
Bar charts 74
Bitmaps 183

Blank Page 208
Blank Presentation 150, 152, 166
Blank Publication 129, 130
Bold 65
Bookmark 215
Booting up (switching on) 4–5
Borders 34, 36–8, 69, 71–3, 139
Brackets 60
Breaks during work 45
Broadband 225
Browsers
   Favourites 236
   Picture saving 235
   Print 235
   Save 235
   using 227–8
   World Wide Web 225
   see also Internet Explorer
Bullet points 35, 36–8, 159–60, 161–2
By Blank Publications 130, 133

C drive 12
Cable safety 46
Calculations 59–62, 64
Cameras 180–1
Capitals (Caps) Lock 21
Cc (copy) 244
Cells
   active 54
   format 62, 63
   formulas 60
   reference 60
   shift 58
Center 65, 141
Centering text 41
Central processing units (CPU) 3
Chair comfort 45–6
Characters

    size   204
    Spacing   142–3
Charts
    applications   73–4
    axes   87
    comparison   73–4, 85–6
    creation   75–7
    editing   77–8
    Print Preview   89
    printing   89–90
    rows and columns   76
    saving   79, 86
    types   75
    viewing   75, 79, 80
    Wizard   75–6
Checking text *see* Grammar;
    Spelling
Clear   57–9
Clip Art   140–1, 160–1, 162, 206, 210
Clipboard   32–3
Close option   15
Color
    FrontPage   210–11
    PowerPoint   161
    Publisher   131, 139
    text   191
Column charts   74, 76, 78–9
Columns   135
Columns and rows   55–6
Comfort   45–6
Comma   63
Communication online   224–52
Company policy   246–7
Comparison charts/graphs   73–4, 85–6
Computers   2–3
    switching on   4–5
Control Panel   9, 45
Copy   154–5, 156, 183
Copy to Folder   17, 241
Copy option   13, 17, 29, 32
CorelDRAW   176–99
    Acquire Image   181, 185, 186
    Arrange   183, 192
    Bitmap   183
    color   191
    Copy   183
    Crop   179–80, 182–3
    Cut   183
    Delete   183
    digital cameras   180–1, 185–6

    Edit   183
    Ellipse tool   188, 189
    exploring   176–8
    Files   176, 179
    formats   176
    Freehand   187, 189–90
    Get Pictures   181, 186
    importing images   178–84
    Interactive Fill   186, 188–9
    line thickness   189–90
    Look in box   179
    mirror   194
    more practice   193–8
    New Graphic   177, 178
    Paste   183
    Pick   188, 189, 190
    Preview   179
    Print   178, 192
    rectangles   188, 191
    Redo   187
    Resample   179–80, 184
    resizing images   185
    resolution   184–5
    Save   178, 184, 185, 186, 189
    Select Source   181
    text   190–2
    thumbnails   186
    Transformations   183, 192
    Undo   187
Counting words   35, 205
CPU *see* Central processing units
Creation
    charts   75–9
    column charts   78–9
    databases   101–4
    documents   19–22, 24–6
    e-presentation   149–74
    files   16–19
    graphs   53
    images   175–99
    line charts/graphs   80–3
    pie charts   83–4
    spreadsheets   53–98
    web pages   200–23
Crop   179–80, 182–3
Currency   65, 117
Current Slide   164
Cut   13, 17, 29, 154–6, 183

Data
    adding   121
    editing   105–6

    entering   104
    grouping   114
    Labels   90
    non-continuous   81–3
    type   117
    see also Sorting databases
Databases   99–127
    see also Access
Date & time settings   45
Dated within last 2 weeks   230
Decimal places   63
Decrease Decimal   65
Deletion   13
    Access records   105–6
    Address Books   246
    CorelDRAW   183
    Excel   57–9
    Outlook   238, 240, 241
    Undo   58
Demote text   158–9
Descending sorting   108, 118
Design
    FrontPage   203
    PowerPoint   150, 151
    Publisher   131
    view   102, 103, 117
Desktop   5
Desktop publishing (DTP)   128–48
Digital cameras   180–1, 185–6
Disks *see* Floppy disks
Displaying formulas   72
Documents   2–52
    creation   19–22, 24–6
    printing   19–26, 30–3
    saving   24–6
Dongles *see* Memory sticks
Drawing   161, 175–99
    see also CorelDRAW
DTP *see* desktop publishing

E-documentation   2–52
E-image creation   175–99
E-presentation creation   149–74
E-publications   128–48
Editing
    Bitmap   183
    charts   77–8
    CorelDRAW   183
    data   105–6
    Excel   77–8
    graphs   87–8
    line graphs   87

Outlook   238, 240
PowerPoint   154–7
Word   27–9
Ellipse tool   188, 189
Email   236–47
   addresses   232, 244–6
   attaching files   244
   deletion   238, 240, 241
   formatting   242
   management   237–8, 249
   netiquette   242
   receiving   240–1, 242–4
   replying to   248–9
   sending   238–40, 248
   web-based   246
   see also Outlook
Emboldening rows and columns   65
Emphasising text   40–1, 203–5
Enhancement of presentations   157–63
Entering data   104
Entire workbook printing   71
Exact phrase   229, 230
Excel
   applications   53–74
   As new sheet   82
   borders   69, 71–3
   brackets   60
   calculations   64
   charts   75–6, 77–8
   Clear   57–9
   Currency   65
   Data Labels   90
   Decrease Decimal   65
   delete tool   57–9
   editing   77–8
   files   56–7
   Find and Replace   67
   Fonts   63
   formatting   62–5, 78, 87–8, 90
   formulas   59–62
   Headers/Footers   67
   hide tool   57–9
   Increase Decimal   65
   Insert menu   55–6
   loading   54, 55–6
   Margins   66–7
   mathematical operators   59–62
   more practice   91–5
   new spreadsheet   57
   Number tab   63

Page Setup   66–7
   presentation   63, 67–9
   Print Preview   70, 90
   printing   69–73, 89–90
   recalculation   64
   replication   61
   rows and columns   55–6, 65
   saving   62, 79, 86, 88
   shading   69, 71–3
   shift cells   58
   SUM function   60, 62, 68
   Undo   58, 59
   windows   53–4
   Wizard   75–6
   see also cells
Existing File   214

Favorites   236
Faxes   43
Fields   101, 113–14, 117
   see also Records
Files   2–52
   attaching to email   244
   CorelDRAW   176, 179
   creation   16–19
   Excel   56–7
   finding   15–16
   formats   176
   FrontPage   203, 206, 209
   management   16–19
   retrieving   26–7
   Windows Explorer   13–15
Fill Color   161
Find and Replace   67
Find Next   155
Finding files   15–16
Flash drives *see* Memory sticks
Flip   138
Floppy disks   12, 25
Folders
   appearance   14
   management   16–19
   manipulation   17–19
   Outlook   238
Fonts
   Excel   63
   FrontPage   203–4
   Outlook   242
   Publisher   131, 136, 137
   Size   203–4
Footers   34–5, 67, 163, 166
Format

CorelDRAW   176
   Excel   62–5, 78, 87–8, 90
   FrontPage   203, 204, 211–12
   graphic files   211–12
   menu   34
   Outlook   242
   PowerPoint   152, 158, 166
   Publisher   135, 138–9, 141–2
Format Axis   88
Format Chart Area   78
Format Data Series   87, 90
Formulas
   display   72
   Excel   54, 59–62
   replication   61
Forward
   Internet Explorer   228
   Outlook   241, 243
Frames   132–3
Freehand tool   187, 189–90
From File   206
FrontPage   201–23
   Background   203, 210–11
   Blank Page   208
   Bookmark   215
   checking text   205
   Clip Art   206, 210
   colors   210–11
   Create New Document   215
   design   203
   Display   213
   emphasising text   203–5
   Existing File   214
   exploring   201–3
   Files   203, 206, 209, 213
   Font   203–4
   Format   203, 204
   From File   206
   Grammar   205
   HTML   202, 216
   Hyperlink   212–16
   images   210–11
   Insert   203, 207–10, 215
   Look in box   208
   Maximise   202, 208, 213
   more practice   216–22
   Normal tab   202, 203, 214, 215
   Open   203
   Page   202, 208
   Picture   203, 210–11
   Preview   214
   Print   203, 206, 210, 216

Products   214
Remove Link   214
Save   203, 206, 209, 215
Save As   206
Spelling   205
text   203-5, 207-10, 213
toolbars   207
Web Page   214
Word Count   205
World Wide Web   214
Full Page   130, 133

Games   10-11
Get Pictures   181, 186
Google search engine   232, 233-4
Grammar   205
Graphic file formats   211-12
Graphic images   186
Graphic User Interface (GUI)   11
Graphs   53
    applications   73-4
    comparison   85-6
    editing   77-8, 87-8
    printing   89
    Save as   86, 88
Gridlines   81, 82
GUI see Graphic User Interface

Hard drives   12
Hardware   4
Headers and Footers   34-5, 67, 163, 166
Help   46-7
Hide tool, Excel   57-9
History   236
HTML   200, 202, 216, 221-2
http (Hypertext Transfer Protocol)   226
Hyperlinks   212-16, 226-7
Hypertext Markup Language (HTML)   200, 202, 216, 221-2
Hypertext Transfer Protocol (http)   226

Icons   5
Illustrations   160-1
    see also Images; Pictures
Images
    changing   206
    creation   175-99
    FrontPage   210-11
    graphic   186

importing   178-80, 182-4
Publisher   138-9
resizing   185
Importing text/pictures   140-2, 178-84
Inbox   237, 240-1
Increase Decimal   65
Indents   40, 142-3
Information location   12-16
Input   7-11
Insertion
    Access records   105-6
    AutoText   32, 35
    Excel menu   55-6
    File   239
    FrontPage   203, 207-10, 212, 215
    hyperlinks   212
    New Slide   150
    paragraphs   40
    pictures/text   137-8
    PowerPoint   150, 151, 152
    Publisher   130, 137-8
    Table   33
Interactive Fill   186, 188-9
Internet   224-5
    see also World Wide Web
Internet Explorer   224-5, 227-30
    Back   228, 230
    Dated within last 2 weeks   230
    Exact phrase   230
    Forward   228
    Search   230
    Show   230
    using   227-8
Internet Service Providers (ISPs)   225

Justifying text   41

Keyboards   3, 4, 7-8

Languages   200
Laptop computers   3, 4, 8
Layout   38, 41-3, 130, 132, 134
Left-handed mouse users   9
Legislation   246-7
Letters & Faxes   43
Light for work   46
Line charts   80-3
Line graphs   74, 80-3, 87

Lines
    PowerPoint   161
    Publisher   139, 142-3
    spacing   39, 142-3
    thickness   189-90
Links see Hyperlinks
Lists   35, 142-3
Look in box   61, 71, 90, 134
    CorelDRAW   179
    FrontPage   208
    Publisher   140

Management
    email   237-8, 249
    files/folders   16-19
Margins   39, 66-7, 106-7, 132
Master page   133
Master slides   165-7
Mathematical operators   59-62
Maximise   202, 208, 213
Memory sticks   12
Microsoft see individual applications
Mirror   194
Modifying report design   114
Mouse   8-9, 10-11
Move   17
My Computer   5

Netiquette   242
New address entry   245
New Contact   245
New Distribution List   245
New Graphic   177, 178
New Message   245
New Slide   151, 152
Non-continuous data   81-3
Notepad   20, 221
Number format   63
Numbering lists   35
Numerical searching   112-13
Numerical sorting   107-8

Offences   247
Online communication   224-52
    ideas   250
    more practice   247-9
    see also Email; Internet Explorer; Outlook
Operating systems   3, 12
Orientation   158
Outbox   237, 240

Outlook   236–47
　Address Books   237, 244–6
　Background   242
　Copy to Folder   241
　Delete   238, 240, 241
　Edit   238, 240
　features   237
　Folder   238
　Font   242
　Format   242
　Forward   241, 243
　Inbox   237, 240–1
　Insert File   239
　Outbox   237, 240
　Paragraph   242
　Print   241
　receiving email   242–4
　Reply   241, 243
　Save   237, 240, 241
　sending email   238–40, 243, 248

Page   202, 208
Page Setup   66–7, 106–7, 130–2, 133–6
Pages
　hyperlinks   226–7
　printing options   70
　world wide web   200–23
Paint program   175–6
Paragraphs   39, 40, 242
Passwords   4, 5, 43–5
Paste
　CorelDRAW   183
　PowerPoint   154–5, 156
　Word   13, 17, 29, 32
Pen drives *see* Memory sticks
Percent   63
Phrase replacement   38
Pick   188, 189, 190
Pictures   130, 137–9, 140–2, 203
　see also Images
Pie charts   73–4, 83–4
Placeholder   166
PowerPoint   149–74
　alignment   159
　applications   149–50
　Apply to All   167
　background   158, 162
　Blank Presentation   150, 152, 166
　bullet points   159–60, 161–2
　Clip Art   160–1, 162
　Color   161
　Copy   154–5, 156
　Current Slide   164
　Cut   154–5, 156
　Demote text   158–9
　drawings   161
　editing   154–7
　enhancement   157–63
　Fill Color   161
　Find Next   155
　Format   152, 158, 166
　headers and footers   163, 166
　illustrations   160–1
　Insert   151, 152
　lines   161
　master slides   165–7
　more practice   167–72
　New Slide   151, 152
　orientation   158
　Paste   154–5, 156
　Placeholder   166
　presentation ideas   172
　Preview   162
　printing   163–5
　Promote text   158–9
　Redo   152–3
　Replace   155, 156
　saving   154, 157, 162, 167
　Slide Design   150, 152
　Slide Master   165–7
　slide order   156
　Slide Show   152, 154, 157, 162–3
　Slide Sorter   156
　Spelling   153, 162
　text   158–9
　Tools   153
　Undo   152
　View   154, 157, 163
Presentation   149–74
　applications   149–50
　Excel   63, 67–9
　ideas   172
　new   150–4
　see also PowerPoint
Preview
　CorelDRAW   179
　FrontPage   214
　PowerPoint   162
　reports   115, 116

Print
　browsers   235
　CorelDRAW   178, 192
　FrontPage   203, 206, 210, 216
　Outlook   241
　web pages   235
Print Preview   30
　CorelDRAW   192
　Excel   70, 89, 90
Printing   4, 19–26
　Access   106–7
　charts   89–90
　choices   30
　documents   30–3
　Excel   69–73, 89–90
　graphs   89
　margins   106–7
　page options   70
　Page Setup   106–7
　PowerPoint   163–5
　printers   23
　Publisher   143
　reports   114
　text   19–26, 30–3
　Word   19–26, 30–3
Products   214
Programs menu   6
Promote text   158–9
Publisher   128–48
　alignment   137
　Arrange   130, 138
　Art   139
　Blank Publication   129, 130
　Border Art   139
　By Blank Publications   130, 133
　Center   141
　Character Spacing   142–3
　Colors   131, 139
　Columns   135
　designing   131
　exploring   130–1
　Flip   138
　fonts   131, 136, 137
　Format   135, 141–2
　frames   132–3
　Full Page   130, 133, 134
　images   138–9
　importing text/pictures   140–2
　Indents and Lists   142–3
　Insert   130, 137–8
　Layout Guides   130, 132, 134
　lines   139, 142–3

Look in box   134, 140
margins   132
master page   133
more practice   143-6
objects toolbar   139
Open   140
Page Setup   130-2, 133-6
pictures   130, 137-9, 140-2
printing   143
Quick Publications   129
Rotate   138
Save   136, 142
Search   141
spacing   142-3
templates   133
Text   134, 135, 137-9, 140-2
window   129
Wizard   145
Zoom   136

Querying databases   107, 109-11, 118-20, 123
Quick Publications   129

Recalculation   64
Receiving email   240-1, 242-4
Records   101, 103, 104, 105-6
  see also Tables
Rectangles   188, 191
Recycle Bin   5
Redo   30, 152-3, 187
Reference cells   60
Remove Link   214
Rename option   13
Replace   38, 67, 155, 156
Replication of formulas   61
Replying to email   241, 243, 248-9
Reports
  Access   113-16, 120-1
  databases   123
  modification   114
  preview   115
  printing   114
  Wizard   113-16, 120-1
Resample   179-80, 184
Resizing images   185
Resolution   184-5
Retrieving files   26-7
Right-handed mouse users   9
Rotate   138
Rows and columns   55-6, 65, 76

Safe working practices   45-6
Sans serif fonts   136
Saving
  Access   110-11, 119
  Address Books   246
  browsers   235
  CorelDRAW   178, 184, 185, 186, 189
  databases   110-11, 119
  documents   24-6
  Excel   62, 79, 84, 86, 88
  FrontPage   203, 206, 209, 215
  Outlook   237, 240, 241
  Picture As...   235
  PowerPoint   154, 157, 162, 167
  Publisher   136, 142
  Word   22, 24-6
Screen print   45
Screens   11
Search engines   229-34
Searching
  with Altavista   232-3
  databases   107, 111-13
  for files   15-16
  with Google   233-4
  Internet Explorer   230
  Publisher   141
  World Wide Web   229-34
Security see Passwords
Select Source   181
Sending email   238-40, 243, 248
Serif fonts   136
Shading   34, 36-8, 69, 71-3
Shift cells   58
Shortcuts   8, 46
Show   79, 81, 82, 230
Shutting down   6-7
Site search engines   229-34
Size of characters   204
Slide Design   150, 152
Slide Master   165-7
Slide order   156
Slide Show   152, 154, 157, 162-3
Slide Sorter   156
Software   3
  see also Applications
Sorting databases   107-8
Sound-alike matching   229
Sound volume adjustment   45
Space for work   45
Spacing   142-3
Spelling   26, 153, 162, 205

Spreadsheets   53-98, 100
  see also Excel
Start button   6, 8
Storing information   12-16
Strain reduction   46
SUM function   60, 62, 68
Support websites   118
Surfing World Wide Web   226
Switching off   6-7
Switching on   4-5
System settings   45

Tables
  Access   101, 104, 116-18, 124
  Word   33, 36-8
  see also Excel; Records
Tabs   40
Task Pane   53
Templates   43, 133
Testing hyperlinks   213-16
Text
  alignment   41
  centering   41
  checking   205
  color   191
  CorelDRAW   190-2
  editors   20
  emphasis   40-1, 203-5
  file inserting   207-10
  justifying   41
  manipulation   28-30, 31-3
  Notepad   20
  PowerPoint   158-9
  Publisher   134, 135, 137-9, 140-2
  rectangles   191
Text to Display   213
Thickness, lines   189-90
Thumbnails   186
Time & date settings   45
Title tab   79, 80-1
Transformations   183, 192

Undo   17, 30
  CorelDRAW   187
  Excel   58, 59
  PowerPoint   152
Unhide   58
Universal Resource Locators (URLs)   235
User accounts   44
User names   4, 5

Value   90
View Show   154, 157, 163
Viewing charts   75, 79, 80

Web pages   200-23
  creation   205-7
  definition   200-1
  hyperlinks   226-7
  Print   235
  saving   235
Web-based email   246
Websites   118
  searching   229-34
  structure   226-7
  see also Internet Explorer; World Wide Web
Window definition   11
Windows Explorer   12-15, 16-19
Windows Help   46-7
Wizards   75-6, 145
Word
  appearance   38, 41-3

borders   36-8
bullets   36-8
Clipboard   32-3
counting words   35
document creation   20-2, 24-6
editing   27-8
floppy disk saving   25
indents   40
layout   38, 41-3
Letters & Faxes   43
line spacing   39
loading   6
margins   39
more practice   47-9
paragraphs   39, 40
phrase replacement   38
printing text   19-26, 30-3
retrieving files   26-7
Save   22, 24-6
shading   36-8
starting   6
Tables   33, 36-8

tabs   40
templates   43
text manipulation   31-3
Word count   35
word replacement   38
Word Count   35, 205
Working off-line   236
Working practices   45-6
World Wide Web (WWW)   224-52
  access   225
  browsers   225
  company policy   246-7
  legislation   246-7
  pages   200-23
  searching   231-4, 247-8
  surfing   226
Writing HTML   221-2
WWW *see* World Wide Web

Yahoo search engines   232, 234

Zoom   136